A Concise History of the Wind Band

OTHER BOOKS BY DR. DAVID WHITWELL

On General Education
On Music Education
Music Education of the Future
The Sousa Oral History Project
The Longy Club 1900–1917

The History and Literature of the Wind Band and Wind Ensemble Series
A Concise History of the Wind Band
Volume 1 The Wind Band and Wind Ensemble Before 1500
Volume 2 The Renaissance Wind Band and Wind Ensemble
Volume 3 The Baroque Wind Band and Wind Ensemble
Volume 4 The Wind Band and Wind Ensemble of the Classic Period (1750–1800)
Volume 5 The Nineteenth-Century Wind Band and Wind Ensemble

For a complete list of the works of Dr. David Whitwell visit:
whitwellbooks.com

Dr. David Whitwell

A Concise History of the Wind Band

THE HISTORY AND LITERATURE OF THE WIND BAND AND WIND ENSEMBLE SERIES

EDITED BY CRAIG DABELSTEIN

WHITWELL PUBLISHING • AUSTIN, TEXAS, USA

A Concise History of the Wind Band
Second Edition
Dr. David Whitwell
Edited by Craig Dabelstein
www.whitwellbooks.com

Whitwell Publishing
815-A Brazos Street #491
Austin, Texas, USA
www.whitwellpublishing.com

Copyright © David Whitwell 2010
All rights reserved

Composed in Bembo Book
Published in the United States of America

A Concise History of the Wind Band (Paperback) ISBN 978-1-936512-06-5

Foreword

The purpose of this book is to supplement the information one receives in undergraduate music history courses and texts, where virtually no mention is made of wind bands.

During recent years musicologists throughout the world have finally begun to devote serious study to the wind band and an extensive literature has begun to become available regarding individual civic, court, military, and church wind bands and their traditions. Today one can see that the wind band and its music, like that of any other musical medium, has its own continuous and logical development. Contrary to the impression often given in general music history texts and older general music history texts, wind bands provided music for the highest levels of society in all periods and were used no more and no less frequently for *tafelmusik* and other background music than any other kind of ensemble.

As this work is intended as a general text book and to make it easier to read for the student I have left out footnotes, however, for those interested in further research, the *History and Literature of the Wind Band and Wind Ensemble* series of books are comprehensively footnoted.

David Whitwell
Austin, Texas

Contents

PART I   ANCIENT AND MEDIEVAL WIND MUSIC

1 *Wind Music before the Christian Era*   3
2 *Wind Instruments and the Early Christian Church*   27
3 *Civic Wind Bands*   39
4 *Court Wind Bands*   49

PART II   THE RENAISSANCE

5 *Court Wind Bands*   75
6 *Civic Wind Bands*   107
7 *Church Wind Bands*   127

PART III   THE BAROQUE

8 *The Birth of the Hautboisten and Harmoniemusik*   149
9 *Court Wind Bands*   159
10 *Military Bands*   177
11 *Civic Wind Bands*   187
12 *Church Wind Bands*   197

PART IV   THE CLASSIC PERIOD

13 *Court Wind Bands*   207
14 *Military Bands*   227
15 *Civic Wind Bands*   237
16 *Music of the French Revolution in Paris*   245

PART V   THE NINETEENTH CENTURY IN EUROPE

17 *Military Bands*   267
18 *Civic Wind Bands*   301
19 *Court Wind Bands*   315
20 *Church Wind Bands*   325

PLATES   331

PART I

Ancient and Medieval Wind Music

1   *Wind Music Before the Christian Era*

ONE CAN ONLY WONDER when man began to communicate by music made from wind instruments, which were made from natural objects such as tree branches, cane, bones and shells and required only simple technology. In the oldest of man's own records, the cave paintings from the last Ice Age (approximately 100,000 BC), performance on wind instruments is not only present, but is in some cases being used in formal rituals. The oldest specimens of musical instruments are also wind instruments, from the Upper Paleolithic Period (30,000 to 10,000 BC), and interestingly enough these are the very same three kinds of flutes still known today: the transverse flute, fipple flute, and panpipes.

In general, it is from the Neolithic Period (10,000 to 2,500 BC) that one finds specimens of drums and from the Bronze Age (2,500 to 650 BC) examples of trumpets made of metal.

Bone flute dated in the Upper Paleolithic from Geissenklösterle, a german cave on the Swabian region. Replica. [Source: José-Manuel Benito]

The Ancient Civilizations

It is very difficult to appreciate today the musical practice of the important Near East civilizations, which existed even before those of Ancient Greece, as any form of written record is extremely rare. One of these, a seal cylinder from the court of the Sumerian King, Gudea (2,600 BC), however, mentions the playing of flutes in his court.

Early instrument specimens include flutes and primitive horns and some scholars believe the concept of the vibrating reed instrument first appeared here, as the earliest names are Semitic in origin.

Opposite page: Dancers and a double-pipe (aulos) player from the tomb of Nebamun at Thebes, ca. 1400 BC

In Ancient Syria one finds the double-bodied reed instrument (known as aulos in Greece) at about the same time the instrument appears in the civilizations to the west. It is from this area that we have one of the earliest extant interviews with a performer of this instrument. The early rhetorician and biographer, Flavius Philostratus, writing in the early third century AD, reports an interview with the most famous player of that time, Canus of Rhodes. It is interesting that he mentions already the same uses of music in society that we know today.

> (The purpose of my music is) that the mourner may have his sorrow lulled to sleep by the pipe, and that they that rejoice may have their cheerfulness enhanced, and the lover may wax warmer in his passion, and that the lover of sacrifice may become more inspired and full of sacred song.

This famous early performer also left some interesting comments on performance practice:

> Namely reserves of breath and facility with the lips consisting in their taking in the reed of the pipe and playing without blowing out the cheeks; and manual skill I consider very important, for the wrist must not weary from being bent, nor must the fingers be slow in fluttering over the notes.

The earliest references to the Far East are almost exclusively of percussion instruments. The Emperor Chao-hao of China (2,598 BC) prescribed the use of small drums to play for the changing of the watchmen. Kastner tells a nice story from China in the second century BC. It seems an emperor named Lieu-Pang became irritated by the resistance he encountered in sieging a city and decided to reduce it to ashes. One night, as he made a tour of the walls to find an ideal place to attack, he heard a concert of voices and instruments from within the city. He was surprised and, after listening for a while said to his officers, 'It must be that these people are very well ruled, since they love music. I consider their resistance as a mark of their attachment to their duty; thus I will revoke my order and give them life and liberty.'

Similarly, the Indians, even in battle, used only percussion instruments, in particular timpani and whips which gave a 'deafening and frightening noise.' We are told they played on the skin, but also on the sides of the instrument for signal purposes.

According to several early sources, it was this Indian tradition of using percussion in battle which spread into Parthia, a kingdom in the eastern part of Alexander the Great's empire. The Parthians had instruments made of hollowed out wood and covered with skin and brass bells which made a 'deafening noise resembling the cries of ferocious beasts mixed with thunder.' According to Plutarch, the very sound of these instruments contributed to the Roman's defeat in one of their many battles with the Parthians.

> During this time, the enemy arrived, made more terrible by their cries and their victory chants; they put themselves to simultaneously. hitting a multitude of timpani, at the great surprise of the Romans, who were waiting for a completely different kind of attack.

The Wind Music of Ancient Egypt

Ancient Egypt represents the oldest civilization for which we have a written record, in the form of the iconography of the royal tombs. In the oldest periods of these representations, the Old Kingdom (ca. 2,686 to 2,181 BC) and the Middle Kingdom (ca. 2,133 to 1,786 BC), one finds a clear pattern of performance on long end-blown flutes, reed pipes, and simple percussion instruments for ritual and entertainment purposes.

In the paintings of the New Kingdom (ca. 1,567 to 1,085 BC) the trumpet appears, but only in a military association. In Tomb 90 of the Theban necropolis, for example, one sees an instrument which appears approximately two and one half feet in length, held parallel to the ground. During this same period the double-pipe (*aulos*) appears, usually in association with entertainment scenes. The instrument is pictured sometimes with hands crossed over and sometimes with the hands playing the nearest pipe.

No further development seems to occur until the arrival of the short transverse flute, called *photinx*, in approximately the fourth century BC.

The Hebrew Wind Music of the Old Testament

While the Old Testament contains numerous descriptions of the use of wind instruments, these descriptions may be more valuable to us today if they are taken as representative of a general practice and not as specific historical accounts. This is because even though the principals of the Old Testament may be presumed to have been actual people, who in some cases can be rather accurately dated (David, ca. 1,000 BC, or Solomon, ca. 950 BC, etc.) one must remember that the accounts of these people, the Books of the Old Testament, were written generations, and sometimes centuries, after the people and events they describe. As with any account which lived through generations of oral retelling before being placed in a written form, one must allow for the possibility of error or exaggeration. An example of the latter is surely Josephus's account of Solomon's dedication of the first Temple, which he assures us included a performance by 200,000 trumpets! In addition, of course, there are tremendous linguistic problems, especially with regard to the musical instruments of the Old Testament. In the oldest versions of Daniel 3:5 and 3:15, which describe the musical ensemble of Nebuchadnezzar, one finds the names of instruments which can no longer be identified by modern scholars. Accordingly each generation who translates this passage simply takes the names of instruments known to contemporary read-

Roman soldiers removing a candlestick and Jewish ceremonial trumpets from the Temple of Jerusalem after sacking the city in 70 AD (from the Arch of Titus in Rome).

ers. In the case of the King James Version (Authorized Version, AV), therefore, one finds a renaissance band including cornett, sackbut, psaltery, dulcimer, etc.

In spite of these problems, however, if one considers the function of winds in a more general way, perhaps the Old Testament provides a fairly accurate insight into the use of wind music by ancient peoples. One of the most valuable accounts, from this perspective, is the extensive description of the use of trumpets found in Numbers 10.

> The Lord said to Moses, 'Make two silver trumpets; of hammered work you shall make them; and you shall use them for summonsing the congregation, and for breaking camp. And when both are blown, all the congregation shall gather themselves to you at the entrance of the tent of meeting. But if they blow only one, then the leaders, the heads of the tribes of Israel, shall gather themselves to you. When you blow an alarm, the camps that are on the east side shall set out. And when you blow an alarm the second time, the camps that are on the south side shall set out. An alarm is to be blown whenever they are to set out. But when the assembly is to be gathered together, you shall blow, but you shall not sound an alarm. And the sons of Aaron, the priests, shall blow the trumpets. The trumpets shall be to you for a perpetual statute throughout your generations. And when you go to war in your land against the adversary who oppresses you, then you shall sound an alarm with the trumpets, that you may be remembered before the Lord your God, and you shall be saved from your enemies.
>
> On the day of your gladness also, and at your appointed feasts, and at the beginnings of your months, you shall blow the trumpets over your burnt offerings and over the sacrifices of your peace offerings.

One finds here many specific occasions for trumpet playing, the identity of the performers, the suggestion that specific signals existed and would have been recognized, and even perhaps the suggestion of two-part music. The instrument in question, by the way, is, as the first sentence demonstrates, a metal trumpet, as is characteristic with the oldest books of the Old Testament (Numbers, Exodus, and Judges, all dating from approximately 1,250 to 1,210 BC). It is in the more recent books (I & II Chronicles, I & II Kings, Isaiah, Ezekiel, I & II Samuel, and Joshua) that one begins to find the replacement of the trumpet by the ram's horn, reflecting perhaps both the scarcity of metals in the desert and a desire to rid themselves of Egyptian associations.

The references to the trumpet found in the Old Testament tend to describe the sound simply as a 'blast.' In the Dead Sea Scrolls, however, where it is the ram's horn instrument being used, we find such intriguing descriptions as 'a low, quavering subdued note.'

In Exodus one finds interesting references to percussion instruments, and mention of the sister to Moses being a percussionist.

Aside from religious associations, one finds in the Old Testament references to wind instruments in numerous civic functions, including processions, banquets, coronations, and as civic watchmen.

In the military sphere the trumpet is frequently found, as in almost every society. There are the usual references to the trumpet being used for signals in battle, but more interesting are the two great battles in which trumpets played a primary role.

The earliest of these stories is the famous surprise attack by Gideon when, at night, he surrounded the enemy and gave them the impression that a much greater army was accompanying him.

A coin from the Jewish Bar Kokhba revolution showing two silver trumpets

> So Gideon and the hundred men who were with him came to the outskirts of the camp at the beginning of the middle watch, when they had just set the watch; and they blew the trumpets and smashed the jars that were in their hands. And the three companies blew the trumpets and broke the jars, holding in their left hands the torches, and in their right hands the trumpets to blow; and they cried, 'A sword for the Lord and for Gideon!' They stood every man in his place around about the camp, and all the army ran; they cried out and fled. When they blew the three hundred trumpets, the Lord set every man's sword against his fellow and against all the army; and the army fled.

The more famous passage tells the story of the use of trumpets to blow down the walls of Jericho.

> And seven priests shall bear seven trumpets of ram's horns before the ark; and on the seventh day you shall march around the city seven times, the priests blowing the trumpets. And when they make a long blast with the ram's horn, as soon as you hear the sound of the trumpet, then all the people shall shout with a great shout; and the wall of the city will fall down flat.

And so, we are told, it did!

Opposite page: Julius Schnorr von Carolsfeld (1794–1872), The Battle of Jericho.

The Wind Music of Ancient Greece

Our understanding of the philosophy and literature of the men of the city-states which we call Ancient Greece is possible only because much of this literature is extant. On the other hand, very little actual music has survived from this civilization and hence we can only observe the significant role it played in society by reading about it in Greek literature.

It is clear that beginning with Pythagoras and his school (sixth century BC) music exercised an almost unique power on the Greek mind. The Pythagorean's understanding of the nature of music contained one basic error, which resulted for a time in a society giving music a higher status than perhaps it has ever had since. The Pythagoreans, having discovered the mathematical relationships among the tones of the natural scale and having observed the easy correspondence between rhythm and mathematics, incorrectly designated music as one of the 'exact' sciences, to be included alongside geometry, arithmetic, and astronomy.

It was only a matter of time, of course, before the Greeks began to realize that music is not an 'exact' science, that the contemplation of music does not reveal conceptual insights, but rather non-conceptual, experiential insights. One sees Aristotle (fourth century BC) raising questions regarding the nature of music, some of which are being asked still today: 'Does music have a fundamental value or is it only an entertainment?' and 'Is it necessary for school children to learn to actually play an instrument or is it enough to only be educated to appreciate music as listeners?'

The commonly known instruments during the time of Aristotle were the trumpet, two kinds of reed instruments, the flute, small harp prototypes, and a type of lute.

The trumpet, called *salpinx*, was a straight cylindrical tube, perhaps in several sections, and its earliest mention is in Homer's *The Iliad* (eighth century BC) in connection with a civic watchman. Most references to the trumpet in Greek literature, however, are relative to its use for giving military signals. Xenophon, for example, writing of the famous 'Retreat of the Ten Thousand' after the defeat of Cyrus in 401 BC, suggests a broad range of signals may have already been in use.

Warrior playing the salpinx. Attic black-figure lekythos, late sixth–early fifth century BC.

> When the trumpet gives the signal to rest, get ready your baggage; at the second signal, lead the beasts of burden; at the third, follow your general.

The use of military trumpet signals were apparently so standardized that on occasion armies could employ the tactic of giving false signals to fool the enemy.

> Pericles, general of the Athenians, laid siege on a city which defended itself vigorously. By sounding the trumpets at night and creating great cries on the side of the city which faced the sea, the enemy, fearing a surprise attack from this side, ran through another gate freeing the entrance for Pericles.

Among the most interesting accounts of Greek trumpet music are those found relative to the trumpet contests of the early olympics. Apparently a trumpet event began with the 96th Olympiad, in 396 BC, but were not musical contests so much as physical ones in nature—perhaps a hint to their nature can be found in the modern olympic motto, 'citius, altius, fortius,' or 'faster, higher, stronger.' We know the names of some of these famous trumpeters: Timaios of Elis, Dionysios of Ephesos, Heradorus of Megara, and even a lady trumpeter, Aglais of Megacles. Popular interest in the private lives of these great players resulted in literature which reveals, for example, that a typical meal consumed by Heradorus consisted of six pints of wheat bread, twenty pounds of meat, and six quarts of wine!

The instrument most frequently discussed in Greek literature is not the trumpet but the aulos, a double-pipe found in numerous sizes and often played with a leather band around the head to aid cheek pressure. We can not be sure if this instrument was a single or double reed instrument, but the latter seems suggested by its frequent description as having an 'exciting' tone. Aristotle, in fact, said it was too exciting to be used in educational music and that the proper time for its use was in the relief of passions.

Because the double-pipe could play melodies it was even more important to the Greek armies than the trumpet. Why, asks Agesilaus, King of Sparta (444–361 BC), do the Spartans go into combat to the sound of the double-pipe? Because, he says,

Youth playing the aulos, detail of a banquet scene. Tondo of an Attic red-figure cup, ca. 460 BC–450 BC. [Photographer Jastrow, 2008]

> One can observe, as they advance thus, measure for measure, which are the cowards and which are the brave; because the rhythm of the anapests gives arder to courageous men, the same as it betrays the fainthearted; thus when the foot hesitates to follow the cadence of the double-pipe, the coward finds himself exposed in front of all eyes.

A more practical purpose on the battle field was the ability to move troops in co-ordination to a musical beat. Plutarch thus describes the armies of the Spartan General, Lycurgus:

> It was a magnificent and terrible sight to see them marching to the tune of the double-pipes, with no gap in their lines and no terror in their souls, but calmly and gaily led by music into the perilous fight. Such men were not likely to be either panic-stricken or over-reckless, but steady and assured, as if the gods were with them.

Indeed no less than an oracle of the Gods predicted victory for the Spartans so long as they thus marched to the sound of the double-pipes. In a very famous battle, that of Leuctra, in 371 BC, against the Thebans, they failed to use the double-pipes and lost. Modern historians speak only of the greater military tactics of the Thebans, but for the ancient historians the failure to use the double-pipes was sufficient reason for the defeat.

The Greeks also used the double-pipes to accompany dance, an essential part of the training of young boys for military duty. One of the most famous of these dances was the *pyrrhiche*, whose four parts included the basic movements necessary to attack and defense. First, the *podisme* consisted of very fast feet movement, preparing one to catch the enemy as he fled, or to escape pursuit. The second part, the *xiphisme*, was a kind of simulated combat. The third part consisted of very high leaps, which prepared the soldier for clearing walls and ditches. The final part, the *tetracome*, was tranquil and majestic.

The Greeks even trained their horses to respond to double-pipe melodies, some for tactical purposes and some for entertainment purposes, and some of the most extraordinary stories in early Greek literature center on battles lost when the horses responded to the wrong double-pipe melodies. An example is a story about a battle between the people of Cardia and the Bisaltians, the leader of whom was named Naris, who,

> when a child, had been sold in Cardia, and after serving as a slave to a Cardian had become a barber. Now the Cardians had an oracle that the Bisaltians would come against them, and they would often talk about

it as they sat in the barber-shop. So Naris, escaping from Cardia to his native land, put the Bisaltians in readiness to attack the Cardians, and was appointed leader by the Bisaltians. All the Cardians had schooled their horses to dance at their drinking-parties to the accompaniment of the double-pipes, and rising on their hind legs and, as it were, gesticulating with their front feet, they would dance, being thoroughly accustomed to the double-pipe melodies. Knowing these facts, Naris purchased a pipe-girl from Cardia, and on her arrival in Bisaltia she taught many double-pipers; accordingly he set out with them to attack Cardia. And when the battle was on, he gave orders to play all the pipe-melodies which the Cardian horses knew. And when the horses heard the piping, they stood on their hind legs and began to dance; but since the whole strength of the Cardians lay in their cavalry, they were beaten in this way.

The double-pipes also were fundamental to all the celebrations of daily Greek life: weddings, social gatherings, entertainments, and funerals. It was in this secular tradition that the great tradition of choral odes, accompanied by double-pipes, evolved. By about the third century BC, however, some writers were complaining that more attention was being given the double-pipes than the singers. One, Pratinas, grew quite angry when the double-pipes usurped the attention of the audience.

> What uproar is this? What dances are these? What outrage hath assailed the alter of Dionysus with its loud clatter? ... 'Tis the song that is queen ... the double-pipe must be content to be leader in the revel only, in the fist-fight of tipsy youngsters raging at the front door. Beat back him who has the breath of a mottled toad, burn up in flames that spit-wasting, babbling raucous reed, spoiling melody and rhythm in its march.

Some of these choral odes had instrumental preludes, which one might think of an as early Overture for wind ensemble. Semus of Delos mentioned this practice.

> Since the term 'concerted music' is unknown to many persons, I must tell its meaning. It was a kind of contest in harmony, double-pipe music and dance rhythm exactly corresponding, with no singer adding words to the performance.

Amphitheatre at Delphi, Greece [Source: Luarvick, 2008]

We may assume that cult-religious performances included the double-pipe as well. Both Athenaeus and Strabo write of their use in the sacrifices at Delos during the worship of Artemia Chitones by the Syracusans, by boys dancing on Mount Helicon and in the cult of Dionysus.

> ... and bent its Bacchic revelry with the high-pitched, sweet-sounding breath of Phrygian double-pipes.

There were also double-pipe playing contests, which over a period of time had developed from artistic events into popular ones. Athenaeus (second century BC) complains,

> Today, however, people take up music in a haphazard and irrational manner. In the early times popularity with the masses was a sign of bad art; hence, when a certain double-pipe player once received loud applause, Asopodorus of Phlius, who was waiting in the wings, said, 'What's this? Something awful must have happened!' ... And yet the musicians of our day set as the goal of their art success with their audiences.

This direction may have begun much earlier, for Aristotle took a dim view of these contests, noting, 'The vulgarity of the spectator tends to lower the character of the music.'

One example of the repertoire for these contests is described by Strabo, who heard it at a contest at Delphi. He writes of a five-movement composition which describes a battle between

Apollo and a dragon. There was a prelude; preparation for the battle; the battle; the victory; and the death of the dragon, with 'the double-pipe players imitating the dragon as breathing its last in hissings.'

Given the wide role of the double-pipe in Greek society, these contests, and the fact that the instrument was apparently not easy to play (one Greek myth has the Goddess Minerva throwing the instrument away when she discovered that the exertion in playing it deformed her face), it is no surprise there was a thriving profession of double-pipe teachers. Greek literature reveals the names of many of these teachers and their treatises, but unfortunately none have survived.

There was another reed instrument found in Ancient Greece, a single-pipe instrument which was probably a variant of the aulos. This instrument seems to have been played exclusively by young lady entertainers at elaborate private banquets. After the guests had been given course after course the girls, often together with a variety of other entertainers, appeared to perform. Later in the evening, after sufficient drinks had loosened both the purse and the appetite of the guests, the girls were auctioned off. Persaeus gives an interesting example from the third century BC:

> There was a philosopher drinking with us, and when a single-pipe girl entered and desired to sit beside him, although there was plenty of room for the girl at his side, he refused to permit it, and assumed an attitude of insensibility. But later, when the single-pipe girl was put up for the highest bidder, as is the custom in drinking-bouts, he became very vehement during the bargaining, and when the auctioneer too quickly assigned the girl to someone else, he expostulated with him, denying that he had completed the sale, and finally that insensible philosopher came to blows, although at the beginning he would not permit the single-pipe girl even to sit beside him.

One such banquet, documented at length by Hippolochus, was given by Caranus, of Macedonia, for twenty of his friends to celebrate his marriage. We are told that as the guests entered they received as gifts gold tiaras and silver cups. The first course included duck, ringdove, chicken, and a goose; the second course featured rabbit, more geese, young goats, pigeons, turtle-doves, partridge, and other fowl. The custom was for the guests to sample this and then pass the rest back to their servants. More gifts followed, and then drinks.

Now the single-pipe girls entered, together with other entertainers. 'To me,' writes Hippolochus, 'these girls looked quite naked, but some said that they had on tunics. After a prelude they withdrew.' Another round of gifts: jars of gold and silver, perfume, and a great silver platter with a roast pig, filled with a variety of small fowl. Again gifts were distributed: more perfume, more gold and silver, and breadbaskets made of ivory.

Next more entertainers appeared, including naked female jugglers who performed tumbling acts among swords and blew fire from their mouths. This was followed by more gifts: a large gold cup for each guest, a large silver platter filled with baked fish, a double jar of perfume and gold tiaras twice the size of the first ones. The sounding of a trumpet announced the end of the banquet and the enriched guests, according to Hippolochus, all went out to look for real estate agents!

Plato complained that it was those who could not carry on a decent conversation who were responsible for 'driving high the market price of the single-pipe girls.'

The transverse flute is not mentioned in Greek literature (caution: early English translators usually translate the aulos as 'flute'), although one wonders why as it was found both to the East and to the West. Only the panpipe flute is mentioned in the original sources, and always of course in a rural setting.

There is no room here for a discussion of the many associations with wind instruments and the Gods found in the Greek myths, but one story must be told as it demonstrates in yet another way the importance of music in the Ancient Greek civilization. Philetaerus, writing in the fourth century BC, exclaimed, 'Zeus, it is indeed a fine thing to die to the music of the double-pipes!' Being able to arrange such an event, he believed, demonstrated conclusively to the Gods that one appreciated music. In such a case, should one go to 'Hades,' one would be permitted 'to revel in love affairs,' whereas 'those whose manners are sordid, having no knowledge of music,' are condemned to spend eternity carrying water in a fruitless effort to fill 'the leaky jar.'

Wind Music of the Etruscans

The Etruscans (Latin: *tusci*) inhabited the western region of Italy, known today as Tuscany. These peoples, of East Mediterranean origin, migrated in the eighth and ninth centuries BC, and formed a strong cultural entity until their absorption into the Roman Empire in 27 BC.

Because they traded with the Greeks, they form an important link between the city states of Greek antiquity and the Roman Empire. This is quite evident, for example, in the ancient history of the trumpet, which several writers claim was an invention of the Etruscans.

> Athenaeus: 'Horns and trumpets are an invention of the Etruscans.'
> Diodorus of Sicily: 'It remains for us now to speak of the Tyrrhenians (Etruscans) … they were the inventors of the *salpinx*, as it is called, a discovery of the greatest usefulness for war and named after them the 'Tyrrhenian' trumpet.'
> Aeschylus: 'Herald, give the signal and restrain the crowd; and let the piercing Tyrrene trumpet, filled with human breath, send forth its shrill blare to the folk!'
> Sophocles: 'I hear thy call and seize it in my soul, as when a Tyrrhenian bell speaks from mouth of bronze!'
> Euripides: 'Then the Tyrrhenian trumpet blast burst forth, like fire, as the signal for the fight.'

This has been puzzling to scholars, because the salpinx trumpet can be found in both Greece and Egypt before the migration into this part of Italy. What then, are these early writers referring to? It seems possible, on the basis of iconography, to suppose that it was the Etruscans who developed the two new 'trumpets' familiar in Roman music, but not found in earlier Greek traditions. The *cornu*, a great hoop-shaped instrument of bronze or iron, with transverse grip (looking somewhat like a capital 'G'), is seen pictured in virtually every Roman military icon. The second, and a bit less frequently seen, is the *lituus*, with a bell bent backwards (looking like a horizontal letter 'J'). Both of these instruments appear in the iconography of Etruria considerably earlier than that of Rome.

The Etruscans also seem to have experimented with the double-pipe of Greece, adding to it a kind of bell. This new looking instrument may have had a new name at this time. The Roman, Varro, wrote (first century BC) that *Subulo* was a word given by the Etruscans to their 'reed-pipe' players.

A relief on Trajan's Column in Rome, Italy, showing the cornu and buccina.

The Etruscans seem to have particularly cultivated wind instruments and one sees them in many icons of public processions. A late fifth century BC funeral urn (Chiusi, Museo Civivo, Nr. 2260) shows a double-pipe player leading a wedding procession. Cornu and lituus players can be seen in funeral processions in the tombs of Bruschi and Tifone, near Tarquinia. Professional double-pipe players also performed during the lying-in-state, sacrificial rites and magic lamentations for the dead.

No doubt winds were used in all cult and quasi-religious ceremonies. Vergil mentions the cornu as being, together with wine and forecasting from animal entrails, a basic tool of the priest.

> That gentle ground to gen'rous grapes allow.
> Strong stocks of vines it will in time produce,
> And overflow the vats with friendly juice,
> Such as our priests in golden goblets pour
> To gods, the givers of the cheerful hour,
> Then when the bloated Tuscan blows his horn,
> And reeking entrails are in chargers borne.

As in Greece, these wind instruments are also part of life on a more day-to-day basis. Alcimus wrote that the Etruscans, 'knead bread, practice boxing, and flog their slaves to the accompaniment of the double-pipe.' Another writer, Eratosthenes, confirms that boxing matches were accompanied by the double-pipe.

As we might expect, accounts exist regarding the use of wind instruments in hunting in Etruria. Such an account by Claudius Aelianus (second century AD) must be regarded as either exaggerated or of a school of the most charismatic double reed players who ever lived!

> There is an Etruscan story current which says that the wild boars and the stags in that country are caught by using nets and hounds, as is the usual manner of hunting, but that music plays a part, and even the larger part, in the struggle. And how this happens I will now relate. They set the nets and other hunting gear that ensnare the animals in a circle, and a man proficient on the double-pipes stands there and tries his utmost to play a rather soft tune, avoiding any shriller note, but playing the sweetest melodies possible. The quiet and stillness easily carry (the sound) abroad; and the music streams up to the heights and into ravines and thickets—in a word into every lair and resting place of these animals. Now at first when the sound penetrates to their ears it strikes them with terror and fills them with dread, and then an unalloyed and irresistible delight in the music takes hold of them, and they are so beguiled as to forget about their offspring and their homes. And yet wild beasts do not care to wander away from their native haunts. But little by little these creatures in Etruria are attracted as though by some persuasive spell, and beneath the wizardry of the music they come and fall into the snares, overpowered by the melody.

Indoor entertainment, especially the dance, also depended on this instrument. Livy wrote that Etruscan dancers were popular in Rome.

> The *ludiones* summoned from Etruria, dancing to the melodies of the reed-pipe (*tibia*) player without any singing … performed movements which were in no way unseemly, in the Etruscan manner.

The Wind Music in the Roman Empire

In the Roman army one would have found the straight trumpet of the Greeks, now called *tuba* (the player: *tubicine*), but also new trumpet types: the *cornu*, *lituus*, and *buccina*, all appearing as early as the period of Servius Tullius (ca. 578 BC).

In practice a system seems to have existed by which the cornu gave signals to the smaller units of the army after having received them from the louder trumpets (which are always described in Roman literature as 'brazen' or 'strifeful' and are pictured in iconography always played by players with extremely puffed cheeks). Both Plutarch and Polybius speak of these instruments being used in great numbers by the military and this seems to be confirmed in an extant record of an Augustan Legion in Numidia which maintained thirty-nine trumpet and thirty-six cornu players.

Percussion is rarely mentioned in literature which discusses the Roman army, although one interesting reference in Tacitus speaks of soldiers participating in a cult ceremony with the 'boom of brazen gongs and the blended notes of trumpets and cornu.'

In the important cult ceremonies of the Roman citizens one frequently reads of a double-pipe similar to that of Greece, now called tibia, as well as a small drum (*tympanum*) and cymbals. One of the most important of these cult festivals was the celebration of the Goddess, Cybele, held on April 4, the origin of which lay in an ancient myth of the God, Saturn, who was told by an oracle that he would be deposed by his son. He attempted to prevent this by eating all his offspring, but his wife finally tricked him into swallowing a stone covered in infant garments, while her servants beat on empty helmets and shields to cover the cries of the actual child. Thus it follows that it was the percussion instruments who, as noise makers, were featured in this festival, as one sees in a typical account by Ovid.

> Eunuchs will march and thump their hollow drums, and cymbals clashed on cymbals will give out their tinkling notes: seated on the unmanly necks of her attendants, the goddess herself will be borne with howls through the streets in the city's midst.

Reliefs on Trajan's Column in Rome showing players of the trumpet and cornu

A larger variety of wind instruments were used in the more famous festival of Dionysus, but again more for noise than for musical purposes. Now, as Pliny writes was also the case with religious sacrifices, the purpose of the wind band was to cover the cries of the victims! The historian Livy (59 BC to 17 AD) describes these Dionysus celebrations as secret, occult rites performed at night.

> There were initiatory rites which at first were imparted to a few, then began to be generally known among men and women. To the religious element in them were added the delights of wind and feasts, that the minds of a larger number might be attracted. When wine had inflamed their minds, and night and the mingling of males with females, youth with age, had destroyed every sentiment of modesty, all varieties of corruption first began to be practiced, since each one had at hand the pleasure answering to that to which his nature was more inclined. There was not one form of vice alone, the promiscuous matings of free men and women, but perjured witnesses, forged seals and wills and evidence, all issued from this same workshop: likewise poisonings and secret murders, so that at times not even the bodies were found for burial. Much was ventured by craft, more by violence. This violence was concealed because amid the howlings and the crash of drums and cymbals no cry of the sufferers could be heard as the debauchery and murders proceeded.

The double-pipe players were especially in demand for funeral rites and according to Ovid it became such a status symbol that the government had to draw up a regulation limiting their number to ten in these processions.

Before leaving the discussion of cults, we must mention that two of the instruments enjoyed their own 'holy days.' Although the trumpets were not used as extensively as the double-pipes in religious and cult ceremonies, they nevertheless enjoyed certain status because of their association with the leaders of the state and its armies. Accordingly, each March 23 and May 23 a festival day called the *Tubulustrium* occurred. This ceremony was a blessing of the instruments, or as Ovid wrote, 'to purify the melodious trumpets.' Varro indicated that he believed this ceremony took place in the Shoemaker's Hall.

The double-pipe players, present at everyone else's cult celebration, themselves enjoyed a special double-pipe holiday, held each June 13, called 'lesser *Quinquatrus.*' This festival commemorates an occasion when the double-pipe players of Rome went on strike, enraged at some ordinance of the government which reduced their wages. On this occasion (third century BC) all the double-pipe players left Rome and retired to Tibur. They were missed.

> The hollow double-pipe was missed in the theatre, missed at the altersi; no dirge accompanied the bier on the last march.

Apparently negotiation did not result in their return to Rome so the government devised a plan to trick them into returning. A wealthy citizen in Tibur threw a great party in their honor and when they were 'reeling with heady wine' their host arranged for wagons to return them to their lodging. But instead the wagons took the sleeping double-pipe players to Rome and in order to help them save face upon their unexpected arrival they were given masks and long gowns. Hence the double-pipe festival in Rome was always celebrated with the double-pipe players parading through the streets wearing masks and long gowns.

The double-pipe was also found in many kinds of entertainment activities available to Romans. They seem to have been frequently found at banquets, as they were in Greece. Martial (first century AD) wrote a poem listing all that he could offer if a friend would attend a banquet. After listing a wide variety of food, he promises,

> It's a poor sort of dinner; yet, if you deign to grace it,
> You'll neither say nor hear
> One word that's not sincere,
> You can lounge at ease in your place,
> Wearing your own face,
> You won't have to listen while your host reads aloud from some thick book
> Or be forced to look
> At girls from that sink, Cadiz, prancing
> Through the interminable writhings of professional belly-dancing.
> Instead, Condylus, my little slave,
> Will pipe to us something not too rustic, nor yet too grave.

At some banquets, perhaps on more formal occasions, the double-pipe was put to more serious purpose. According to the historian Valerius Maximus (first century AD), during banquets the elders would compose, to the accompaniment of the double-pipe, their ancestors' outstanding deeds in song, so that by this they might make the younger men more eager to imitate them.

This instrument was also used in the Roman theater and of course in the arena, called the Circus. There is an extraordinary account of the latter by Polybius (second century BC) in a description of a special performance organized by the Roman General, Lucius Anicius, to celebrate his defeat and capture of King Genthius of the Illyrians.

> Having summonsed the most distinguished artists of Greece and constructed a very large stage in the Circus, he first brought on the double-pipe players; there were Theodorus of Boeotia, Theopompus, Hermippus, Lysimachus, all of them the most distinguished. Posting them, then, at the front of the stage with the chorus, he directed them to play all together. As they started to perform their music to accompany the dance motions which corresponded to it, he sent word to them that they were not playing in the right way, and ordered them to whoop up the contest against one another. Since they were puzzled at this, one of the officials indicated that they should turn and advance upon one another and act as if they were fighting. Quickly the players caught the idea, and taking on motions in keeping with their own licentious characters they caused great confusion. For the double-pipe players by a concerted movement turned the middle choruses against those at the ends, while they blew on their double-pipes unintelligible notes, and all differing, and then they drew away in turn upon each other; and at the same time the members of the choruses clashed noisily against the players as they shook their gear at them and rushed upon their antagonists, to turn again and retreat. And so in one case, a member of the chorus girded himself, and stepping out of the ranks he turned and raised his fists as if to box against the double-pipe player who plunged against him; and then, if not before, the applause and shouts that arose from the spectators knew no bounds. Furthermore, while these were contending in a pitched battle, two dancers entered with castanets, and four boxers mounted upon the stage accompanied by trumpeters and horn players. All these contests went on together, and the result was indescribable.

To accomplish all this wind instrument performance, players early in the Roman Empire began organizing themselves into associations very much like the guilds of medieval Europe. There were separate guilds (called *collegia*) for trumpet, horn, double-pipe, and bagpipe players. According to Plutarch, these began in the seventh century BC, and in any case we know the double-pipe guild was one of the oldest professional organizations in Rome.

These guilds were modeled on the Italian municipality, having a hierarchy of magistrates. They also had their own deities, festivals and sought patrons.

Funerary inscription about members of the guild of the tibicens (collegium tibicinum). Stone, first half of the first century BC. From the Esquiline Hill in Rome, 1875. [Photographer Marie-Lan Nguyen, 2009]

Two final notes: first, the panpipe flute is found here as it was in Greece, a rural instrument, outside the wind practice of government or aristocratic circles. In a passage by Vergil, one notes that the players complained that playing the panpipe (*fistula*) 'chafed their lips.'

Some members of aristocratic families played wind instruments themselves for pleasure, including at least two of the Emperors. Early writers maintain that Elagabalus (third century AD) played the double-pipe and cornu, while the famous Nero was a performer on the bagpipes. Can it be, therefore, that Nero did not 'fiddle while Rome burned,' but rather blew?

2   *Wind Instruments and the Early Christian Church*

After the wind music of the Roman Empire and before the numerous wind ensembles which can be documented in the later Middle Ages, the traditions and techniques of wind performance were kept alive by that musician known as the minstrel.

In the larger story of wind music, he takes on a significance even greater due to the role he unwittingly played in the development of instrumental music in the early Christian Church. The objection to his 'character' was one of the reasons the Church denounced all instrumental music, and indeed there are churches today who still do not permit this form of music. It is because of this relationship that the history of wind bands in the church must begin with the minstrel.

The Early Medieval Jongleur

During the latter part of the fourth century AD, as the effective protection of the Roman Empire was evaporating and the 'barbarians,' the German tribes, Huns, and Goths, began to flood into Central and Southern Europe, the first period of mass migration on the continent began. As the peoples of Europe began to pass from region to region, they were accompanied by a broad range of entertainers and fellow travelers: jugglers, storytellers, actors, musicians, and performers of magic.

During the early Middle Ages the musician was usually called jongleur (from the Latin *Ioculator*, meaning 'one who makes merry') by the early scribes. These jongleurs wandered from village to village and from castle to castle performing wherever they could find donations. For centuries they were probably entertainers in a broad sense, as we can see in a catalog of skills claimed by one of them.

> I can play the lute, vielle, pipe (shawm), bagpipe, panpipes, harp, fiddle, guittern, symphony, psaltery, organistrum, organ, tabor, and the rote. I can sing a song well, and make tales to please young ladies, and can play the gallant for them if necessary. I can throw knives into the air and

Opposite page: A caricature of a minstrel from a series by Nicholas de Larmessin, late seventeenth century

catch them without cutting my fingers. I can jump rope most extraordinary and amusing. I can balance chairs, and make tables dance. I can somersault, and walk doing a handstand.

A twelfth-century educational treatise, called *Enseignamens*, for the would be jongleur offers a similar broad list of skills. It warns him to be prepared to, 'learn the arts of imitating birds, throwing knives, leaping through hoops, showing off performing asses and dogs, and dangling marionettes.' Even those who thought of themselves as being primarily musicians probably had to include extramusical attractions to satisfy the audience. Joinville, in the thirteenth century, relates a performance by three trumpet players:

Miniature from 'Jongleurs', Ms. latin 1118; f. 112. Bibliothéque National de Paris.

> When they began to play their trumpets you would have thought it was the voice of swans coming from the water, and they produced the sweetest and most gracious melodies, a marvel to hear. And these same minstrels did wonderful acrobatic feats. A towel was put under their feet and, holding themselves rigid, they turned a complete somersault, their feet returning to the towel. Two of them turned their heads to face behind them, and the eldest also, and when he turned it round again he crossed himself, for he was afraid of breaking his neck in the act of turning.

The lucky few received temporary employment by a noble, but most lived a meager existence from donation to donation. Who is not filled with the deepest sympathy upon reading the early poet Rutebeuf's heartbreaking description of the poor jongleur?

> I cough with cold and with hunger gape,
> Through them I die and am finished with.
> I am without coverlet or bed;
> Lord, I know not where to go.
> My sides feel the straw—
> A bed of straw is no bed,
> And in my bed there is nothing, but straw …
> Lord, I would have you know
> I have not wherewith to buy bread.

Although we know little of this early jongleur, we can see that his contribution was a great one. As he traveled from country to country, he wove an evermore unified cultural language that laid the way for a truly European music culture.

The Late Medieval Minstrels

A street in Paris, the *rue de Jugleurs*, was renamed during the fourteenth century, *rue des Ménétriers*, and reflects the new name by which the wandering musician came to be known. The minstrel (from the Latin *ministerialis*, meaning 'office-holder or functionary') is increasingly identified as an instrumentalist and in particular a player of wind instruments (usually flute, shawm, trumpet, or bagpipes). His identification as a wind player can be seen in the variant terms for singers (*ménétriers de bouche*, or 'mouth minstrels') and string players (*ménétriers de cordes*), in iconography, and in literature. An early English scribe, for example, comments,

> For the most parte all maner mynstrelsy
> By wynde they delyver thyr sound chefly.

By the late Middle Ages the better minstrels were beginning to be employed by nobles or by towns, which were just beginning to establish real independent identities. Iconography usually pictures the minstrels dressed in short coats or capes with hoods. If employed by a noble or a town, the cape included a coat of arms, which offered an important form of protection when they traveled.

One important fact we know of these minstrels is that they exchanged international literature and instruments during the astonishing minstrel 'schools,' called *scolae ministrallorm*. These schools can be documented from the twelfth century and seemed to have peaked during the late fourteenth and early fifteenth centuries. They were held throughout France, the Low Countries, and Germany during Lent (when no minstrel performances were allowed) or on a more informal basis whenever large numbers of minstrels gathered in the same town for a large celebration or church council.

It is possible to document the fact that large numbers of minstrels attended these schools, some 1,500, for example, in the case of one held in Italy in 1324. Perhaps one record of these schools is Chaucer's *House of the Dead*, for how else could he have imagined the large numbers of musicians he mentions? He begins with a category of musicians who played 'sondry gleës' and says they were more numerous than the stars in the sky! Next he discusses in more detail three large groups of harps, trumpets, and shawm players ('pipe' was a synonym for shawm), referring to some of the latter as Dutchmen.

> Then saugh I famous, olde and yonge,
> Pypers of the Duche tonge,
> To lerne love-daunces, springes,
> Reyes and these straunge thinges.

Finally, Chaucer describes a band ('loud minstrels' was a synonym for wind band before the Baroque) of woodwinds numbering in the tens of thousands!

> Tho saugh I stonden hem behinde,
> Afar fro hem, al by themselve,
> Many thousand tymes twelve,
> That maden laude minstralcyes
> In corne muse and shalmyes,
> And many other maner pipe
> That craftely begunne to pipe,
> Both in doucet and in redek
> That ben at feastes with the brede
> And many floute and lilting-horne,
> And pypes made of greene corne,
> As have thise litel herdegromes
> That kepen bestes in the bromes.

One can not mention Chaucer without reference to his classic, *Canterbury Tales*. It was the absence of regular minstrels that caused this famous group of pilgrims to begin their telling of stories to one another. There was the miller, 'a Baggepype wel koude he blowe,' but in particular it is the flute playing squire who attracts our attention. Both in dress and in his numerous skills, he seems to be a surrogate for the otherwise missing minstrel.

> Singinge he was a floytinge al the day;
> He was as fresh as is the month of May.
> Short was his goune with sleves long and wide,
> Wel coude he sit on hors, and fayre ryde.
> He coude songes make, and wel endyte,
> Juste and eeke daunce, and well purtreye and wryte.

Chaucer says he could ride a horse well, draw well, dance, compose and notate his music. How many flute players today are so broadly educated?

An illumination from Tacuina sanitatis (Tables of Health), fourteenth century

The Decline of Minstrelsy

During the fourteenth century one finds those minstrels who have permanent employment in towns, or with nobles, distinguishing themselves from their wandering brothers by use of the term 'minstrel of honor.' This new self-identity was an important step toward their acceptance by society at large.

The true wandering minstrel in the later Middle Ages had virtually no legal rights. In some places he could not transmit his possessions to heirs or even claim the rights to his own compositions. In a few areas special courts (called 'Curia Vigiliae' or 'Curia de Gayte') were established to deal with the minstrels, but even these probably offered little satisfaction. In the earliest comprehensive German law book, the *Sachsenspiegel*, for example, one reads that even if a minstrel won a case in court and demanded justice, he was permitted only to 'beat the shadow' of his adversary! The wandering minstrel was also excluded from the rites of the Church and so one reads a plea by the minstrels of Elsass that they should be given the holy sacrament and treated as other Christians in spite of their being instrumentalists.

In order to help overcome these prejudices, the minstrels residing in towns took a positive step in forming guilds modeled after those of the other medieval crafts. The earliest of these minstrel guilds was the *Nicolai-Brüderschaft* of Vienna, founded in 1288, which can be said to be a direct ancestor of the Vienna Philharmonic. The first guild in France was the *Confrérie de St. Julien des ménestriers*, chartered in 1321 by thirty-seven minstrels, of whom eight were women. This guild soon built its own chapel and a hospital for older members.

Such guilds not only offered the opportunity to care for the welfare of their members, but offered a framework for limiting performance opportunities in the town to its own members. This, of course, represented a further exclusion of the wandering minstrel and throughout the late Middle Ages one finds more and more civic edicts aimed at the wandering minstrel. By 1547 one finds a national law in England in which such a wandering person was limited to a residence in any town of three days, with penalties such as the branding of a 'V' on the forehead or the loss of ears! A sad end for one who contributed nine-tenths of all medieval literature!

Wind Bands in the Church

In the beginning the Christian Church was intolerant of instrumental music as a matter of security. During the period of persecution, the services were held in secrecy, an environment not conducive to instrumental music, and thus, in contrast to the rich discussion of instruments in the service in the Old Testament, one finds not a single reference in the New Testament to the use of instrumental music in the service.

As a matter of conscience, the Church objected to the participation of jongleurs as they viewed the entire class of traveling entertainers as having unworthy reputations. Even as late as the thirteenth century, Conrad of Zurich included them in a category with evil-doers and prostitutes. In addition the Church was dedicated to eliminating pagan elements in general from the lives of the faithful and thus could hardly afford the inclusion of these popular musicians.

A painted panel on the organ balcony at Abbey Eglise Saint-Pierre et Saint-Paul, Gonesse, France, dating from 1508

But the laws of the Church are sometimes difficult to keep and, judging by the stream of interdictions which begin in the eighth century, one must believe the policy of the exclusion of instrumentalists was not strictly observed.

Part of the Church's difficulty, in this regard, was a theological dilemna: Having taken a stand against instrumentalists, how does one explain the frequent references to instrumental music in the Old Testament? Most early Church writers attempted to circumvent this problem by taking these references as being mere symbols, thus Augustine's interpretation of the famous passage in Psalm 150:5, 'Praise the Lord with cymbals, praise him with loud cymbals':

> Cymbals touch each other in order to play and therefore some people compare them to our lips. But I think it better to think of God as being praised on the cymbals when someone is honored by his neighbor rather than by himself.

One of the many factors which contributed to a change in the position of the Church was the acceptance of the organ, beginning as early as the seventh century. The very sound of the organ—so much like a wind band in texture that most of the individual pipes are named for wind instruments—must have helped prepare the way psychologically for the acceptance of the 'real' wind band.

During the thirteenth century one begins to find frequent payments, or food and shelter, to minstrels for performances in the individual monasteries and priories. One attractive story says that in 1224 a Benedictine house in England received with joy two visitors assumed by their dress to be minstrels. When it was discovered that the guests were in fact visiting friars, they tossed them out! Perhaps the private enjoyment of these entertainers helped a gradual redefinition of the classification of these peoples by some Church leaders which one finds at the same time. St. Thomas Aquinas (1225–1275), for example, made the distinction that the profession of *histrio* (actor) was not in itself unlawful, only one who exercised this profession in an unfitting manner should be considered a sinner.

Certain popular traditions which were associated with the Church also demanded wind music. Funerals and dancing, for example, the latter of which was frequently done on Church property during the thirteenth century, surely included the minstrels.

Another persuasive argument for opening the doors of the Church to instrumental music must have been the quality of ceremonial music heard outside the church. The Church was in competition for the burger's awe and the early church leaders must have wondered why the devil had all the good tunes! One must remember, in this regard, that Church princes were often persons who were reared in aristocratic families and accustomed to the trappings of the court. It would be natural for them to desire that their own coronations, for example, be as impressive as those of their secular brothers. Thus when the popes began using wind bands in their coronation processions, beginning with Pope Gregory IX, in 1227, it must have signaled an acceptance for such Church related activities.

By the fourteenth century one begins to find numerous references to private wind bands maintained by archbishops and bishops in the German-speaking countries, again following the example of their secular brothers. The most complete documentation for this part of fourteenth-century Europe comes from Salzburg. Here the Archbishop Pilgrim von Puchheim (1365–1396) ruled, 'a more worldly than spiritual lord, witty, splendour-loving, enthralled by the arts.' His villa, called the Freudensaal, was dedicated to poetry, music, and conversation and was one of the most important salons in Europe. He maintained 'trumetterey' in addition to other instruments. His resident composer, the famous Hermann, Monk of Salzburg (ca. 1350–1410, the first poet-musician to write in German), has composed two- and three-part wind ensemble pieces, labeled, '*ist gut zu blasen*.' These compositions are among the very earliest of all extant wind ensemble works.

A sculpture from the cloister of the Eglise Santa Maria La Real Sasamon, Burgos, Spain, thirteenth century

Whenever a great Church council was held, these bishops took their private wind bands with them for, again following the secular model, these bands were a kind of aural coat of arms. Eyewitness reports of the Council of Constance, 1414–1418, for example, mention hundreds of these wind players accompanying the Church officials. Even the Pope arrived with a shawm and trombone band, although they may have been hired just for this appearance as they were reported to have played in 'wild discord.'

Another step toward acceptance of wind bands in the actual church service was the employment of musicians in official church processions through the town streets, as for example those of the festivals of Corpus Christi or of the Virgin Mary.

The appearance of wind bands in any sort of service inside the church no doubt began with the private wind bands of nobles accompanying them in their family ceremonies, such as weddings. When one reads that during the marriage ceremony of Charles the Bold, with Margaret of York, in 1468, an ensemble of shawms and trombones performed a motet and a chanson, it is clear that a new attitude on the part of the church is now established.

Another appearance by wind bands inside the church, if not a religious service, was their involvement in the medieval church dramas, known as 'mystery' and 'miracle' plays. These events usually began with a trumpet fanfare followed by a parade with wind band and actors to the church building. The play itself often began with three fanfares, but the dramatic structure itself always included specific associations: recorders with shepherds, percussion with Hell, and wind bands with aristocrats, etc. A depiction of the last judgement seems also to have always used wind bands and it has been suggested that there was a connection with breath as a symbol of life (Genesis) and the resurrection (Kings II).

All of these influences, together with the frequent availability of the wind bands, did eventually lead to their acceptance in the service itself. This seems to have become an accepted practice by the fifteenth century, certainly in the case of the special feast days. In the Low Countries it became a custom for the wind band to play the first Mass read by each new priest. But there is evidence which suggests that wind bands were used on a more regular basis for accompanying the singers in polyphonic music, as is clearly stated by Tinctoris, in *De Inventione et Usu Musicae*, with regard to the Cathedral at Chartres. Some authorities date this practice even as early as the polyphonic music of the thirteenth century.

It was this regular use of the wind band in the service during the fifteenth century which set the stage for the extraordinary wind music composed for the church in Italy during the sixteenth century. For the moment, however, the fifteenth-century parishioner could finally fully appreciate Psalm 98:

> With trumpets and the sound of the horn
> Make a joyful noise before the King, the Lord!

3 *Civic Wind Bands*

THERE IS RATHER SUBSTANTIAL DOCUMENTATION for real civic wind bands in medieval Western Europe dating from about the twelfth century, but this may only be the point by which such documentation begins to survive. Given the similarity of the functions of the later medieval civic musicians with those of the ancient civilizations, it would seem logical to assume that in some areas, in Italy, for example, these traditions had in fact continued throughout that long period for which no civic records survive.

By the later Middle Ages these civic wind band functions seem nearly the same throughout Europe. First, and foremost, was the watchman-musician who looked over the town from a tower (Frankfurt had one hundred and forty such towers in the thirteenth century) built for this purpose. In a medieval town without light, during the night there was genuine fear for human predators and rouges, but especially for fire—which could destroy the entire town. It is thought that the watchmen at first used bells to warn the sleeping citizens, but after the twelfth century one finds musicians instead, for they could produce a much more detailed musical-signal than a mere bell-ringer. They soon took on broader duties such as playing regular fanfares to announce the time (since one could not see the clock in the dark) and playing 'aubades' to warn lovers of the approach of dawn. In English these musical watchmen were called 'waits,' which can perhaps be traced to the Anglo-Saxon, 'Wacian,' or the old German, 'wahta.'

As paid civic employees, these musicians were soon called upon to supply other important civic duties, including music for official banquets, accompanying the town announcer, playing as prisoners were paraded through the streets to the whipping post or for prostitutes to their public flogging, or for civic entertainments such as carnivals. These musicians could also be hired by individual citizens to help in their weddings or to celebrate their graduation from the university.

By the fifteenth century these civic bands had evolved into ensembles of shawms and slide-trumpets or trombones and had begun to play regular public concerts. These concerts were

Opposite page: Heinrich Aldegraver (1502–1555), Crumhorn players

not only the first in the modern use of the word, but perhaps one might even think of them as the beginning of 'art music,' in the sense that it was music to be listened to with no other functional purpose.

The documentation, for the Middle Ages, is of course incomplete, but the writer hopes that the following examples will, taken as a whole, serve to suggest the nature of these early civic bands.

Italy

One of the earliest references to Italian civic music is of an institution which would exist in that country until the seventeenth century, the *carroccio*. In its earliest mention, in the eleventh century in Milan, it was a wagon, used for field Masses, large enough for a priest, the civic flag, and eight civic trumpeters. In times of peace the *carroccio* became a feature of civic parades, such as the one in 1268 carrying shawms, percussion and a trumpet which welcomed the Queen of Sicily to Milan.

Most Italian towns seems to have had only these civic trumpeters until the fourteenth century. It is interesting to read a document, dated 1232, from Florence, which reveals that these musicians had already two official uniforms, one for summer and another for winter. In Siena, a document of 1262 also speaks of uniforms, housing, and a monthly salary based on the amount of performance.

A modern resconstruction of the Carroccio, in the course of the historic parade of 2007

By the fourteenth century one finds a much more extensive tradition. In Florence there were now three separate civic ensembles, a three-member shawm band (*pifferi*) which played daily at the city hall, a six-member trumpet ensemble (*trombetti*), and an ensemble called *trombadori*. In Bologna, in 1336, the civic shawms gave their first performance of the day at 3:00 AM, reflecting the fact that medieval life was closely timed to the available daylight. Even the smallest of towns valued such music, thus one finds a document from Treviso, dated 1395, relative to the purchase of a new trumpet, which mentions, 'for the presence of artists increases the honor of the whole community.'

During the fifteenth century many of the civic bands are known by the name, '*Concerti*,' a tradition they would maintain until the Classic Period. In fifteenth-century Florence

The Pifferari playing before the Virgin, Rome, unknown artist

one now finds a larger ensemble of three shawms and two trombones, whose obligations included performing concerts each Sunday at the city hall. Beginning with the employment of a German-speaking shawmist in 1401, a strong preference for foreign musicians now characterizes this ensemble. In fact, the trombonists, now members of the pifferi ensemble, were German-speaking during the entire fifteenth century. One of these, Master Augustine of Augsburg, who served in Florence from 1489 to 1493, may have been the same person who appears later in the wind band of Maximilian I.

'Wedding,' attributed to Giovanni di Ser Giovanni (1406-1486). The ensemble consists of a trombone and three shawms.

Documentation for similar ensembles, and similar concerts, can be found in Siena, Lucca, Perugia, and Turin (where one reads of regular hour-long concerts). Among the surviving iconography of these civic bands is Bellini's famous *Procession in Plazza S. Marco* (1496), where one sees a ten-member band of trumpets, shawms, and sackbuts, in uniform, parading through Venice.

Detail of band members from the middle left of Gentile Bellini's 'Processione della Vera Croce a Piazza San Marco a Venezia', 1496

During the fifteenth century in Italy the civic wind band was experiencing a wide expansion of duties, including playing for the formal civic banquets, for the civic carnival, for horse races and archery contests, for private weddings and even for students for parades to celebrate their achieving the doctorate degree.

England

In England the civic wind bands were called 'waits' after their performance as civic watch-musicians employed for security. Indeed the earliest extant document on this subject in England, an order by Henry III, warns of 'a full remedy of enormities in the night.'

By the fourteenth century one finds references to a number of individual civic bands and in London there were also wind bands hired by individual guilds to represent them in the larger civic celebrations. An extant document of 1391, for example, indicates the Goldsmith Company (guild) even maintained its own collection of instruments.

During the fifteenth century there seems to have been six-member civic bands in nearly all towns of any size. These bands each had their own distinctive uniforms, some of which can still be seen today in British museums. These bands seem highly organized, each with an official leader called 'chief,' or 'headman,' and paid from tax funds. No doubt the pay was small, although one near-contemporary remarked, 'Observe that in those dayes they payd there mynstrells better than thyre preistes.'

As in Italy, during the fifteenth century the civic wind bands in England began to perform a wide variety of duties. Among these duties were their service as substitute actors, as we see in a 1483 Shrewsbury payment, 'For the livery of the Common histriones called the waytes of the town.'

The Low Countries

If the reader will remember the importance of the Burgundian lands in the political affairs of Europe during this time, he will not be surprised to discover a very highly developed tradition of civic institutions as well, including civic wind bands (called *stad pijpers* or *scalmeyers*, after their basic instrument, the shawm).

By the fifteenth century the average size was a four-member band of two shawms, bombard or tenor shawm, and sackbut (called *tromper*, often mistranslated as 'trumpet'). Occasionally one reads of more extensive organizations, such as the one under contract in Ghent in 1430 which consisted of no fewer than sixteen sackbuts, three trumpets, and eighteen shawms!

In addition to performing the usual watch duty, civic fairs, etc., a special obligation in the Low Countries was the annual parade, part civic and part religious, called the *Ommegang*. These were great events in the life of the towns and often one reads of numerous visiting bands participating. For example the *Ommegang* of 1405 in Termonde had seventeen visiting bands totaling sixty musicians. In Mechlin in 1414 there were twenty-four trumpeters and fifty-eight shawm players and in 1418 no fewer than 215 visiting musicians.

Eyewitness reports of concerts by these civic bands often supply clues to their repertoire. First, the accounts nearly always make a distinction between the trumpets, who 'blew' (*gheblasen*) and the shawms, who 'played' (*ghespeelt*). An interesting report of the Mechlin band performing in the market place, during the fifteenth century, speaks of Overtures (*overijssche*), although more frequently one finds references to transcribed vocal polyphony, as in the example of the Brussels civic wind band performing 'various chansons' during a banquet in 1495. A more detailed example of the latter is found in an actual contract of the Bruges band, in reference to their public concerts:

> Each of them are obligated to play at the front of the old hall at the customary place on all Sundays and Holy Days at 11:00 before noon and at 6:00 in the evening … ; they are to play two chansons (*liedekens*) or motets (*moteten*) at each performance; each performer is to appear in uniform and sign the work book.

Another document, from 1484–1485, mentions that the city fathers paid one of the priests of the cathedral to compose motets specifically to be played by the Bruges town band.

France

Rather little information is extant regarding civic wind music in individual towns in France before the sixteenth century, but what there is suggests the same kinds of activity as in the other countries. One reads of watch music during the fourteenth century in Marseilles and Paris, where an edict of 1372 makes 'unofficial' trumpet playing after the curfew hour a crime. A contract from Lille, in 1480, suggests performances from the town tower everyday at morning and evening 'for the honor

A May-Day cavalacde near the town of Riom from 'Les Très Riches Heures du duc de Berry,' 1410

of the city,' indicating a more musical approach perhaps. One wealthy citizen in Paris, in 1418, is described as walking the streets with a private 'watch' band before him to frighten potential muggers. There are also the usual accounts of civic bands, or trumpet ensembles, playing in processions, for the town crier, or to welcome visiting nobles.

Of particular interest is the extant by-laws of the first civic minstrel guild in Paris, the *Confrérie de St. Julien* founded 14 September 1321. This document speaks of 'the science and music of minstrelsy,' thereby implying an even older tradition. Much of this document deals with the ethics of playing contracts: one may not leave an engagement to take another until the first one is finished; once one is contracted to play a particular job, one may not have another minstrel take his place—unless one is ill or in prison; and if one is hired to play for a wedding, one can not—on the side—also contract to be the head cook or to supply food, nor deprive any third person of their commission.

There were some restrictions on advertizing: one may not walk through the streets of Paris advertizing his availability, rather potential customers should be directed to the guild headquarters. This was perhaps aimed more at the control of visiting, foreign minstrels than toward the guild members themselves.

The by-laws also discuss the subject of apprenticeship. An apprentice may not accept a performance without his master's knowledge and the apprentice who is caught playing in a tavern is expelled.

These statutes were extended several times to reflect the changing profession. A new statute in 1372 exempts minstrels from having to play 'serenades' at night, unless they were inside, in order to protect the musicians from robbers. In 1395 a statute allows singers ('mouth-minstrels') to join the guild, but forbids them from singing songs which satirize the pope, king, or any of the great men of France, under penalty of prison with bread and water!

Further new statutes in 1407 go into more detail regarding the control over new members, in particular the apprentices. A young candidate had to go to the home of one of the members, 'masters,' to sign a formal contract and the apprentice program, which in theory lasted six years, concluded with the performance of a 'chef-d'oeuvre.'

The leader of the guild was called the 'king,' as was often the case on the continent. The title itself can only be understood in the sociological perspective of this feudal and monarchial era. Moreover, in some ways the leader exercised powers like a real king: he had the right to judge without appeal, he was the last resort in all that concerned the exercise of the craft, and he levied fines for offenses against the laws of the guild and controlled the apprentice program.

The Nuremburg Town Band, a mural by Durer in the Town Hall, ca. 1500

The German-Speaking Countries

Extant documentation suggests that civic wind bands, known as *Stadtpfeifers*, in this area were common by the thirteenth century and references from both Hamburg and Breslau suggest the four-man band was typical. Guilds were established during this century in Vienna and Lübeck. One formed in Danzig, in the fourteenth century, defined the privileges for the members, established a seven-year apprenticeship program, and permitted itinerant minstrels to remain in town only two weeks. The leaders of these guilds were called 'king,' or '*spilgraf*.'

By 1303 Bremen and Brandenburg had six- and eight-member civic wind bands, but the more typical ones were apparently not yet so large.

During the fifteenth century the instrumentation for the four-member band was three shawms with sackbut or slide-trumpet. These bands appear in many towns and some wealthy cities again had larger bands of up to nine players.

The duties of these German civic musicians also included the traditional watch duty. A civic ordinance of 1452 in Köln states that the watch musician at the outbreak of fire must first play his trumpet and then ring the fire bell. During the night he was required to perform hourly and warned to stay awake. In Weissenfels, in 1483, the tower musicians were to perform every hour during the day, every fifteen minutes during the night, and 'Abblasen' at seven or eight o'clock in the morning, at eleven o'clock, and at eight or nine o'clock in the evening. This Abblasen, usually the playing of chorales or other spiritual music, is the tradition one reads so much about during the sixteenth and seventeenth centuries in Germany. The 'Sunday concert,' which was so common in the other countries is mentioned in a fifteenth-century document from Basel. From the repertoire of the Nuremberg civic wind band we have a very important collection of their music from ca. 1490 known as the *Lochamer Liederbuch*.

Here as well, the civic musicians earned extra pay by playing for private weddings. This was apparently an important status symbol for the bridegroom in early times, for one reads of the city limiting the number of musicians one may use to six during the twelfth century in Mulhouse, to eight in 1303 in Bremen, and in Munich in 1322 a regulation limits the number to eight for wealthy citizens, to four for the less affluent, and to two for the poor. A regulation in Köln, in 1439, states that on the evening before the wedding one may hire no more than four musicians and they must be paid one Mark each. On the wedding day itself, again the limit is four musicians, but now they must be paid two Marks for a whole day and one Mark for a half-day. No musician should accept more than one wedding per day.

There is little documentation before the sixteenth century to reveal the nature of the fines assessed against those *Stadtpfeifers* who broke the municipal statutes governing their professional lives. For the serious offender, perhaps the musician was subjected to something similar to the device which one can see today in the torture tower (Folter-tor) in Rothenburg-on-the-Tauber. It has a heavy iron collar which was fixed to the poor wretch's neck and to this collar was attached an iron imitation of a musical instrument with a mouthpiece which fits just under the chin. The bad musician's fingers were held down over six finger holes by means of a metal bar, which fastens down tightly. Probably he was then chained to a post in a public square!

The Nuremberg Stadtpfeifers ca. 1449, playing for a dance by the butchers' guild at their annual Schembart Carnival.

4 *Court Wind Bands*

THE ART OF THE WIND BAND reaches a great climax in the aristocratic life of the fifteenth century, both in its artistic achievements and in its importance to society in a more functional way. The roots of this climax can be traced partly to the enthusiasm for instrumental music gained from the experiences of the crusades and the rapid development of organized instrumental music in the towns. Mostly, however, it was probably due to the high level of achievement of the final stage of the wind instrument minstrel. By the fifteenth century the shawm and sackbut band is frequently described by eyewitnesses as a very proficient and musical ensemble. For the most part during this century, the professional instrumental musician played a wind instrument, the strings were still the instrument of the amateur and the itinerant musician (hence the frequent description of the 'beer fiddler').

What do we know of fifteenth-century court instrumental music? To begin with, one must be very cautious of poetic literature of the fourteenth and fifteenth century, and to some degree iconography, for poets and artists both, perhaps as a demonstration of skill and knowledge, tended to portray one of each instrument known to them. A typical example is the Scottish, *Buke of the Howlate*.

> All thus our lade thai lovit, with lyking and lysh,
> Menstralis and musicianis, mo than I mene may.
> The psaltery, the sytholis, the soft sytharist,
> The croude and monycordis, the gittyrnis gay;
> The rote, and the recordour, the rivupe, the rist,
> The trumpe and the talburn, the tympane but tray;
> The lilt pype and the lute, the fydill in fist,
> The dulset, the dulsacordis, the schalme of assay;
> The amyable organis usit full oft;
> Claryonis lowde knellis,
> Portatius and bellis,
> Cympaclanis in the cellis,
> That sound is so soft.

Opposite page: The indoor wind band from the court of Maximilian I

Hence one can can gain the mistaken impression that the medieval ensemble was a large one consisting of one of each kind of instrument. But literature is not history and the historical record reveals a clear organizational principle of court music, a distinction between the 'loud' ensemble (*haut*, *stark*, or *alta*) and the 'soft' ensemble (*bas*, *bajo*, or *still*).

The 'loud' band was always a pure wind band, consisting usually of shawms and sackbuts, but sometimes with trumpets, bagpipes, and percussion. This ensemble is accurately identified by Johannes Tinctoris, in his treatise, *De Inventione et Usu Musicae* (ca. 1487).

> For the lowest contratenor parts, and often for any contratenor parts, to the shawm players (tibicines) one adds trumpet players (tubicines) who play very harmoniously upon the type of instrument which is called trompone [sic] in Italy, *sacquebouts* in France. Together it is called *alta*.

The 'soft' ensemble most often consisted of families of flutes or recorders, with lute-types and keyboards. Contrary to the impression often given by later musicologists that 'table music' meant wind music, in earlier periods it was in fact often the 'soft' ensemble which played for private aristocratic dinners. One contemporary even suggested that this was because 'soft' music helped digestion!

> Encore est chose convenable que tu aies des ménestreux a bas instrumens pour aucune recreations, faisant digestion de ta personne royale.

In practice the choice was dictated by function, not aesthetics: loud music for large palace rooms and the out-of-doors and soft music for private use in smaller palace rooms.

It was for performance in fifteenth-century palace rooms that we have today an extant vast repertoire of multi-part chansons and motets. Frequently this music survives in four-parts with text in only some voices and with some voices without text. Further, the music given in the voices without text usually appears quite different, with entirely different rhythmic values, than the music of the voices which have text. A number of works have the titles of well-known chansons but have no text at all in any voice.

Earlier music historians knew there was no tradition for string instruments playing these voices with 'missing' text, but at the same time their ignorance of early wind band practice prevented them from believing that these text-less voices could have been played in the palace by wind instruments. Consequently, in earlier publications, scholars went to great lengths to 'explain' the voices with missing text. Some contended that the lower text-less voices were 'vocalized' by some of the singers, or perhaps they adapted the text to these voices. In the case of the hundreds of multi-part chansons with no text at all in any voice some scholars professed to believe that the singers must have known the texts by heart. But in the case of the Petrucci volumes alone this would mean all the singers knowing by memory hundreds of texts in several languages!

Such explanations are, of course, quite unreasonable and today it is generally accepted that these text-less voices were performed by wind instruments and many recent recordings reflect this. Consequently we are beginning to understand that there is a vast 'lost' repertoire of fifteenth- and sixteenth-century wind music performed before the highest levels of society. But we hasten to add that the evidence was always there for the objective historian to see. The French poet, Martin le Franc (d. 1461), for example, in his *Champion* wrote of this kind of music being performed by both 'loud' and 'soft' combinations of wind instruments.

> But I'm told by those who know
> with so fine a melody
> few of them could discant
> as Binchois and Dufay.
> For these men a newer way have found
> in music loud and soft
> of making lively concordance
> through feint, pause, and nuance

During the fifteenth century, one occasion where one always heard the pure wind band was the formal, aristocratic dance, as is accurately reflected in the anonymous poem, *Echecs amoureux* (ca. 1375).

> Whenever that they were fain to dance
> And frolic, gathered in a crowd,
> The dancers called for music loud—
> It was this that always pleased them best,
> And ever added to their zest.

The most important of these dances was the basse-dance and it was in part the form of the dance itself which made the shawms and slide-trumpet or sackbut the ideal source of music. The 'basse-dance' was actually a general term representing a number of different dances, each differing in tempo, meter, and in the actual dance steps. It was based on known melodies, notated only in whole notes. When the dance leader would call for a specific form of the basse-dance it was the slide-trumpet player who played the melody, in slow moving notes cast in the appropriate meter and rhythms. The two or three shawms who constituted the rest of the ensemble engaged in rapid figuration over the melody. Thus, while we have many descriptions of this rich polyphonic repertoire, little actual music (beyond the slide-trumpet melodies) has survived, because, being improvised, there was never a need to notate it.

Basse-dance at the court of Burgundy

Other court functions also were reserved for the wind band, among these were welcoming ceremonies and outdoor entertainments such as tournaments, jousts, and hunting. Needless to say, these same players provided the music for the battle field. But also the indoor entertainments which were held in large rooms also used the wind band, including masquerades and mummer's plays and above all the formal banquet. The musical ritual for the banquet included special music to announce the time for the event was at hand, special music to remind the guests to wash their hands, special music to accompany each course of food brought into the hall, and dinner music which often alternated with vocalists.

Thus the wind band had a social role to play in most of the activities of the noble's day and when he traveled it became an aural coat of arms. It is easy to see, therefore, why not only nobles employed such wind bands, but even the Church bishops found them basic to their private needs.

England

The association between English aristocracy and wind instruments can be documented back to the primitive trumpet-prototypes, known as *buccine*, of the early Middle Ages, the 'war-horn' of the eighth-century *Beowulf* for instance. But even with the first of the modern kings, William the Conqueror, one finds descriptions of these instruments which seem to imply a higher level of musical organization. An account of his siege of Rochester in 1088, for example, implies recognizable literature.

> When Bishop Eudes was forced to surrender, he obtained the king's permission to quit the city with all arms and horses. Not satisfied with this, he further endeavoured to seek the favour, that the king's military music should not sound their triumphant fanfares during the capitulation.

It was during the reign of his son, William 'the Red' (1087–1100) that the English made their first crusade (1096–1099) and encountered for the first time the far wider variety of instruments, and higher organization, of the peoples of the East. According to contemporary Arabic historians, the instruments they heard were: metal trumpets (*anāfir*, which is also the cognate of 'fanfare'), horns (*būgāt*), shawms (*zumūr*), small timpani (*kūsāt*), drums (*tubūl*), and cymbals (*kāsāt*). These bands were organized both with respect to the field function and according to the rank of the officer. They gave precise signals for troop movement, gave heart to their own troops, and through their size and noise tried (apparently very successfully) to scare the enemy!

> They came on with irresistible charge, on horses swifter than eagles, and urged on like lightening to attack our men; and as they advanced, they raised a cloud of dust, so that the sky was darkened. In front came certain of their admirals, as it was their duty, with clarions and trumpets; some had horns, others had pipes and timbrels, gongs, cymbals, and other instruments, producing a horrible noise and clamour. The earth vibrated from the loud and discordant sounds, so that the crash of thunder could not be heard amidst the tumultuous noise of horns and trumpets. They did this to excite their spirit and courage, for the more violent the clamour became, the more bold were they for the fray.

The West soon began to adapt these ideas and by the Third Crusade (1189–1192), under Richard I, 'Coeur de Lion,' an accompanying scribe speaks of Richard's armies now having added the shawms, some percussion, and the metal trumpet (called *trumpae*, the first cognate form of the modern word). Not only this, but the organization of his military music was now far more advanced.

> It had been resolved by common consent that the sounding of six trumpets in three different parts of the army should be a signal for a charge, viz., two in front, two in the rear and two in the middle, to distinguish the sounds from those of the Saracens, and to mark the distance of each.
>
> ...
>
> Meanwhile the trumpets blew, and their sounds being harmoniously blended, there arose a kind of discordant concord of notes, whilst the sameness of the sounds being continued, the one followed the other in mutual succession, and the notes which had been lowered were again resounded.

These have been descriptions of Richard's trumpets as used with the land forces, but the organization of his fleet also took into account the need for trumpet signals. An eyewitness explains that the fleet was arranged in a great pyramid, with three ships in the first row, thirteen in the second, fourteen in the third, twenty in the fourth, thirty in the fifth, forty in the sixth, and sixty in the seventh.

> Between the ships and their ranks there was such care in the spacing of the fleet that from one rank to another the sound of a trumpet could be heard, and from one ship to another (in the same rank) the voice of a man.

By the fourteenth century one begins to find regular court musicians who appear to be performers of other wind instruments. Edward I (1272–1307) seems to have employed minstrels only as the occasion demanded (notably four hundred and twenty-six for his daughter's marriage!), but Edward II (1307–1327) employed two regular minstrels, probably shawmists, in addition to two trumpeters.

> There shalbe ij trompeters & two other minstrels, & sometimes more & sometimes lesse, who shall play before the Kinge when it shal please him. Thei shal eate in the chamber or in the hal as thei shalbe commaunded; thei shal have wages & robes each according to his estate at the discretion of the steward & thresorer.

This gentle king banned football in 1314 because it was so violent and once ordered a stop to the practice of torture in the examination of suspects or witnesses, but was immediately reprimanded by Pope Clement V:

> We hear that you forbid torture as contrary to the laws of your land. But no state law can override canon law, our law. Therefore I command you at once to submit those men to torture!

With Edward III (1327–1377) a regular five-member shawm ensemble (called 'pipers') appears in his Household Ordinance of 1348, together with five trumpets, two Clarions, one each of citolers, nakerers, fidelers, and taberett players, and three wait musicians. It was such 'pipers,' or shawms who accompanied the dance described in an account of a mumming given in honor of the young Richard II in 1377.

> And then ye prince caused to bring ye wyne and they dronk with great joye, commanding ye minstrels to play and ye trompets began to sound and other instruments to pipe etc. And ye prince and ye lordes dansed on ye one syde, and ye mummers on ye other a great while.

One sees this verb 'to pipe' in reference to shawms again in an extraordinary document of Edward IV (1461–1483) which gives our best picture of these early court bands in England.

> Mynstrelles, xiii, whereof one is verger, that directeth them all in festivall dayes to theyre stations, to bloweings and pipynges, to suche offices as must be warned to prepare for the king and his houshold at metes and soupers, to be the more readie in all servyces; and all these sitting in the hall togyder; whereof sume use trumpettes, sume shalmuse and small pipes, and sume as strengemen (strangers?), comyng to this courte at five festes of the yere, and then to take theyre wages of houshold after iiijd ob. a day, if they be present in courte, and then they to avoyde the next day fter the festes be done. Besides eche of them anothyr reward yerely, taking of the king in the resceyte of the chekker, and clothing wynter and somer, or xxs. a piece, and lyverey in courte, at evyn amonges them all, iiij gallons ale; and for wynter season, iij candels wax, vj candells peris', iiij talwood, and sufficiaunt logging by the herberger, for them and theyre horses, nygh to the courte. Also havyng into courte ij servauntes honest, to beare theyre trumpettes, pipes, and other instrumentes, and a torche for wynter nyghts, whyles they blowe to souper, and other revelles, delyvered at the chaundrey; and allway ij of these persons to continue in courte in wages, beyng present to warne at the kinge's rydinges, when he goeth to horse-backe, as ofte as it shall require, and by theyre blowinges the houshold meny may follw in the countries. And if any of these two minstrelles be sicke in courte, he taketh ij loves, one messe of grete mete, one gallon ale. They have no part of any rewardes gevyn to the houshold. And if it please the kinge to have ij strenge Minstrelles to contynue in like wise. The Kinge wull not for his worshipp that his Minstrelles be too presumptuous, nor too familier to aske any rewardes of the lordes of his londe, remembring De Henrico secundo imperatore (1002–1024) qui omnes Ioculatores suos et Armaturos monuerit, ut nullus eorum in eius nomine vel dummono steterint in sericio suo nihil ab aliquo in regno suo deberent petere donandum; sed quod ipsi domini donatores pro Regis amore citius pauperibus erogarent.

Henry V (1413–1422) was himself a musician and it is no surprise that he supported musicians when possible. Following the signing of a treaty in 1420, for example, he ordered that every visiting musician participating in the celebration should be given a gold coin. No doubt it is an exaggeration, but one eyewitness reported that musicians appeared 'by the hundreds and thousands.' In his own court he maintained eighteen minstrels and during the lulls in his battles he arranged to have an ensemble of eight or ten musicians perform an hour-long concert at sunrise and sunset every day.

By the end of the fifteenth century in England one finds a large number of permanent instrumentalists, organized into the kinds of separate ensembles traditional in the sixteenth century. The funeral of Henry VII (1485–1509) included a four-man sackbut and shawm ensemble, an ensemble of persons (known to be shawm players) called 'The Mynstrells,' a nine-member ensemble called the 'kyng's trompytts,' another six-member trumpet group, with five additional minstrels and three percussionists.

France

So traditional were some of the duties of aristocratic wind players that one finds a ninth-century account of food being served to the music of clarions and minstrels, for the wedding of Louis I (814–840), which varies little from similar accounts in the fifteenth century.

It was during the reign of Louis IX, 'Saint Louis' (1226–1270), that the most important French participation in the crusades took place and once again the instruments of the East made a strong impression.

It is difficult to trace the development of French court music during the fourteenth century, as a series of kings changed rapidly and few records seem to be extant. Judging by the late fourteenth-century poetry, however, it would seem that there was an abundant musical life in the court.

There is a bit more contemporary description and iconography for the first king of the fifteenth century, Charles VI (1380–1422). An account of one of his banquets in 1393 speaks of 'soft' background music, food served with trumpet fanfares, and a special performance by the singers of the royal chapel together with the 'wind minstrels,' who undoubtedly were his own wind band.

Accounts from the reigns of the final three kings of the fifteenth century, Charles VII, Louis XI, and Charles VIII, speak mostly of ceremonial trumpets. During the sixteenth and seventeenth centuries such accounts always include the timpani, an instrument unknown in the West until the late fifteenth century. They were seen for the first time in Paris in 1457, accompanying envoys of King Ludislaus of Hungary visiting Charles VII. An eyewitness exclaimed,

> One had never before seen drums like big kettles, carried on horseback.

The last of these kings, Charles VIII, after reading a chivalric romance, decided to make a crusade in 1494. He progressed no further than Milan, but his exposure to the ideals of the Renaissance there helped set the stage for a dramatic improvement in the arts in France early in the sixteenth century.

Spain

Spain was not yet a unified nation during the Middle Ages, consisting of separate kingdoms, the most important of which were Aragon and Castile.

The Aragon kings of the twelfth century, such as Pedro III (1276–1285) maintained only the trumpet and percussion players for ceremonial use common to this period. Under Jaime II (1291–1327) a wider range of instrumentalists are employed and one finds payments to visiting minstrels from throughout Western Europe.

The greatest musical court of the Aragon kings belonged to Juan I (1350-1396), who not only also entertained minstrels from many nations but hired his own wind band members from those countries where this tradition was more established. A document of 1388 indicates that his five-member shawm band included players from Flanders, France, and Germany.

Sancho IV (1284–1295) maintained a very large court which included minstrels, trumpeters, and players of Moorish drums. There are some interesting insights from this period found in an encyclopedia on theology, *Libre de contemplacio en Deu* (ca. 1272) by Ramon Lull. First, in a list of the social standing of the various professions, one can see how the musician ranked in the eyes of his thirteenth-century contemporaries. The list begins with the pope (God's representative on earth), followed by kings, knights, pilgrims, judges, lawyers, doctors, merchants, seamen, minstrels, shepherds, painters, farm laborers, and artisans. Yet he finds that, while the poor shiver in rags outside the palace door, the minstrels were clothed in royal clothing, banquet with kings, and are loaded with gold and silver. He observed that no king ruled as he should, few judges were not corrupted by gold, and few minstrels would not lie for money!

It is apparent that during the fifteenth century Castile enjoyed the extravagent court life found elsewhere on the continent. There is a wonderful glimpse of this in an account of the bride to Enrique IV (1425–1474) as she made her journey to the court city of Valladolid. En route she was entertained by the Count of Haro, who welcomed her with his wind band and gave her a great banquet with his minstrels playing throughout. Determined that no visiter should accrue any debt during these festivities, the count set up a fountain which gushed a stream of pure silver available to anyone.

All this paled in comparison, however, to the events of the fourth day of the bride's visit. The count had a large field near the palace turned into a kind of fifteenth-century Disneyland, which included a transplanted forest—together with puzzled dear, boars, and bears—and a man-made lake stocked with fish. Behind this lake a huge building of twenty levels was created, all carpeted with green sod. Here the guests took their places on the various levels to enjoy a banquet, while watching hunters kill the helpless game in the artificial forest and anglers pull fish out of the lake. After the meal, the party danced until breakfast, where each lady found a gold ring set with jewels by her plate. The count also distributed two great sacks of coins among the exhausted minstrels.

If this was not interesting enough for the court wind player, there was still another duty in Castile—the performance of a fanfare the moment when a royal bride ceased to be a virgin. In the case of Enrique IV, the trumpets took their places by the door of the bridal chamber, waiting for word from one of the three notaries who were standing inside by the bed. The trumpets never played and history has since named Henry, 'the impotent.'

The most important of the Castile rulers were Fernando V (1474–1516) and Dona Isabel (1474–1504), the patrons of Columbus. Isabella, according to a document of 1498, maintained a true wind band, together with three organists and five trumpeters. Ferdinand also had a wind band (*ministrils alta*) which he gradually increased in size from six in 1491 to eleven in 1511.

Italy

During the period between the fall of the Roman Empire and the eleventh century there are few extant records to help us understand the connections between our ancient and modern civilizations. Life went on, of course, and it may be that there was considerable musical activity during the entire period. One reads, for example, of the Greek Exarch, Longinus, being welcomed in Venice in 568 AD by 'bells, flutes, and other instruments.'

It seems clear that from the time the popes began to use wind bands to celebrate their coronations, from the thirteenth century, a rapid development in aristrocratic instrumental music occurred. By the fifteenth century even the popes had private wind bands and ceremonial percussionists, called '*i Musici Capitolini e i tamburini del Popolo Romano.*' Leading Cardinals, as well, employed shawm bands for their banquets and dances in their palaces.

In Ferrara, the court wind band tradition began with the Marquis Niccolo III (1393–1441) who maintained a shawm band and trumpet choir. In 1426 Philip the Good, of Burgundy, made him a present of instruments for his wind band, consisting of '2 quatre grans instrumens de menestrelz (probably bombards), quatre douchaines et quatre fleutes,' all garnished with leather and in cases.

The next ruler, now the Duke of Ferrara, Borso d'Este (1450–1471), maintained this shawm band (called '*piffari*') and we can see how important it was through an extant letter by his wife. Earlier she had received a letter from Bianca Maria Sforza requesting permission to borrow the wind band for a forthcoming wedding, a request which she could not honor.

> Because the wedding will occur in April, which coincides with our own festival in honor of San Zorzo, the piffari are needed, indeed most needed to help honor our Saint. If the illustrious Bianca Maria Sforza would therefore accept our excuse we would be most content and if there are any other possibilities of repaying the declined favor we would be most happy.

Detail of the court wind band (bottom right) from the Borso Bible, 1460

The brother and successor to Borso, Ercole I (1471–1505), was one of the great patrons of art in fifteenth-century Italy (and two of his daughters, Isabella and Beatrice d'Este, were among the most extraordinary women of the Middle Ages). His musical establishment was much larger, as it included a separate shawm band, a trombone ensemble, trumpet choir, and '*musici*,' who were perhaps singers. These musicians were apparently well paid, as we see when we compare the rate of pay for one of the woodwind players, Corado de Alemagna (26 Lire) with engineer-builders (26 Lire) and physicians (22 to 30 Lire).

The court in Bologna had a similar wind band and one reads of their participation in a great pageant in 1490 during which appropriate goddesses pleaded with a 'doctor of the university' as to whether Wisdom or Fortune wielded the greater influence over the affairs of men (the answer was Fortune). This wind band joined '100 trombita e 70 pifari e trombuni e chorni e flauti e tamburini e zamamele' in the celebration of the wedding of Lucrezia, daughter to Duke Ercole of Ferrara, and Annibale Bentivoglio of Bologna in 1487.

Francesco Sforza, who established the Sforza dynasty in Milan in 1450, maintained a large trumpet choir (eighteen in 1463) together with other wind players. His son, Galeazzo Maria Sforza, who ruled between 1466–1476, was given to pleasure, luxury, and the seduction of the wives of his friends and indeed was murdered by a relative of one of the wronged ladies. He took a personal interest in the recruiting of the best players from Germany and Flanders for his wind band (*piffari e tromboni et trombetti*). As with all nobles at this time, the Duke always traveled with his personal wind band and there are several extant accounts of these costs. On one occasion, in 1471, for some perceived misbehavior he had his entire wind band thrown in jail and had to borrow the wind band of the Marquis of Mantua for a journey to Florence!

The marriage celebrations of another family member, Constanze Sforza, in 1475, included the performance of the kind of large polychoral composition which one associates with the sixteenth century. An eyewitness reports that the Mass was celebrated in the cathedral with the concurrence

> of numerous organs, shawms, trumpets, and drums, accompanying two separate groups of many singers, the one alternating with the other, and there were about sixteen singers in each.

One reads of a similar performance celebrating the marriage of Bianca Maria Sforza with Maximilian I, in 1493, in a letter written by the bride's mother, Beatrice d'Este.

> When we were all in our places, the Most Reverend Archbishop of Milan entered in full vestments, with the priests in ordinary, and began to celebrate the Mass with the greatest pomp and solemnity, to the sound of trumpets, piffari, and organ-music, together with the voices of the chapel choir.

The sister to Beatrice, Isabella d'Este, was married to Francesco II Gonzaga of Mantua and developed one of the most cultured of all Italian courts. The leading modern authority on this court, Iain Fenlon, writes of the importance of the court wind band in Mantua.

> From its origins as a simple band used on ceremonial occasions, this ensemble seems to have been transformed during the period of Isabella d'Este into a highly skilled and more versatile ensemble performing more sophisticated music. Throughout the sixteenth century frequent references to the *alta cappella* confirm that it remained an important feature of court life and a central institution of court music.

In Florence, Lorenzo 'Il Magnifico' (1449–1492) also maintained both a shawm band and a trumpet choir. One reads of yet another of the arduous demands on the court wind band when, at two o'clock in the morning, Lorenzo decided to throw snow balls at the window of Marietta Strozzi. Even this required the attendance of his personal wind band!

We can not leave Italy without mentioning another citizen of Florence, Leonardo da Vinci. As everyone knows, his sketches cover virtually every facet of fifteenth-century design. Among these sketches, one discovers he also gave some thought to the chief problems of wind instrument construction of his day: the addition of diatonic notes on the trumpet and the problem of making tone holes in woodwind instruments where the human hand could reach them. In his sketches it is apparent that he was thinking in the direction of attempting to add keyboards to these instruments!

Burgundy

The Dukes of Burgundy had the constant political aim of having their titles changed from duke to king, an honor only the pope or the Holy Roman Emperor could bestow. While they never achieved this, their determination to at least live as kings helped make their courts the cultural center of Western Europe for nearly a century.

The first of these dukes, Philip the Bold (1363–1404), had a great interest in instrumental music, buying instruments on his trips, rewarding visiting minstrels, and sending his own instrumentalists to minstrel schools in Ghent (1378) and Germany (1386)—where he instructed them to buy instruments while on their trip. A famous early scribe, Froissart, heard this duke's wind band in person during a voyage he made with the duke in 1390.

> Much great beauty and pleasure to hear from the resounding trumpets and clarions, and other minstrels performing on bagpipes, shawms, and timpani.

John the Fearless (1404–1419) was a rather bad character (who made possible the sobriquet 'the Good,' by which his son was known), but he too had a large musical establishment. In addition to a trumpet choir he had a true indoor wind band, for which an order for a complete set of instruments in 1413 provides the basic instrumentation: two shawms, two bombards 'with key,' a 'contre' (a bass to the bombards) and a trumpet 'to be played with the other instruments' (in other words, a slide-trumpet).

The next duke, Philip the Good (1419–1467), was perhaps the most influential noble of the fifteenth century with respect to art and music. So elaborate were his court entertainments, that we see them imitated even by such powerful figures as Maximilian of Austria and Henry VIII of England.

He was keenly interested in music and perhaps no other aristrocrat of the fifteenth century so richly rewarded visiting minstrels. Such was his reputation in this regard that even the minstrels of the lands with whom he was at war would slip behind the lines to play for him. In so doing he constantly looked for the best players to add to his court, personally auditioned them, and, being convinced of his own expertize, usually retained them for life.

The records of his court reveal that he usually maintained a choir of five or six ceremonial trumpets and a wind band identical with that of his father. Of course when he traveled to other cities, or held important festivities, he always added to these numbers from the local civic wind bands. Thus, for example, when he celebrated the arrival of his bride, Isabel of Portugal, in 1430, one scribe reports

> more than 120 silver trumpets, plus other trumpets, minstrels, players of organ, harp and other instruments without number; the force of the music made the entire city vibrate.

One can gain a glimpse of the careful organization of his own court music in the ritual accompanying his departure on a trip. On the morning of such a trip the trumpeters would play at the duke's window to awaken him and then split up into groups to play in the streets of the city (perhaps to awaken the citizens so they could wave goodby). After returning for breakfast, they would play to have the horses made ready (an important safety measure, to accustom the horses to the noise of the instruments), and play for the assembly, etc. When the traveling party was ready, the trumpets would be joined for the trip by the '*haults instrumens*,' the wind band of shawms and bombards.

These musicians also accompanied Philip to his many battles, of course, and one of these must be mentioned. During the siege of Bouvignes, the duke had constructed an enormous wooden cat, taking an inspiration from the famous horse of the Trojan Wars. With ten pair of wheels, the great cat carried two hundred soldiers under cover. A chronicler tells us they forgot to oil the wheels of this huge cat and the subsequent 'meeowing' would have been heard for many miles, had it not been for the noise of the shouting and the duke's trumpets.

Perhaps the event of Philip's reign most often mentioned by historians was a great banquet held in 1454. This was one of several periodic gatherings of a chivalric order, called the *Toison d'Or*, created by Philip at the time of his wedding. The banquet in 1454 took on unusual significance in Philip's mind, as its purpose was to initiate a new crusade to Constantinople which had fallen to the Turks the previous year.

Philip sat under a canopy of velvet and gold, his noble guests at long tables with individual cushions embroidered with their coats of arms. The service was gold; the glassware was of crystal with jewels encrusted. In addition there were a number of specially created structures and tableaux in the hall, among them a model church with stained glass windows and a bell in its steeple and a dragon spouting fire as it flew across the room and then mysteriously disappeared. The most remarkable was a great pastry pie, large enough to contain twenty-eight musicians. Contemporaries differ in their descriptions of the music made inside the pie, due to the poor acoustics, but it would be a good guess to suppose the duke's wind band was there.

After the guests were seated, a chanson was sung by musicians from inside the model church. Several other chansons and motets were sung during the banquet, including Dufay's 'Lamentatio sanctae matris ecclesiae Constantinopolitanae.' Alternating with the vocal works were an extraordinary variety of other types of music: a performing horse, walking backwards, carrying two trumpeters wearing the duke's colors; four trumpeters in white robes played gold trumpets; and at various times a 'German cornett,' a four-part recorder performance and a pipe and tabor from inside the pie!

This was followed by Philip's public oath to to make his crusade, a procession of torch-bearers and musicians with gifts for the guests, and finally a dance. One who was present got tired and left early, just before four o'clock in the morning!

The wedding music of Philip's son, Charles the Bold, included a 'long trumpet fanfare,' a motet performed by three shawms and a slide-trumpet, and a motet and chanson performed by an ensemble of sackbuts, shawms, and bombards with 'excellent effect.'

Charles continued the wind band of his father, but his reign was short. Extraordinarily cruel even in an age inured to violence, Charles lost his realm and his life on the field of battle in 1477. As he left no male heir, the territories passed through his daughter, Mary, to her husband, Maximilian I, of the Hapsburg Empire.

The German-Speaking Countries

The greatest of the early German kings was, of course, Charlemagne (742–814 AD). Charlemagne had a strong interest in his minstrels and paid them with choice land. It is said that one jongleur, who guided Charlemagne over Mt. Cenis in 773, was given as a reward all the land over which his *tuba* (trumpet) could be heard when played from a hill.

According to one source, Charlemagne had a collection, called 'Frohliche Jagd,' of his musical hunting signals prepared, but the music is not extant. His minstrels accompanied him in battle and perhaps it was one of his battles celebrated by the later Minnesinger, Wofram von Eschenbach.

> There were sounds of busine
> And drums were thrown and beat
> A thousand drum sticks and no *krumbes*
> And the noise of 800 pusinen one heard.

The first of the German emperors for whom there is specific information relating to his wind musicians is Frederick II (1194–1250). His musical establishment seems to have been influenced by the crusades, for it included a corps of young Negro boys who served as his trumpeters and a contemporary who visited him reports being shown 'various musical instruments' which had been returned from those battles. A fragment of a document, which was lost in the last war, contained a reference to the purchase of a sackbut and is one of the earliest known references to that instrument.

According to the German scholar Johannes Reschke, by the fourteenth century there were many military bands in this area. A document of the court of Duke Albert IV in Vienna, in 1398, lists his musicians as three flutes, three shawms, trombone, two trumpets, three timpani, and a 'leyrer,' fidler, and lute player.

The first important emperor of the fifteenth century was Sigismund, an attractive man proficient in seven languages. His musical establishment was poor due to his serious financial situation—apparently the other German princes, his sole source of funds, were rather niggardly. An icon showing his arrival at the Council of Constance shows the shawm band not in his uniforms, suggesting he could only afford to hire such musicians for special purposes.

The reign of Frederick III is documented in a book written by his son, Maximilian, called the *Weisskunig*. The two hundred and fifty-one woodcuts which it contains picture all the varieties of court wind music which have been discussed above. During this period one also finds the individual dukes of Northern Germany and Denmark also maintaining private wind bands.

Maximilian I (1459–1519) is often called 'the last knight' and is indeed the last great noble of the medieval tradition. He was reared in Flanders where he came to know the art of the Van Eycks and Memling and the music of Dufay. He combined the musicians of his father with those of Burgundy to form one of the best musical establishments of the Middle Ages.

His court wind players are best documented in one of the world's richest and most unusual monuments of art, the one hundred and thirty-seven woodcuts known as the *Triumph of Maximilian I*. The procession represented by these woodcuts begins with an ensemble of four fifes and five drummers on horseback. This was the basic military band of Maximilian and an accompanying text has a fife player saying,

> I, Anthony of Dornstätt, have played my fife
> For Maximilian, great in strife,
> In many lands on countless journeys,
> In battles fierce and knightly tourneys,
> At grave times or in holiday,
> And so in this Triumph with honor I play.

(Gladly and oft my fife I blew
In proper style, with honor true,
Serving the Imperial arms
In knightly joust and war's alarms.
Always prepared, the fifer blows
Tunes gay and stern, as this Triumph shows.)

Plates 19 and 20 show Maximilian's indoor wind band, with two shawms, two crumhorns, and the trombonist, Neyschl, seated on a large wagon. Another large wind ensemble, called the 'Burgundian Fifers' (Plates 77–79) consists of ten trombones and five each of shawms, bombardons, and rauschpfeiffen.

Plates 19 and 20 showing the indoor wind band

COURT WIND BANDS 69

Plates 25 and 26 show the church music, singers with a cornett and trombone. Both the plates and the accompanying text demonstrate once again that polyphonic church music was not unaccompanied.

The Trumpets and Timpani from 'The Triumph of Maximilian'.

> The cornets and trombones we placed
> So that the choral song they graced,
> For His Imperial Majesty
> Has often in such harmony
> Taken great pleasure, and rightly so,
> As we have had good cause to know.

Plates 25 and 26

Plates 115–117 picture the royal trumpeters, twenty-five trumpets and five players of timpani, two per man, all on horse.

In addition to this iconography, there is a very interesting account by a visiting French journalist which describes Maximilian dining alone in 1492.

> His Majesty sits in a hall covered with tapestry, without another person except his court jesters. At every meal, mid-day or evening, there were 10 trumpeters and 10 other kinds. There were two large timpani of fine copper covered with ass skins and standing in two baskets. In the middle sat a man with a thick stick which he let loose in beats on (the timpani) so that the tone was in unison with the other instruments, as is used in Hungary or Turkey, it was amazing and humorous to hear.

This account reminds us that the timpani entered Western European music not as 'rhythm' instruments, but as an instrument which could supply the harmonic bass of the trumpet choir.

Finally it should be noted that for the Congress of Vienna, hosted by Maximilian in 1515, he arranged for the performance of a fanfare by forty-five trumpets, forty-five trombones, and six timpanists.

The reader may also have noticed that in the ensembles of Maximilian the new renaissance instruments are beginning to appear for the first time. Thus, Maximilian, as the 'last knight,' represent both the end of an era and the beginning of another.

COURT WIND BANDS 71

Rauschpfeifen and Shawms from 'The Triumph of Maximilian'.

PART II
The Renaissance

...oga... ... in siuito che tuttauia se opponi sma a esso
...uire il quale sara utile adogni istrumento di fiato et ch...
...to ,, coposta per sylvestro di ganassi dal fontego sona...

5 Court Wind Bands

IN GENERAL MUSIC HISTORY TEXTS THE 'RENAISSANCE' is given as beginning with the fourteenth century because of developments in harmony and notation which took place at that time. In considering the history of the wind band, however, it is the beginning of the sixteenth century when things really change and thus in this book it is only that century which we call the 'Renaissance.'

In particular, shortly after the year 1500 there were significant leaps forward in the craft of the wood worker. The availability of the lathe made possible woodwind instruments with more artistic shapes and new skills in boring made possible the making of more than one bore in a single piece of wood. This led to the possibility of making instruments which produced lower sounds, the *piece de résistance* of which was the Great Bass Rackett, with nine bores, which while only scarcely a foot in height produces sounds lower than any modern instruments. At the same time the development of alloys changed the making of brass instruments.

In the sixteenth century the making of woodwinds, in particular, became a test of the ability of the wood worker (anyone could make a chair). Wood workers everywhere in Europe began to create new wind instruments and to make the traditional ones in many different sizes. In the same way silver smiths now competed in creating silver trumpets in fancy shapes and today in Europe these instruments are often found in the silver collections rather than in the music instrument collections.

Most important was the organization of these instruments by families called 'consorts,' which replaced the old 'loud–soft' principle of the Middle Ages. The preference for consorts of the same instrument made possible a homogenous, matched ensemble sound and, with new lower members of these families, a darker ensemble sound in contrast to the more shrill, heterogeneous medieval sound. The consort principle also helped with the significant problem of intonation, for now one could obtain a matched set of instruments from the same maker.

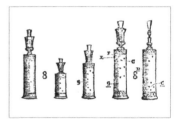

Various sizes of Racket in Michael Praetorius's 'Syntagma Musicum'

This woodcut by Johann Christoff Weigel, Abbildung der Gemein-Nützlichen Haupt-Stände (1698), shows an instrument maker working on woodwind instruments. It is possibly an image of Johann Christoph Denner in his workshop.

Opposite page: Detail from Silvestro Ganassi's 'La Fontegara' showing members of the Doge's wind band performing as a recorder consort, 1535

Variety in instrumental color, during performance, was achieved by the alternation of these consorts, a practice which explains the extremely large collections of instruments owned by many nobles during the sixteenth century.

So enthusiastically was this new consort principle adopted by nobles everywhere for their musical establishments, that one Englishman went so far as to suggest that the best equipped household would even have the dogs in its kennel organized in a consort!

> If you would have your kennels for sweetness of cry then you must compound it of some large dogs that have deep, solemn mouths ... which must as it were bear the bass in consort, than a double number of roaring and loud-ringing mouths which must bear the counter tenor, then some hollow, plain, sweet mouths which must bear the mean or middle part and so with these three parts of music you shall make your cry perfect.

Can one take this seriously? Probably not, but then one reads of this idea again in Shakespeare's *A Midsummer Night's Dream*, where 'My hounds,' says Theseus, 'are,'

> Slow in pursuit, but matcht in mouth like bells,
> Each under each. A cry more tunable
> Was never holla'd to, nor cheer'd with horn.

After mid-century this principle began to break down with the appearance of 'broken consorts,' which were often consorts consisting of several instruments of two families. This occurred due to certain inherent weaknesses in some consorts, which therefore invited substitutions. For example the trombone consort (which lacked an agile upper voice) and the cornett consort (which lacked a good bass) were combined to make one of the most popular 'broken consorts' of the sixteenth century.

String instruments begin to appear in court records by about the middle of the sixteenth century and these too were often combined with wind instruments in broken consorts. Although strings begin to appear, the wind band remained the preferred ensemble for much of the sixteenth century. This preference should be no surprise if one remembers that the renaissance mind still tended to measure every instrument against 'God's instrument,' the human voice. As Marcello Castellani points out,

> a consequence of the aesthetic ideal of the Italian Renaissance, which attributed the role of voice-imitation to instruments. This ideal was so well-rooted that even the instrumentalists were called *cantori*. It is not to be denied that Renaissance wind instruments, not so much for their tone color as the way in which the performer breathed and produced the sound, could imitate the human voice better than could the string instruments.

For many court functions the pure wind band remained the favored ensemble. Chief among these, of course, was the music for the dance, which had been so long associated with wind music. As a contemporary stated, nothing could be more natural than wind music and dancing, 'And noe number can be truer, than musick-wynd with dancinge.'

Pure wind bands are also often mentioned in reference to performances during banquets and for the *intermedii* of theatrical plays, as well as for tournaments and ceremonial needs. Wind instruments also began to be used more by the military during the sixteenth century, replacing the drums in the performance of 'signals' for troop movement.

England

The story of sixteenth-century England begins with Henry VIII (1509–1547), who among other things was also a musician. He played the flute, lute, harpsichord, sung at sight, and composed. During his reign there was a rapid accumulation of instruments in the royal collection, including nearly two hundred and fifty wind, fifty string, and a large number of keyboard instruments. This was a collection for indoor use and included among the winds were one hundred and fifty-four flutes, twenty-two cornetts, twenty-one crumhorns, seventeen shawms, and eleven bassoon-types. The trumpets, trombones, and percussion instruments mentioned so frequently in accounts of ceremonial occasions are missing from this collection and were apparently housed elsewhere.

King Henry VIII's wind band in the musicians' gallery at Whitehall

The royal musicians at the beginning of Henry VIII's reign included three distinct wind ensembles: a nine-member ensemble called 'The Styll shalmes,' a four-member ensemble called 'Sakbudds and shalmes of the Privee Chambre,' and fourteen trumpets.

Of all the indoor entertainments available to the king, Henry seemed to enjoy most appearing with his nobles in elaborate disguises. An eyewitness to one of these, a ride during which Henry was 'surprised' by 'Robin Hood and his men,' provides a typical description.

> Then Robyn hood desyred the kynge and quene to come into the grene wood, & to se how the outlawes lyue. The kyng demaunded of ye quene & her ladyes, if they durst aduenture to go into the wood with so many outlawes ... the hornes blewe ... there was an Arber made of boowes with a hal, and a great chamber and an inner chamber very well made & couered with floures & swete herbes, which the kynge muche praysed.

One may suppose the leading nobles also maintained personal wind bands. The most important of these court figures was Cardinal Wolsey and we have a contemporary description of his personal wind band performing during a mumming presented for visiting French ambassadors in 1518.

> And when the banket was done, in came vj mynstrels, richely disguysed, and after them followed iij gentelmen in wyde and long gounes of Crymosyn sattyn, everyone havyng a cup of golde in their handes, the first cup was ful of Angels and royals, the second had diverse bales of dyce, and the iij had certayn payres of Cardes. These gentelmen offered to playe at monchaunce, and when they had played ye length of the first boorde, then the mynstrels blew up.

Another contemporary describes the Cardinal's wind band, seen when the king borrowed the band on the morning following a banquet given in his honor, and hints rather darkly of possible foul play (on the part of the royal wind band?) in the sudden death of one of the shawm players.

> The next day the King took my Lord's minstrels, and rode to a nobleman's house where there was some image to whom he vowed a pilgrimage, to perform his devotions. When he came there, which was in the night, he danced and caused others to do the same, after the sound of my Lord's minstrels, who played there all night, and never rested, so that whether it were with extreme labour of blowing, or with poison

(as some judged) because they were commended by the King more than his own, I cannot tell, but the player on the shalme (who was very excellent on that instrument) died within a day or two after.

Many of Henry's wind players were foreign musicians who were enlisted for service in the court. The results of one such recruiting effort can be seen in a letter from the Chamberlain, Court-Master of the English merchants in Antwerp, to Paget, First Secretary of the Court. He reports that with the help of local merchants he has found five musicians, one of whom can make all sorts of instruments. Four of the musicians are young and would like to join the king's service, but own no instruments. The fifth, who owns the instruments, has with some difficulty been persuaded to go with them. If paid wages and expenses in advance they agree to stay in England until the new year. One of many examples of proof that it was the wind players who were thought of as 'professional' musicians can be seen in the further report that there were also some Italians in the town, but they could play only the viols and therefore, 'are no musicians.'

An extant document, addressed to one of these foreign musicians, suggests that the wind band played in intimate, indoor situations as well as the great ceremonial ones.

> … paied to phillip [van Wilder] of the pryvat chambre for ij sagbuttes ij tenor shalmes and two treble shalmesse. 10.10s.

When the king traveled the wind band was always present. Perhaps the most discussed of these trips was the one to France in 1520, for a meeting with Francis I known as the meeting of the 'Field of Cloth of Gold.' A typical reference mentions the wind band going with Henry to perform before the Queen of France.

> … the Drumslad plaiers and other minstrels arayed in white, yelowe, and russet Damaske, these minstrels blew and played and so passed through the strete of Arde.

'The Field of Cloth of Gold' by James Basire in 1774, after a sixteenth-century oil painting in the Royal Collection.

The second-half of the reign of Henry VIII one associates with his notorious trading of wives. The first of these new wives, Anne Boleyn, was given an extraordinarily lavish coronation celebration, partly to hide the fact that she was six months pregnant. The public celebration began with a great water procession led by a great 'Dragon continually mouyng & castyng wyldfyer' and a group of 'terrible monsters and wylde men castyng fyer, and makyng hideious noyses.' Next came the mayor's barge, in which there were 'Shalmes, Shagbushes & diuers other instrumentes, whiche continually made goodly armony.' Each of the forty-eight major guilds of London had their own barge, and each with its own 'mynstrelsie,' which one can take to be a wind band. The following day a procession was made through the streets of London and one reference uses a frequent synonym for a trombone ensemble, 'solemn music.'

> [In a nearby tower] was suche several solemne instrumentes, that it seemed to be an heauenly noyse, and was muche regarded and praised.

The funeral of Henry VIII included a number of separate wind ensembles: a large group of trumpets, seven 'Mynstrells,' five 'Musytyans' (known by their names to have been wind players), four 'Shackebuttes,' five 'Fluttes' (probably shawms, as the English scribes tended to follow the custom in Italy and the Low Countries of confusing 'piper' [shawm] with 'flute'), as well as a drummer and a bagpipe player.

Documents from the brief reigns of Edward VI and Mary Tudor suggest that the basic separate ensembles of trumpets, shawms, and trombones continued until the reign of Elizabeth I. Indeed, Mary Tudor's account books for her New Year's gifts for 1543 mention separate consorts of trombones, percussion, an Italian wind consort, a flute consort and a Recorder consort.

The forty-five year reign of Elizabeth I was one of such success and style that today we know the entire period by her name. She was well educated and according to her tutor, 'she speaks French and Italian as well as she does English, and has often spoken to me readily and well in Latin, moderately in Greek.' Elizabeth herself took this ability in stride, noting, 'it is no marvel to teach a woman to talk; it is far harder to teach her to hold her tongue.' She was also skilled on the harpsi-

Portrait miniature of Elizabeth I playing the lute, ca. 1580 by Nicholas Hilliard

chord, but, according to one who heard her play, 'she was not used to play before men, but [played only] when she was solitary to shun melancholy.'

During her reign Elizabeth employed large numbers of woodwind players, a trombone consort, eight treble string players, drummers, and a player of bagpipe and lute. The ceremonial trumpets were always present, of course, and are frequently described as playing while the food was brought into the hall at state banquets. A German guest in 1598 mentions, 'twelve trumpets and two kettle-drums made the hall ring for half-an-hour together.' In Elizabeth's army there were also trumpets, although in the regular foot company it was the fife and drum which supplied the music. These players, however humble their music, were carefully selected as one can see in a contemporary ordinance.

> [The fife and drummers are to be] of able personage to use their instruments and office, of sundrie languages; for oftentimes they bee sente to parley with their enemies, ... which of necessitie requireth language.

Some of the most colorful accounts of aristocratic wind bands during the reign of Elizabeth I are associated with summer journies, a tradition she began soon after her coronation. Her desire to make these 'progresses' was in part to be seen by her subjects, in part to keep an eye on her powerful vassal lords, and, no doubt, in part to escape the discomfort of London in the summer. Large numbers of her court, not to mention her personal belongings and furniture, accompanied her and so great was the subsequent cost to her hosts that many prayed she would not pass their way.

Perhaps the most celebrated of these trips was her 1575 visit to Kenilworth Castle, which was inhabited by the Earl of Leicester. Upon her entry upon the castle property, she was welcomed by a 'gigantic porter,' who stood before six great statues ('made up') of trumpet players. Hidden behind each statue was a real trumpeter, but many of those present were fooled.

Kenilworth Castle by Wenzel Hollar (1607–1677)

> [The porter] cauzed his Trumpetoourz that stood upon the wall of the gate thear, too soound up a tune of welcum: which, besyde the noble noyz [the queen's wind band], was so mooch the more pleazaunt too behold, becauz theez Trumpetoourz, beeing sixe in number, wear everyone an eight foot hye, in due proportion of person besyde, all in long garments of sylk suitabl, eache with hiz sylvery Trumpet of a five foot long, foormed taper wyse, and straight from the uppor part untoo the neather eend: whear the diameter was a 16 ynchez over, and yet so tempered by art, that being very eazy too the blast, they cast foorth no greater noyz nor a more unpleazaunt soound for time and tune, than any oother common Trumpet, bee it never so artificially [skill-fully] foormed. Theese armmonious blasterz, from the foreside upon the wallz, untoo the inner; had this muzik maintened from them very delectable, while her Highness all along this Tylt-yard rode.

In the tournament field in the courtyard a lake had been constructed for a pageant based on the 'Lady of the Lake.' Here a 'floating island' drifted toward the shore upon which the queen waited. The island, blazing with torches, supported two nymphs who addressed the queen in poetry regarding the history of the castle and its owners. This was concluded with a performance by a large wind band.

> This Pageaunt was cloz'd up with a delectable harmony of Hautboiz, Shalmz, Cornets, and such oother looud muzik [wind music], that held on while her Majestie pleazauntly so passed from thence toward the Castl gate.

During the subsequent days the queen was entertained with dancing, hunting, fireworks, and concerts, one of which was by musicians in a boat on the artificial lake playing 'sundry kinds of very delectabl muzik.' There were more pageants, of course, and the most extraordinary of these occurred on the Monday of the second week of her visit. Returning from another hunt, the queen encountered on the lake a mechanical mermaid, eighteen feet long, swimming along with Triton and his trumpet ('Neptune's Blaster') on its back. Following this came a mechanical dolphin, large enough to contain a complete consort hidden in its belly! Accounts of the instrumentation of this consort vary, as the musicians were hidden from view, but the account of one present uses the word 'Noise,' which was always a synonym for the wind band. Sitting on top of this twenty-four foot long dolphin was a God, who sang another song of welcome and praise.

> O Noble Queene, give eare to this my floating Muse;
> And let the right of readie will my little skill excuse.
> For heardmen of the seas sing not the sweetest notes;
> The winds and waves do roare and crie, where Phoebus seldome
> floates; etc.

One who listened in awe to this consort in the belly of the dolphin was very moved.

> [The God] beegan a delectabl ditty of a Song well apted to a melodious noiz; compounded of six severall instruments, al coovert, casting soound from the Dolphin's belly within; Arion, the seaventh, sitting thus singing without. Noow, Syr, the ditty in mitter [meter] so aptly endighted [written] to the manner, and after by voys [voice] so deliciously delivered; the Song by a skilful artist into hiz parts so sweetlie sorted; each part in hiz instrument so clean and sharpely toouched; every instrument agayn in hiz kind so excellently tunabl; and this in the eeving of the day, resoounding from the calm waters, whear prezens of her Majesty, and longing to listen, had utterly damped all noyz and dyn; the hole armony conveyd in tyme, tune, and temper thus imcomparably melodious; with what pleazure … with what sharpnes of conceyt, with what lyvely delighte, this az ye may; for, so God judge me, by all the wit and cunning I have, I cannot express, I promis yoo … A, muzik iz a nobl art!

One valuable source of information for the day-to-day traditions of wind music during the reign of Elizabeth I is the rich body of literature for the Elizabethan stage. Since one of the important 'new' concepts of writing for the stage was the intent to make the characters and situations life-like, one can take the many references to wind music as reflective of actual practice. As Gustave Reese, in his *Music of the Renaissance*, confirms,

> certain dramatic situations had corresponding musical formulas. And it is quite evident that these were taken from contemporary real-life practices in Elizabethan England.

The most conspicuous example of these relationships lies in the appearances of the trumpet. The trumpet, while the most frequently mentioned of all instruments, is never included when 'music' is called for, nor is it found accompanying references to the military (this being fife and drum or bagpipe). Rather, the trumpet was reserved exclusively for associations with royalty, most frequently to announce the arrival of some great person. If he were a king, often the timpani as well were present, as in the case of Hamlet (act 1, scene 4, line 8).

> (A flourish of trumpets, and two guns go off)
> HAMLET. The king doth wake to-night and takes his rouse,
>   Keeps wassail, and the swagg'ring upspring reels,
>   And as he drains his draughts of Rhenish down,
>   The kettledrum and trumpet thus bray out
>   The triumph of his pledge.

Stage references to the trumpet often mention specific kinds of literature, most frequently 'flourishes' and 'alarums,' there being more than seventy such occurrences in Shakespeare alone. The precise musical nature of these pieces is not known today, but two specific kinds of flourishes, 'tucket' and 'sennet' are thought to derive from the Italian, 'toccare' and 'sonare.' The sennet seems to have been the longest of the flourishes.

When the dramatic action dwelt with those moments of aristocratic life in which the trumpets played so inseparable a part, the playwright would build the sounding of the instrument into the very heart of the dialog.

Thus in Shakespeare's *Tragedy of King Richard II* (act 1, scene 3) one finds such a scene which would have seemed incomplete to the sixteenth-century audience without the trumpet, a trial by combat.

> (Flourish, Enter King ... Then Mowbray in armour, and Herald)
>   ...
>
> (Tucket. Enter Hereford and Herald)
> 1ST HERALD. Harry of Hereford, Lancaster, and Derby Stands here ...
> 2ND HERALD. Here standeth Thomas Mowbray, Duke of Norfolk, ...
> MARSHAL. Attending but the signal to begin, Sound trumpets, and set
>   forward, combatants.
>   (A charge sounded)
>   Stay, the king hath thrown his warder down.
> RICHARD. Let them lay by their helmets and their spears
>   Withdraw with us and let the trumpets sound,
>   While we return these dukes what we decree.
>   (A long flourish)
>   ...

> And for our eyes to hate the dire aspect of civil
> wounds ploughed up with neighbours' swords;
> Which so roused up with boistrous untuned drums,
> With harsh-resounding trumpets' dreadful bray.
> Cousin, farewell - and uncle, bid him so,
> Six years we banish him and he shall go.
>   (Exit. Flourish)

A similar duel in *Troilus and Cressida* (act 4, scene 5) realistically includes the command to blow a Greek trumpet.

> AJAX. Thou, trumpet, there's my purse.
> Now crack thy lungs, and split they brazen pipe; …
> Come, stretch thy chest, and let thy eyes spout blood;
> Thou blow'st for Hector.

Lesser nobility and minor dignitaries are sometimes introduced by cornetts, as if the instrument itself were considered, in Elizabethan England, a 'lesser trumpet.' In the plays of Marston, for example, one reads, 'The cornetts sound a synnet and the Duke goes out in state.' The cornetts were also used when the stage requirement necessitated an unusually long flourish, suggesting perhaps that the aristocratic trumpet repertoire of memorized signals were mostly brief in length.

The horn is mentioned exclusively with reference to hunting scenes and in a few cases an actor will describe these hunting signals in detail. For example, in the play *The Return from Parnassus* one finds,

> When the fox is earthed you must blow one long, two short; the second wind, one long two short. Now in blowing every long containeth seven quavers, one short containeth three quavers … (When you return home) you must sound the relief three times … Your relief is your sweetest note … You must sound one long and six short; the second wind, two short and one long; the third, one long and two short.

The shawm (Hautboy) ensemble, conforming with its known role in the palace, is almost always found indoors in an atmosphere of hospitality or entertainment, often a banquet. Thus in the stage direction for the beginning of act 1, scene 7, of *Macbeth*, the shawms appear with the food.

> (A lobby in Macbeth's castle. Hauboys and torches. Enter a Sewer, and divers Servants with dishes and service.)

The various members of the flute family also conformed to their use in daily Elizabethan life, with the fife in military scenes and the pipe and tabor for the dance (*The Tempest*, act 3, scene 2). The recorder consort is almost always found in church scenes, especially if there were an association with mourning.

These plays, by the way, began with the ancient tradition of three fanfares played on trumpets. The musicians, usually members of civic wind bands, were situated in special 'music rooms' located behind, above, or below the stage itself.

The most important body of wind band literature from the Elizabethan period is the early consort collection (1599) by Antony Holborne, *Pavans, Galliards, Almains, and other short Aeirs both grave and Light, in five parts, for Viols, Violins, or other Musicall Winde Instruments*. The Elizabethan 'or other' in the title meant 'or else.' Although the title reflects a broad possibility of instrumentation, in order to encourage sales, in all probability most of the music was written for the wind band of Sir Richard Champernowne, for whom Holborne was earlier employed. Some scholars believe that some of these pieces were used in specific Elizabethan plays, a repertoire otherwise not thought to be extant.

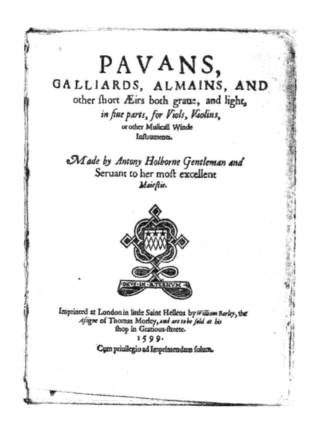

Title page of Anthony Holborne's 'Pavans, Galliards, Almains and other short Aeirs' published by William Barley, 1599

France

Little is known of the wind band of Louis XII (1498–1515), the first French king of the sixteenth century, perhaps due to his confessed stinginess toward ceremonial extravagence. There is one small masterpiece which was surely written for his band, the *Vive Le Roy* by Josquin. Louis himself was a singer and there exists a composition by this same composer with a part labeled, 'vox regis,' consisting of a single pitch repeated throughout!

A much more significant king, in terms of both France and the Renaissance, was Francis I (1515–1547). It was under Francis I that France's most important early wind bands were established. These bands, together with their administrative organization, would remain in place until the Revolution at the end of the eighteenth century.

The court musicians were organized under two administrative sections, the *Chambre* and the *Écurie*. Under the *Chambre* there were *Les officiers domestiques*, which included singers, organists, and lute players. A separate category, *Les cornets*, usually referred to two virtuosi, nearly always from Italy. Here also were the performers of ceremonial music, the *Les flutes hautbois et trompettes* and *Les fifres et les tabourins*, players not considered virtuosi and thus paid less.

King Francis I of France, ca. 1538, previously attributed to Joos van Cleve

Under the administrative wing called the *Écurie* there was a group which included the royal trumpets, five fife players and six trumpeters called *Les fifres et les trompettes*. It was here that the most important early wind band in France was formed, the *Joueurs d'instrumens de haulxbois et sacqueboutes*. This ensemble would become the famous *Les Grands Hautbois* under Louis XIV, an ensemble which all wind bands in the late Baroque would imitate. The earliest complete listing of the names of the members of this wind band, dated 1529, gives eight players with Italian names. During the sixteenth century a few French names appear, but for the most part this would remain an ensemble of Italians. It is probable that this ensemble existed from the beginning of the reign of Francis, for accounts of his coronation mention a wind band of shawms and sackbuts. Surely they were also the band which provided the music for the Mass attended by Francis and Henry VIII during their historic meeting in 1520, which an eyewitness describes as being played by 'organ, sackbuts, and cornetts.'

The interest of Francis in his own wind band is complimented by his gifts to visiting bands. In 1538 alone, he rewarded a visiting band of cornetts, belonging to the Queen of Hungary; an oboe band of the Duke of Mantoue; and no fewer than four bands (two of trumpets and two of oboes) of Pope Paul III.

Although modern recordings usually employ string ensembles, it is more appropriate to think of the publications of 'Danseries' before 1550 by Pierre Attaingnant and Nicolas du Chemin of Paris as representative of the repertoire of the wind band of Francis. We know the wind band remained the basic 'dance band' before 1550 and two of the compilers of these collections were members of the king's musical establishment, Claude Gervaise and Jean d'Estrée—the latter always identifying himself as an oboist (shawmist) in the king's wind band. This view is supported by Caroline Cunningham, the leading scholar of the music of d'Estrée.

> The iconography shows a gradual swithchover from pure wind bands, both loud and soft, to various combinations of strings, both viols and violins, amplified as the century goes on by plucked instruments: lute and keyboard.

There is also strong contemporary evidence that the Danseries before 1550 were wind band literature. Thoinot Arbeau, writing in his *Orchésography* of 1588, speaks of the dance music of his period as being 'lascivious, shameless ones' and then speaks of the earlier period of Francis I.

> On solemn feast days the pavan is employed by kings, princes and great noblemen to display themselves in their fine mantles and ceremonial robes. They are accompanied by queens, princesses and great ladies, the long trains of their dresses loosened and sweeping behind them, sometimes borne by damsels. And it is the said pavans, played by hautboys and sackbuts, that announce the grand ball and are arranged to last until the dancers have circled the hall two or three times.

After quoting some of these tunes, Arbeau makes a direct reference to the body of published Danseries as being the very body of literature he had in mind when he referred to those played by the wind bands of 'hautboys and sackbuts.'

The 'Orchesography' of Thoinot Arbeau, 1588

You will find plenty in the books of dances printed by the recently defunct Attaignant, who lived near the church of St. Cosmo in Paris, and in the books of the late Master Nicolas du Chemin, printer in the said Paris at the sign of the Silver Lion.

Following Francis I there were four kings with relatively brief reigns, each filled with religious and political strife which left little time to enjoy court entertainments. A document of 1552 proves that Henry II (1547–1559) continued the wind band of his father and perhaps it was his band who performed 'Io lche del Bronzo fui,' one of the *Intermedii* composed by Piero Manucci for three crumhorns and sackbut during Henry's visit to Lyons in 1548.

The boy-king Charles IX (1560–1574) was taken on a grand tour by his mother, Catherine de Medici, in 1564–1566 for the purpose of uniting factions in the provinces and to stage a meeting with Philip II of Spain, which she hoped would resemble the famous meeting of Francis I and Henry VIII of 1520. As it turned out Philip frustrated the plan by sending his wife, Elizabeth (a daughter to Catherine) instead. The journals of this grand tour contain frequent references to the participation of wind bands in the ceremonies which welcomed Charles. The tour began at the palace of his brother in Fontainebleau with a typical pageant.

> As the king entered, he heard a concert of very excellent cornett players. And meanwhile from the end of the main canal came three Sirens, who were three young children having excellent voices and looked so natural that they appeared to be nude, their navels lower than their long gilded braids, in silver and azure, decorated like Dolphins, in the way in which Sirens are ordinarily painted, and swam in the middle of the water upright, with admirable guile. As they came in front of the king, the cornets stopped.

Now a poem was recited, then Neptune appeared drawn by four marine horses to the accompaniment of 'a concert of two shawms and a sackbut.' During the banquet that evening, the first course was served to 'a concert of cornetts and a sackbut.'

Elizabeth's arrival in Bayonne for the meeting with Charles was celebrated with a Te Deum in the cathedral which was accompanied by 'excellent cornetts.' One of the entertainments was a river journey to an 'enchanted island,' which featured various aquatic spectacles including a mechanical whale.

Another was Neptune, riding in a shell boat drawn by marine horses, and accompanied by no fewer than three consorts of six cornetts 'very pleasant to the ear.'

Another contemporary document gives extensive details of the arrival of Charles IX in Paris in 1571 with his Queen, Elizabeth of Austria, for his coronation (which had been delayed ten years due to the political climate). In addition to a large number of civic and military musicians, the king's wind band participated under its leader, the shawmist, Jehan Gentilz. An epic poem, *La Renommée*, by Charles de Navieres, also describes the coronation procession and includes a description of the royal wind band.

> Here the eight oboes and cornetts resounded
> And filled the strains, the music furnished
> Was titillating with sweet harmony to all ears.

The poem also mentions eight royal trumpeters and perhaps suggests their performance of an eight-part work, 'Eight trumpets and eight sounds filled the air.'

With Henry III (1574–1589) the affairs of both state and family fell to the lowest ebb of the century. This was the period Arbeau knew and in which he spoke of dances which were 'lascivious, shameless ones.' A description of his court by Hesketh Pearson offers further insight.

> The Court of Henry III was a mass of corruption. The King had his pimps and minions, and did not much discriminate between male and female bedfellows, frequently following his orgies of lust with public exhibitions of repentance … When some of his male lovers were murdered by the followers of his brother, he gave them state funerals and raised marble monuments over their graves … Rings, bracelets and earrings adorned his person; his body was annointed with perfumes, his face painted and powered; and occasionally he dressed as a woman … waited on by court ladies attired as men.

Although it was under Henry III that the string instruments began to rise to importance in the French court, he also maintained the wind band of his predecessors. An icon of 1579 pictures a nine-member wind band with several sizes of shawms and a list of players in 1580 indicates the full ensemble, 'hautbois, sacquebutes, cornets i bouquin,' had twelve players. This same band performed for the marriage of Henry, King of Navarre, in Notre Dame Cathedral in 1572 and again for his coronation in 1594 as Henry IV.

Spain

The reign of Philip I (1504–1506) was brief and tragic, with his death at age twenty-six and his wife's retreat into madness, but produced two children who became emperors—Charles V and Ferdinand I. His brief reign consisted of almost constant travel, accompanied by his personal musicians. Upon his arrival in Spain he was accompanied by nine trumpeters, three musettes, and four sackbuts and a trip in 1506 included an ensemble called *Jouelx d'Instrumens*, which may have been a wind band.

Charles V, one of the great figures of the Renaissance, maintained a large trumpet corps who are described by an eyewitness to a procession in Valladolid in 1517.

Detail from 'The Engagement of St. Ursula and Prince Etherius,' a panel painting from the Master of Saint Auta altarpiece, Spain, ca. 1520.

> Afterwards came twenty-eight Spanish trumpets, followed by the twelve trumpets of Charles, all dressed in sleeveless violet tunics covered with little silver and gold letter C's sown on … Next came twelve [more] trumpets of Charles playing in 'bon art et mode.'

His indoor musicians seems to have been few in number, but included three of the most famous artists of the century, the cornettist, Augustin de Verona, and the Flemish trombonists, Hans Naghele and Jehan Van Vincle. He apparently augmented his musicians as needed and on at least one occasion borrowed his mother's wind band, her '8 ministriles altos.' His sister, Mary of Hungary, by the way, maintained a huge collection of wind instruments, among them nearly fifty cornetts and some sixteen shawms.

Charles may also have had a sizable collection of instruments for a large number were cataloged upon the death of his successor, Philip II. These instruments, including some thirty cornetts, are listed by consorts.

The German-Speaking Countries

Among the many dukes of the German-speaking lands, one finds some of the sixteenth century's most colorful accounts of personalities and their wind bands. In the court in Munich, in Bavaria, the musical establishment began a period of growth during the first-half of the century with the arrival of Ludwig Senfl, who had been a court musician under Maximilian I. The German scholar, Sandberger, describes the musical function of the wind band at this time.

It was the prevailing condition that zinks [cornetts] and trombones took over the performance of the works of Josquin, Issac, Brumel, Mouton, and Willaert.

Documentation of more extensive court musical activities are extant from the period of Duke Albert V, after Lassus was appointed Hofkapellmeister in 1563. The journal of a court singer, Massimo Troiano, describes a five-member wind band performing as consorts of differing instrumentation for the duke's banquets,

> sometimes with corna-muse, sometimes with recorders or with flutes, or cornetts and trombones in French chansons or other light compositions.

For one occasion Troiano gives the instruments of an interesting broken consort of winds, as 'fagotto, corna-musa, mute cornett, cornett, tenor cornett, flute, dolzaina, and bass trombone.'

Troiano describes in detail the music for a banquet for this duke, on the occasion of his wedding to Renate von Lothringen in 1568. It began with trumpet fanfares followed by the performance of an original eight-part wind band composition,

'Landscape in Spring' by Lucas van Valkenborch, 1587, while living near Vienna under the patronage of the Archduke Matthais. The wind band can be seen entertaining the picnic at right.

the 'Battle-music' of Annibale Padovano, performed on cornetts and trombones. During the first course these same players performed a seven-part motet by Lassus and during the second course a six-part madrigal by Striggio with six large (grosse) trombones, one of which was a bass trombone. Yet another composition was performed by a 'soft' wind band, consisting of a dolzaina, cornamuse, shawm, and mute cornett.

Albert's son, William, was married in the same year to Renée of Lorraine and among the music performed for his banquet was a motet by Lassus, 'Providebam dominum,' played by cornetts and trombones. This William in 1574 purchased trombones, flutes, and crumhorns for the band of his brother, Duke Ernst of Bavaria.

In Austria, to the south, the accounts of court music under Archduke Karl I, of Graz, speak mostly of ceremonial trumpets, although the inventory of his musical collection (which includes consorts of crumhorns and dolzani) suggests he also had a regular wind band. On one occasion the duke's sister heard the trumpet choir perform during a banquet and requested a copy of the music, to which the duke replied that he could not honor the request as the music was not notated. It was typical, of course, for the aristocratic trumpets to perform only memorized repertoire at this time, but it should not be assumed that this literature was only in the form of brief fanfares. Praetorius, for example, records that the 'sonata or *sonada* is also used with reference to music played on trumpets for banquet and dance.'

Archduke Karl II also maintained a large trumpet corps and in one document of 1572 there is the suggestion of some discipline problem.

> [The trumpet corps] must have diligent attention and must also appear for services on Sundays and holidays. Unless one has a better reason not to appear, he or they will receive serious punishment.

The Emperor Ferdinand I established courts in both Munich and Vienna, beginning in 1558. In addition to accounts of his trumpeters, there is an early reference to his trombone consort making a guest appearance before Margaret of Austria, the Regent of the Low Countries, in 1521. An engraving of a court ball in Vienna in 1560 pictures his eight-member wind band playing from a special box in the foreground (according to Köchel there were no strings used in this court before 1543). Ferdinand's son, Maximilian II (1564–1576), moved his court to Prague, where we find his trumpeters divided into categories as 'musical' or 'not musical,' a reference perhaps to the fact that some trumpet players were now learning to read music.

The dukes to the west also supported large musical establishments. Duke Ludwig III of Württemberg (1568–1593) had, in his palace in Stuttgart, one of the largest collections of instruments in Europe. One finds, for example, no fewer than two hundred and twenty flutes, forty-eight recorders, one hundred and thirteen cornetts, fourteen crumhorns, etc., as compared to thirty-nine viols.

Philipps von Hessen also had a large collection of instruments, which included sixty-seven wind, sixteen string, and three keyboard instruments. He also seems to have experienced a discipline problem with his wind band, for an edict given out in 1541 orders them to henceforth play for his dances with an attitude that is, 'willing, unquestioning, and untiring!' One wonders if the band's attitude toward the court dances was in any way related to this court's infamous reputation for drunkenness. At nearby Münster, there was even a bishop who used to get so drunk that his trumpets and drums were kept nearby to wake him.

Philipps von Hessen, like most of the German dukes, spent much of his time hunting and on one day in 1559 killed, together with his guests, more than a thousand boars. This extravagence can be seen in better perspective with respect to the punishment given any starving peasant caught hunting on Philipps' land, the least of which was having the arms tied behind and being drawn upwards by a rope, pulling the arms backwards over the head, and left to hang.

The best known of the Hessian nobles was Moritz, Landgraf of Hesse-Cassel, who also maintained a large collection of instruments. One finds forty-four string, ten keyboard, and one hundred and forty-two wind instruments, the latter organized in consorts with a strong emphasis on the lower family members. His wind band consisted of eight members in 1596, but a few years later a larger ensemble of twelve is described relative to the festivities welcoming the Ambassador of Queen Elizabeth of England.

… musicke of sackbotes and cornets clade in greene tafetie to the ground, six before and six behind, with the most harmonious noyse that could be, answering one another like an eccho. This kind of musicke had a princely ayre.

Moritz was also a great hunter and the importance of this court activity can be seen in the authority given the court official in charge. This Master Huntsman once shot a peasant who had lingered behind in the chase, once struck an ear off another who came up late with his hounds, and once slashed in two the head of a third. He himself was only brought to justice when he made the unfortunate mistake of addressing Moritz in an impolite manner!

Moritz, Landgraf of Hesse-Cassel by Matthäus Merian, 1662

In Northern Germany one finds a duke, Duke Albert of Prussia, who took a very great personal interest in his wind band, which ranged twelve to seventeen members in size between 1540 and 1578. There are numerous extant letters by Duke Albert regarding his personal involvement in the purchase of wind instruments for his band. Most of these refer to the purchase of complete consorts of one or another instrument. For example in a letter, dated 1541, to the instrument maker Seblad von Thyll in Nürnberg, the duke purchased twelve German trumpets, twelve 'Welch' [Italian] trumpets, a tenor and bass pomhart, two Welch cornetts, six cornetts voiced together [a consort], and new mouthpieces for his trombones. Many letters suggest the duke knew his instruments and was a tough bargainer when it came to prices.

With Duke Albert of Prussia we have the largest extant collection of sixteenth-century wind band music, a set of seven part-books (one is failing), ca. 1541–1543, containing one hundred and forty-nine compositions. An extant court document of 1569 mentions another similar set of five part-books for the duke's shawm players which have been lost. Many of these compositions are of course chansons and motets which have been set down in an instrumental version. There is one interesting example where the composer himself made a wind band transcription for the duke. Thomas Stoltzer, a court composer in Hungary, made a wind band version of his 'Erzürne dich nicht,' a massive seven-part composition, and sent it to the duke with the following note:

> It occurred to me in this work to specially serve your Lordship, to whom I owe all I have, and so I have thought of crumhorns and thus have set the psalm so that it completely suits them, which is not the case with every compositions and especially those with many voices.

One must also mention the *Concentus novi* (ca. 1540) composed by the court 'concert trumpeter' (*tubicinae symphoniarum*), Johann Kugelmann, as a further possible example of literature which may have been played by this wind band.

There is also a vary rare manuscript, dated 1598, which gives notated examples of the quasi-secret, memorized repertoire of the North German aristocratic trumpet choirs. These manuscripts, prepared by the court trumpeters Hendrich Lübeck and Magnus Thomsen for teaching purposes, contain all the basic international military signals ('à cheval,' 'la charge,' etc.), but also a number of very interesting 'concert' works called, *Sonaten*, *Sersseneden*, and *Tokkaten*. Among these is the familiar 'In dulci jubilo,' which appears here as, 'In dultzi gubilo.'

Perhaps it should be mentioned here that there is a valuable German publication (1555) on military music, by Lienhart Fronsperger. On the duties of the field trumpeter, he writes,

> Each squadron should have at least one trumpeter serving under his captain and he should be found day and night by his captain's tent ... He should know and be able to variously blow: when one mounts, when one eats, when one dismounts or sets out; also when the enemy is present, alarms, or when one should attack the enemy ... a trumpeter should be bold, manly, intelligent, and honorable, as he may have to serve as an ambassador to the enemy.

To the east, an early sixteenth-century account of the wedding of Duke Johann of Saxony to Sofia of Mecklenburg includes a very interesting reference to the royal wind band, divided into two ensembles to perform a polychoral Mass.

> The bride and bridegroom together with the other princes and princesses heard Mass in the castle chapel; the singers belonging to my Most Gracious and Noble Lord sang two Masses with the help of the organ, three sackbuts and a cornet, and also four crumhorns with the positive organ which were almost joyful to hear.

The Elector August of Dresden (1553–1586) maintained a wind band and there is an interesting extant letter of his, dated 13 May 1563, written to Duke Albert of Bavaria, which refers to his band. Duke Albert had apparently written inquiring about the crumhorns he had heard in the Elector's wind band when it had performed for a meeting of the Electors in Frankfurt. August responded,

> When Your Lordship kindly asked us in an enclosed note to inform you where the crumhorns can be obtained, such as you heard in Frankfurt, our instrumentalists and other servants have reported that some time ago our dear late brother Elector Moritz … bought these crumhorns from a merchant in Nurnberg … Our instrumentalists have no other information except that the Cardinal of Trent also has a case full of crumhorns of this type which are supposed to be better than ours.

Christian I of Saxony maintained a collection of instruments which included (in 1593) more than one hundred and twenty wind instruments. An engraving of 1584 pictures his wind band as eight players of sackbuts, cornetts, tenor shawm, and bass recorder.

Like his contemporaries, Christian I spent much of his time hunting and to save the game for himself he once issued an order that all dogs belonging to peasants entering his hunting fields must first have a forefoot cut off! But he had other interests, as we can see in one of his extant letters to Prince Hans Georg of Anhalt.

> The reason why this letter is so stupid and badly written is that I have not yet altogether got over that last splendid orgy, and my hands tremble so that I can scarcely hold my pen.

Italy

Following the great cultural accomplishments of the fifteenth century, Italy began the sixteenth century with a long period of political strife, countless wars, and domination by foreign lords. As a result many documents have been lost and it is difficult to piece together the story of many of these court wind bands. There was as a consequence of the foreign activity in Italy a great flow of artists from other countries. One eyewitness, for example, reports hearing a Spanish shawm band which gave an hour-long concert both mornings and evenings in Piacenza in 1581.

With the sixteenth century one finds a great deal more information regarding the wind bands of the papacy. The first pope of the sixteenth century, Rodrigo Borgia, who named himself after Alexander the Great, spent most of his time attempting to regain control over the papal states which had fallen under the control of local dictators. To emphasize his station he dressed as a potentate and was often seen accompanied by his 'kettledrums, trumpeters, and minstrels carrying instruments of silver slung on chains of gold.' His daughter, Lucrezia Borgia, is perhaps better known to the modern reader and when a party from Ferrara arrived in Rome to escort her back for her wedding to Alfonso d'Este it was no doubt Alexander's wind band who are described as greeting the party on the steps of St. Peters.

Leo X, having been born a Medici, received his musical education under the great Isaac. He had a good ear, a fine voice, composed well, and it is appropriate that in his portrait by Raphael he is pictured reading a volume of sacred music. We know his musical establishment included several Flemish wind players and that he maintained an Italian shawm band, called '*quattro sonatori di pifferi milanesi.*' According to the diary of the papal Master of Ceremonies, Paris de Grassis, the wind band of Leo X even participated in the services of the Sistine Chapel.

Portrait of Pope Leo X and his cousins, cardinals Giulio de' Medici and Luigi de' Rossi, 1518–19, by Raffaello Sanzio (1483–1520)

The next pope, Clement VII (1523–1534), was also born into the Medici family and also trained in music (it was to distinguish himself from this pope that Jacobus Clemens took the sobriquet, 'Clemens non Papa'). He was caught in the struggle between Francis I and Charles V and history has not treated him well due to his indecision leading to the infamous 'Sack of Rome' in 1527. Perhaps this should be offset to some degree in recognition of his support of the arts in Rome, not the least of which was his patient encouragement of Michelangelo.

We have an extraordinary eyewitness account of the wind band of Clement VII in one of the masterpieces of sixteenth-century literature, the *Autobiography* by Benvenuto Cellini. It is so informative it must be quoted in full.

It happened that at that time one Giagiacomo, wind player [piffero, shawmist] from Cesena, who is now in this capacity with the Pope, a very excellent performer [sonatore], sent word through Lorenzo, trombonist from Lucca, who is now in the service of our Duke [Cosmo I], to inquire whether I was inclined to help them at the Pope's celebration of the Ferragosto [a festival on August One], playing soprano with my cornett in some motets of great beauty selected by them for that occasion. Although I had the greatest desire to finish the vase I had begun, yet, since music has a wondrous charm of its own, and also because I wished to please my old father, I consented to join them. During the eight days before the festival we practiced two hours a day together; then on the first of August we went to the courtyard of the Vatican Palace [the Belvedere], and while Pope Clement was at his banquet, we played those carefully rehearsed [disciplinati] motets so well that his Holiness protested he had never heard music more sweetly executed or with better ensemble [unita]. He sent for Giangiacomo, and asked him where and how he had procured so excellent a cornett for soprano, and inquired particularly who I was. Giangiacomo told him my name in full. Whereupon the Pope said: 'So, then, he is the son of Maestro Giovanni?' On being assured I was, the Pope expressed his wish to have me in his service with the other musicians. Giangiacomo replied: 'Most blessed Father, I cannot pretend for certain that you will get him, for his profession, to which he devotes himself assiduously, is that of a goldsmith, and he works in it miraculously well, and earns by it far more than he could do by playing.' To this the Pope added: 'I am the better inclined to him now that I find him possessor of a talent more than I expected. See that he obtains the same salary as the rest of you; and tell him from me to join my service, and that I will find work enough by the day for him to do in his other trade.' Then stretching out his hand, he gave him a hundred golden crowns of the Camera in a handkerchief, and said: 'Divide these so that he may take his share.' When Giangiacomo left the Pope, he come to us, and related ... all that the Pope had said.

Portrait of Giulio de' Medici (1478–1534), Pope Clement VII, ca. 1530, by Sebastiano Luciani

This passage tells us many things, first, that the ensemble had eight-members. All evidence from the first half of the sixteenth century would suggest a wind band and this seems to be confirmed by the identity of three of its members, a shawm, trombone, and a cornett playing the uppermost voice. It was, of course, the normal practice for such a wind band to perform instrumental versions of motets, but this passage confirms that this did not mean mere sight-reading. Here, we are told, the ensemble—who were no doubt among the finest musicians available, and certainly capable of reading at sight—carefully selected the specific motets, with the emphasis being on their great beauty, and then rehearsed them two hours per day for eight days! What were these rehearsals like? Cellini tells us the motets were 'carefully rehearsed' and the pope's judgement, 'sweetly executed' and 'better ensemble,' suggest these rehearsals must have been very much like ours would be today: adding the articulations necessary for the wind version, listening for balance and ensemble, etc.

For the following Pope, Paul III, one can document no fewer than five separate wind and percussion ensembles. The most important, the basic wind band, is at various times reported as an eight-member trombone ensemble, a cornett and trombone band, or a shawm band. The earliest records of this band, when it was known as the '*i musici di Castel Sant'Angelo*,' were destroyed in the Sack of Rome. The sixteenth-century names for this band follow the tradition at this time of using the word, 'Concerto,' meaning 'ensemble.' Thus one reads of the '*musici del concerto di Campidoglio*,' or the '*Concerto de' tromboni e cornetti del Senato et inclito Popolo Romano*.' In any case, the ensemble was led by a '*Priore*,' who could levy fines and make payments to players. They were housed in the Castel Sant'Angelo and later in the Campidoglio and appeared in all festivities which involved the pope. When he traveled they were often given extra money for horses.

Portrait of Pope Paul III Farnese by Titian (1543)

Giuseppe Zocchi (1711–1767), View of the Tiber Looking Towards the Castel Sant'Angelo, with Saint Peter's in the Distance, ca. 1721–67

Like all other aristocrats the pope had a trumpet ensemble, called '*i trombetti del Popolo Romano*.' This ensemble had its own constitution and contemporary documents speak of older, already lost, constitutions. The principal members were called '*trombetti di numero*,' with two classes of alternate members called '*coadiutori*' and '*sopranumerari*.'

Percussion players were found in both a separate personal ensemble and in the ranks of the pope's militia.

Finally, the pope's Swiss Guards had two percussionists and two shawms for each unit of two hundred men. Although these players no doubt appeared in many papal celebrations, they seem to have been less respected. Not only could they alone not accept outside performance, but they had additional non-musical jobs to perform, among which were cleaning the lamps and fireplaces.

The Court at Ferrara had an eight-member wind band, which is described as a shawm band in 1501 when they accompanied the court to Rome. String instruments appear unusually early in this court and in an account of the music for a banquet in 1529 (celebrating the marriage of Ercole d'Este and Princess Renée of France) one can see the custom at that time of achieving variety in tonal color, which we achieve today through what we call 'orchestration,' by employing consorts of alternating texture. In this case, during the first course one heard voices, together with five viols, keyboard, lute, and large and small flutes. The second course was accompanied by vocal madrigals, the third and fourth with music for voices with mixed consorts. The fifth course was played by a pure wind band of five sackbuts and cornett. The sixth course was again vocal music and the seventh again a wind band, now two dolzaine, crumhorn, large cornett and sackbut.

The Dukes of Ferrara maintained a large collection of instruments, which, according to Bottrigari, were 'always in playing condition and tuned, ready to be picked up and played on the spur of the moment.' The Duke also maintained a famous ensemble of twenty-three nuns of Saint Vito, who were also described by Bottrigari.

> You would see them betake themselves in Indian file to a long table, upon one end of which a large harpsichord is laid. Silently they entered, each one with her instrument, be it a stringed or a wind instrument ... and gathered around the table without the slightest noise, some sitting

down, some standing, according to the nature of their instruments. At last, the conductress (la Madre Maestra) faced the table from the other end and, after having made sure that the other sisters were ready, gave them noiselessly the sign to begin with a long, slender, well polished baton.

Vessella adds that this ensemble was 'suave of harmony, angelic of voice, and very fine instrumentalists.' He notes that each played several instruments, 'and not just cornetts and trombones.'

In Florence, after several short-lived experiments in government, the Medicean family was returned to power in 1512 and whenever possible attempted to recapture the grandeur of the past by staging great regal celebrations, in particular for family marriages.

It is in the Court in Florence that one sees the 'intermezzi' given between the acts of stage plays and which are familiar to music students as one of the roots of modern opera. Perhaps not so familiar to music students is the fact that many of the individual compositions in these Florentine intermezzi were accompanied by wind bands. One sees them, for example, in the intermezzi for Strozzi's *Commedia in versi* (1518), for Landi's *Il Commodo* (1539), Del Mazzo's *I Fabii* (1568), and Bargagli's *La Pellegrina* (1589). A typical example of this practice was the intermezzi for d'Ambra's comedy, *La Confanaria*, given in 1565 as part of the celebration festivities for the marriage of Francesco de' Medici and Johanna of Austria. The first intermezzo presented the characters, Venus, the Three Graces, the Four Seasons, Cupid, and the Four Passions—Hope, Fear, Joy, and Pain. During the second intermezzo Cupid serenaded Psyche to a mixed consort. The third intermezzo pictures Cupid so taken by love for Psyche that he has neglected mortals, resulting in the appearance of characters representing Frauds and Deceptions. Here a madrigal, 'S'amor vinto, e prigion posto in oblio,' by Corteccia, was performed by eight singers, five crumhorns, and a mute cornet. The fourth intermezzo presented various characters representing Discord, Ire, and Cruelty—the result of love having died among mankind. Here another madrigal was performed, accompanied by two trombones, dolziana, three cornetts (one, a tenor), and two tamburi. The tale ends with a sixth intermezzo, set at the foot of Mount

Helicon. One eyewitness reports the performance of a large mixed consort, although another, Duke Ferdinand of Bavaria, mentions only the court wind band:

> After the Fifth Act ... came twelve naked nymphs and as many satyrs who sang and played on large curved pipes [crumhorns] with which harmonized cornetts and trombones.

This may have been a standard instrumentation for this court wind band, for Duke Ferdinand also reports hearing the same instruments perform for during breakfast.

> At the breakfast ... music was played with cornetts, trombones, also with crumhorns; but they only played 'Welsche' [Italian] dances which in my opinion were nothing special.

This band also played outdoors, of course, and in one interesting example, for the arrival of Eleanore of Toledo in 1539, accompanied Corteccia's 'Ingredere felicissimis auspiciis urbem tuam Hel ionora,' with four cornetts and four sackbuts.

The reader will recall the strong wind band practice in the court at Mantua during the fifteenth century and this preference continued during the sixteenth century. The authority on this court, Iain Fenlon, writes 'Francesco's attentions appear to have been directed towards the traditional band of pifferi [shawms]', and the great Italian scholar, Vessella, points out that in Mantua the entire century is filled with references to 'trombetti, tromboni e pifferi.'

Isabella was still present early in the century and Vessella writes that she was so interested in the flute [shawm?] and trombone that, in the privacy of her apartments, she had her own children study these instruments. Even by mid-century the wind band seems to have been the only regular musicians on the court payroll, with the exception of one singer and one lute player. When Duke Ferdinand of Bavaria visited in 1565 he reported hearing a band of four shawms, cornetts, and Pomhart performing during dinner. Another visitor in 1587 reported hearing a wind band of cornetts and trombones playing before and after the Mass in San Pietro's Cathedral.

Verona was not a great cultural center during the sixteenth century, but did seem to specialize in the cultivation of cornett players, as is demonstrated by numerous virtuosi who were exported throughout Europe. At least one aristocrat in Verona, Count Bevilacqua, had a wind band and a large collection of instruments.

In Venice the Doge's wind band continued during the sixteenth century and one can see four of its members performing as a recorder consort in an engraving by a member of the Doge's wind band, Ganassi's *Fontegara* (1535). Two additional sixteenth-century icons picture the Doge's wind players, *The Procession of the Doge in Venice* (ca. 1520) by Amman shows five trumpeters in uniforms and a similar work by Pagani (ca. 1559) shows six trumpeters with straight instruments so long they are supported by children.

The court wind band in Siena, 'Concerto di Palazzo,' can be documented until the fall of the republic in 1559.

6   *Civic Wind Bands*

THE READER HAS SEEN, IN PART I, the development of European civic wind bands from purely functional roles into the more musical ones during the fifteenth century. During the sixteenth century the kinds of performances broaden to include the stage and more frequent appearances in church services and in public concerts. In most countries the sixteenth century represents a great climax in the history of the early civic wind band; only in Germany will this activity continue to develop during the seventeenth century.

The civic wind bands followed the lead of the court bands in adopting both the new sixteenth-century instruments and their use in consorts. This meant that the civic government, like the aristocrats, had to assemble large collections of numerous instruments for the civic musicians to use. Nürnberg, for example, which maintained only four or five civic musicians during the sixteenth century, had ninety instruments in 1575 in its Ratsmusik Musikkammer.

It follows, of course, that this new style placed considerable demands on the players, who now had to be proficient on numerous separate instruments as part of the daily exercise of their profession (as the century progressed they had also to be able to play string instruments and even sing). Thus one reads already in 1502 of two civic musicians in Hall (Tyrol) being fired because they were not sufficiently qualified in playing 'all the winds.' Two (unsuccessful!) applicants for a civic position in Rothenburg in 1540, promised proficiency on,

> trombones, cornetts, flutes, schreyerpfeifen, pipe and tabor, crumhorns, shawms, recorders, strings, organ, and lutes.

It is during the sixteenth century that one begins to find a new kind of civic wind music, private wind bands supported by wealthy middle class merchants. These men, too, had to maintain large personal collections of instruments in order to

Opposite page: Detail from a painting by Abraham Schelhas shows a German wind band providing the music for an aristocratic dance, ca. 1600

'be in style.' The most famous of these men, Raimund Fugger, of Augsburg, had a collection which, in 1566, included eighty-two cornetts, fifty-nine recorders, forty-seven flutes, thirteen fagotti, two Doltzana, nine shawms, and eight crumhorns!

England

English civic wind bands reached their greatest period of development, their climax, and the beginning of their rapid decline during the sixteenth century. The proliferation of these bands, still called 'waits,' continued throughout England; in London one now finds, in addition to the principal London Waits, individual wind bands in each of the major wards of the city, in Finsbury, Southwark, Blackfriars, Tower Hamlets, and the City of Westminster. The official size of most of these bands was five, although apprentices were allowed to perform with the regular members in important public festivities.

In London there was enough demand for wind band music, beyond that played by the royal wind band and the London Waits, to support an independent wind minstrel guild. Their charter in 1500 expresses their chief concern in restricting the performance opportunities in London to themselves.

Raimund Fugger by Vincenzo Catena, 1525

> The continual recourse of foreign minstrels, daily resorting to this City out of all the countries of England and enjoying more freedom than the freemen, causes the Minstrels of the City to be brought to such poverty and decay that they are not able to pay 'lots and scot' and do their duty as other freemen do, since their living is taken from them by these foreigners.

They accused these wandering minstrels of outrageous behaviour, appearing,

> uninvited, sometimes as many as five or six at a time crowding to the end of the tables, playing without skill and causing great pain and displeasure to the Citizens and to their honest friends and neighbors.

A new charter, under Henry VIII, establishes an apprentice system, requires apprentices to pass a special proficiency examination before playing in taverns, hostelries, or alehouses, and warns the regular members not to take jobs away from each other.

> It shall not be liefull to eny Mynstrell ffreman of the said ffelishp to supplante hire or gete out another mynstrell ffreman of the same ffeliship beying hire or spoken to ffor to sue [serve] at eny Tryumphes, Ffeests, Dyns, Sowps, Mariags, Gilds or Brotherhede or eny such other doynge whereby eny such mynstrell shuld have parte of his lyvying under the payne to eny such Supplanter ... of 40 shillings.

An ordinance of 1572 specifically mentions musicians as potential vagabonds and attempts to restrict their travels. Now, traveling without a patron or proper traveling papers could result in his being 'grievously whipped, and burnt through the gristle of the right ear with a hot iron of the compass of an inch about' on first conviction and death on the third conviction!

There are many extant records of civic governments purchasing new instruments, often complete consorts, during this century. An inventory in 1572 of the instruments in 'Custodye' of the famous Norwich Waits included,

> ij Trumpettes; iiij Sacquebuttes, iij haukboyes; v Recorders beeyng a Whoall noyse; and one old Lyzardyne.

In 1583 this same band sought additional funds to expand its collection of instruments, 'they bee at greatter chardges then heretofor by providing of sondry sorts of Instruments which heretofore haue not been by them vsed.'

In terms of instrumentation, the most dramatic change was the introduction of strings near the end of the century, for this sounded the death-knell of the golden age of the pure wind band in England. Representative of this basic change was the publication of Thomas Morely's *First Booke of Consort Lessons* in 1599. Specified for a mixed consort of strings and flute, the editor nevertheless allows other substitutions, 'to the ende that whose skill or liking regardeth not the one, may attempt some other.' This publication is dedicated to the London Waits and the composer makes an interesting distinction between their skill and that of the common musicians of the street.

> For I desire no to satisfe bablers, which are baser than brute beasts in reprouing excellencie, neuer attaine to the first degree of any commendable Science or misterie. But as the ancient custome is of this most honorable and renowned Cittie hath beene euer, to retaine and maintane excellent and expert Musitians, to adorne your Honors fauors, Feasts and solemne meetings: to those of your Lordships Waits ... I recommend the same to your seruants carefull and skilfull handling.

Although specified for the new string instrument style, one should remember that much of this music is arrangements of earlier wait literature and might thus represent literature earlier performed by pure wind bands.

A typical mixed consort of winds and strings, 1590

Most towns made direct tax assessments on the citizens to support the civic wind bands. A typical new tax announced by Leicester in 1581 includes a restriction against wandering minstrels.

> It is agreed that every Inhabitant or housekeeper in Leicester (being of reasonable ability) shall be taxed (at the discretion of Mr. Mayor) what they shall quarterly give to the Waytes towards the amending of their living. In consideration whereof the said Waytes shall keep the town [remain in town], and to play every night and morning orderly [watch duty], both winter and summer, and not to go forth of the town to play except to fairs and weddings, and then by licence of Mr. Mayor. Item, that no strangers, viz. Waytes, minstrels, or other musicians whatsoever be suffered to play within this town, neither at weddings nor fair times or any other times whatsoever.

Nevertheless, individual civic bands often traveled to other cities, where they were invariably rewarded by the host town, as a means of augmenting their income. Nottingham, in the single year 1571–1572, rewarded visiting wait bands from Wakefield, Derby, Newark, Barton upon Humber, Leicester, Chesterfield, Leeds, Oxford, Ratford, and Grantham.

On more rare occasions wait bands had the opportunity to travel abroad. In 1589, the famous Sir Francis Drake requested the loan of the Norwich town band to accompany him on a voyage to Portugal, 'to singe the King of Spain's beard.'

Sir Francis Drake by Marcus Gheeraerts the Younger, 1591

> This day was redd in the Court, a letter sent to Master Mair and his brethern from Sir Francis Drake, wherebye he desyreth that the Waytes of this Citie may be sent to hym, to go the new intended voyage; whereunto the Waytes being here called do all assent, whereupon it is agreed that they should have vi cloaks of stemell cloth made them redy before they go; and that a wagon shall be provided to carry them and their instruments, and that they shall have iiiilb to buye them, three new howboyes and one treble recorder, and xlb to bear their chargys; and that the Citie shall hyre the wagon and paye for it. Also that the Chamberlyn shall pay Peter Spratt xs.3d for a saquebut case; and the Waytes to delyver to the Chamberlyn before they go the citie's cheanes.

Unfortunately on this occasion four of the six Norwich waits who made the trip lost their lives. This reminds us that these players were humans and should not be thought of only as 'historical characters.' No doubt among them were representatives of the best artists of their times, but also some who failed to achieve so high a standard. Extant records make clear that civic governments moved quickly if the personal character of any of these wind players threatened to bring discredit to the town. In 1561, the York city officials warned one, Thomas a Wait, that he must,

> respite to learne and applie himself in the instruments and songs belonging to the sayd wayts, and to leave his unthrifty gamyng upon payne to be putte forth of that office.

These same officials dimissed two waits in 1584, charging,

> their evil and disorderly behavior, to the discredit of this city. Viz. for that they have gone abroad, in the country, in very evil apparel, with their hose forth at their heels, also for that they are common drunkards and cannot so cunningly play on their instruments as they ought.

In several cases the entire civic wind band was fired, as in the case of the Leicester Waits in 1563.

> The Waits because they cannot agree together are therefore now dismissed from being the Town Waits from henceforth.

The wait bands continued to perform some type of watch duty as well as for all important civic festivities. An eyewitness describes the London Waits, seen among other musicians in a procession in 1575.

> Then a set of hautboys playing … sixteen trumpeters … the drum and fife of the city … and after, the waits of the city in blue gowns, red sleeves and caps, everyone having his silver collar about his neck.

These same London Waits are praised by an eyewitness who heard them in a procession in 1558.

> Uppon the porche of Saint Peters church dore, stode the waites of the citie, which did geve a pleasant noyse with their instruments.

When the Norwich Waits, 'placed with loude musicke [wind music], who cheerefully and melodiously welcomed hyr Majestie into the citie,' it is said that Queen Elizabeth was so delighted with their performance that she gave each of them a new instrument and a house on King Street as well!

In towns by the sea the civic waits always played to welcome the arrival of ships and in Liverpool this tradition included performing at the door of the homes of the sailors and their families.

A new function which the English waits performed during the sixteenth century was the performance of music for the theater. Records from early during the century suggest the waits sometimes took speaking parts as well (a few of which survive), but during the period of Shakespeare their function was to perform the music referred to in the stage directions of these famous plays. Thus we find an application by the Norwich Waits in 1570 to obtain permission to perform regularly in the theater.

> The whole company of waytes of this Citie did come into this Court and craved that they might have leve to play comodies and Interludes and other such pieces and Tragedes which shall seem to them meete; which petition is granted, they not playing in the Tyme of Divine Service and Sermons.

The English civic wind bands also continued to give public concerts during the sixteenth century. In London regular hour long concerts began in 1571, on Sunday evenings, from a turret of the Royal Exchange Building, a tradition which continued until a more puritan feeling in 1642 prevented music on Sundays. An earlier description of similar concerts, from Norwich in 1553, is found in the following notice by the mayor's court.

> … that the waits of the City shall have liberty and license every Sunday at night and other holidays at night betwixt this and Michaelmas next coming to come to the guildhall, and upon the nether leads of the same hall next the council house hall betwixt the hours of seven and eight of the clock at night blow and play upon their instruments the space of half an hour to the rejoicing and comfort of the hearers thereof.

Another occasion for performances by the London Waits was for the private lawyers celebrations. These usually included elaborate pageants, one of which in 1562 had the theme of the hunt. Among the participants, trumpets, drums, fifes, and 'musick' are described in an indoor procession and performing while 'the fox and cat by the hounds are set upon, and killed beneath the fire.' In other words, after the captive fox and cat were torn into a thousand bloody pieces, dinner was served!

The Low Countries

All evidence points to the fame and success of the Flemish civic wind bands during the first half of the sixteenth century. Their reputation was such that these wind players were in demand, and were found in courts and towns throughout Europe. Even a city so relatively distant as Lisbon used only musicians from Flanders in their civic band from 1495–1521.

The more prosperous towns had five and sometimes six wind players in the town band, but even the smallest towns usually had at least four. In Ghent a six-member shawm and sackbut band can be documented in 1521, a typical instrumentation of which can be seen in a document from a few years later.

> Item, paid to Pieter de Conine, Goldsmith ... for two silver sackbuts, two discant and two tenor shawms ... to be delivered to the six shawms of the city.

Brussels, Bruges, and Mechelen all had bands of the same size and instrumentation. In this area, one finds for all civic bands, large or small, numerous extant documents relating to the purchase of complete consorts ('coker,' for cases) of the new renaissance instruments.

The most important civic wind band in the Low Countries was the Antwerp band, among whose players were the famous trombonists, Hans Nagel and Thielman Susato, whose compositions for this band are one of the 'crown jewels' of renaissance music. Susato was a member of the band from at least 1529 (a fire destroyed earlier records) until 1549 and was apparently a trombonist ('tromper,' in his language), although when he opened his publishing house it was 'under the sign of the crumhorn.'

According to the scholar John Murray, soon after Susato joined the band he transcribed thirty-three volumes of six-part music, running to about four hundred folio pages, for its use—a treasure of early wind band music now apparently lost. The music of Susato which has survived is found in the publications which he began in 1551. The first of these collections, the first publication of multi-part songs in the Flemish tongue, includes an introduction by Susato which gives us an insight into the way these civic musicians looked at their art.

Portrait of Tielman Susato

> Music is a remarkable gift, instituted by order of God and offered to man to be used not for dishonest or thoughtless ends but, above all, to render thanks and praise to the Lord, to shun idleness and make good use of his time, to drive out melancholy and dark thoughts, and in order to restore joy to hearts sorely tried.

As this collection appeared immediately after Susato's departure from active membership in the Antwerp civic wind band, perhaps it is reasonable to suppose that he would first have published those chansons familiar to him through his performances of instrumental versions. In any case, his title page invites such performance.

> The first music books in four parts, including twenty-six new love songs in our Low German tongue, composed by diverse composers, most pleasant to sing and play on all musical instruments.

It is, however, a following publication which claims our greater interest: his famous collection (1551) of instrumental dances in four part-books. Several of these were composed by Susato himself and it is difficult to imagine their source being any other than from the repertoire of the town band.

Another publisher, and principal competitor to Susato, was Pierre Phalèse, who published three large collections of instrumental music, which was probably also intended for use by town bands.

A contract for the members of the Mechelen civic band in 1515 offers a glimpse into the broad range of duties expected by the city. They were to perform on cornetts and other instruments during solemn masses celebrated by order of the magistrates; they were to play at the town hall 'met shalmijen, trompetten ende andere instrumenten,' late mornings, every Saturday, Sunday, holiday, and days preceding public festivities; in the course of banquets organized by the town, they were to perform on string instruments and flutes; they could not refuse to participate in any service required by the town; and in order to maintain a desirable standard of performance, they were ordered to rehearse together at least twice weekly and to obey a leader.

These bands also appeared in all civic processions, including the traditional *ommegangs*. An interesting example of one of the pageants given in one of these processions, this in honor of the visiting Prince Francis, Duke of Brabant in 1581, was one representing the Nine Muses, 'playing on diverse kinds of instruments, and a sweet singer.' Across from the musicians was a 'cave verie hideous, darke, and drierie to behold,' in which lurked the three 'hell-hounds,' Discord, Violence and Tyranie. These three would come sneaking to the mouth of the cave only to hear the music, which caused them to scamper back into the cave. The point of this was to instruct all observers that as long as the realm was interested in the arts, it would not be disturbed by discord, violence, or tyranny!

Four pipers from Leuven in a procession, ca. 1594

Public concerts, such as described in the Mechelen contract of 1505 above, can be seen as well in contracts from Bruges and Mons. In Antwerp the band also played morning concerts as the delegates of the Hanseatic League walked from their factories to the Bourse, as well as during the annual fair. An engraving by Valckenborck pictures a town band situated in a large 'nest' in a tree, playing for the public in the town square.

Several by-laws of the sixteenth-century civic guilds in the Low Countries are extant and a typical one, that of Antwerp in 1541, required the members to swear before a magistrate to use their talents for the well-being of the community, to play and accept engagements whenever they had openings, not to make double bookings or cut short performances, to instruct apprentices in all the instruments 'expected of them by the laws of the town,' and to teach dancing. In Mons, in 1588, a candidate for the guild had to perform before the assembly of 'masters,' following an apprenticeship of two years. To become a 'master,' he had to be able to play, 'two pieces of music on each of said instruments (shawm, cornett, recorder, and violin), such songs as the masters see fit to choose.' In Antwerp in 1555 apprentices were permitted to join with the regular members in performance, thus forming larger wind bands.

France

The famous St. Julien Guild of Paris continued to be active during the sixteenth century and we know each of its leaders ('kings') beginning with Jean Bénard in 1537. During this time the guild instituted a system of 'licenses,' to control visiting minstrels. One of these, issued in 1585 to Yves de Brie, states that he might live in Paris so long as he was 'without fault and created no scandal.' The guild also attempted to bring under its control the instrumental performance in areas outside Paris, through the creation of 'lieutenants' in Paris who would oversee the music in various villages.

There is also more information regarding the apprenticeship requirements for this guild during the sixteenth century. In one respect this guild seems to have been more liberal than most, in that it did not require residence in Paris as a requirement for being an apprentice. The average apprentice was from ten to sixteen years of age and together with his parents or teacher drew up a legal document regarding all the conditions of his service. The duration of this apprenticeship was officially six years, but few seems to have been required to serve so long, and never if one was the son of a 'master.' The apprentice was assigned to a 'master,' who was required to treat the apprentice humanely and to provide for his welfare.

The most distinguished members of this guild were those wind players who were also members of the king's wind band. Most important of these to us was Jean d'Estrée, who was both a shawmist in the king's band and a member of a ten-member civic wind band in Paris. He published four books of danseries, as an editor under the publisher Nicolas Du Chemin, between 1559 and 1564. These dances are melodically oriented, with simple part-writing, suggesting perhaps they were intended for the broader market of small village wind bands, and not the fine professionals who played in court. The demand for exactly this kind of music is clear from a comment by Arbeau (1588).

> Nowadays there is no workman so humble that he does not which to have shawms and sackbuts at his wedding.

An eyewitness account of the civic wind band in Valenciennes (1539) describes the band performing new chansons.

> … des jouers de hautbois qu'il fait moult bon ouyr pour leurs chansons nouvelles.

A similar description of the civic wind band in Lyons in 1548 speaks of a nine-member band of 'dolcians, cornetts and sordun.'

The German-Speaking Countries

The most famous sixteenth-century wind band in Germany was the one in Nürnberg. Indeed it was so often the subject of interest by contemporary artists that one can follow its development in iconography. In 1500 we see a three-man band of two shawms and a slide-trumpet, an instrument which has been replaced in a drawing of 1519. A famous work by Dürer in 1520 pictures four players of shawms and sackbuts and by mid-century the band is seen as five players of cornett, shawms, and sackbut.

Reference has been made above to the fact that the city fathers maintained a very large collection of various consorts of instruments for these players and there are numerous extant documents relative to their purchase. An inventory made in 1598 gives interesting detail for one case of crumhorns.

The Nurnberg civic musicians, ca. 1560–80, an image from the Heldt'schen Trachtenbuch

> Item 1 case with crumhorns, 1 bass with 2 keys, 1 bass with 1 key, 1 tenor with 1 key, 2 tenors without keys, 2 altos and 2 sopranos. Total 9. Note: All there including a small box containing the reeds.

References to the prototype bassoons appear in the Nürnberg records beginning in 1575.

Similar records exist from many towns, including Augsburg, Munich, Leipzig, and Dresden. Even so small a village as Memmingen had a wind band consisting of such fine players that in 1502 the Emperor Maxmilian I pleaded with the town council to send him 'two of your town musicians, Jorg Eyselin and Ulrich Plaser ... who are reputed to be good at playing high and low parts on shawms and trombones.'

There is evidence that the 'Abblasen' tradition, the playing of spiritual music from towers, had begun already by the sixteenth century. The contract for the civic wind band in Dresden in 1572 specified the performance of four-part music from the tower, as well as accompanying the town choir in church 'on feast days, Sundays and at weddings and other occasions when polyphony was performed' (a similar reference to accompanying polyphonic music is found in a contract from Zwickau). A contract from Lübeck requires a chorale at four o'clock in the morning to awaken the farm hands and another to mark the mid-day pause. The band played again at noon to mark the resumption of work and at nine o'clock to indicate the time to sleep.

The ancient tradition of the watch duty continued to be of great importance to the German town fathers, as one can see in an actual oath required of a new civic trumpeter in Wismar, in 1586.

> I swear that I shall be true, obedient and loyal to the honorable council of the town of Wismar, to bear in mind their and the town's best interest, and to avert harm to the best of my ability while on the tower of St. Nicholas where I have been appointed tower watch. I swear to watch carefully day and night, to look after light and fire with all diligence so no harm may come to the town and church from them; in other respects I also swear to behave modestly and peacefully with everyone and to lead an honorable and respectable life, so help me God.

In addition to the trumpet, this watch musician had at his disposal a number of other objects to help alert the town in case of fire, including bells, flags, and lanterns. Perhaps the most unusual of such sixteenth-century references comes from Köln, where the citizens had their time announced with cymbals!

> [They] are to give the time hourly with cymbals, and also every day in the morning around daybreak, at about three or four o'clock, they are to play on flutes, crumhorns, cornetts or shawms; similarly around midday at eleven o'clock and then again in the evening ... at about nine or ten o'clock.

Another account, from Memmingen in 1518, not only reflects the importance of watch duty, but contains a very interesting reference to some kind of early civic wind band contest.

> Jack the town player is to be allowed to go with the other players for ten days to Augsburg, if they wish to win an award with the crumhorns, but in the meantime he must arrange for the watch to be maintained.

There are numerous references to civic wind players being engaged to help in the celebrations of university graduates during the sixteenth century. In the case of the graduation of some Doctors of Theology, in 1591, four wind players were engaged and provided with wine and three persons to carry their instruments. Reports of some of the outdoor engagements suggest larger bands were used, to produce a louder sound. An eyewitness to such festivities in Stuttgart in 1575 reports,

> such a noise of cornetts and crumhorns, of bombards, racketts and shawms that one could not even hear oneself speak.

As in the other countries, the German civic wind band members earned extra pay by performing private weddings and there are many extant civic documents relative to the control and salary for these activities. One interesting document, from Reval (Tallinn) in 1532, gives details of the dance music.

> Item after the evening meal they should play four popular double dances and then they can play a double dance with recorders or crumhorns, as well as a girl's dance and the bride's dance, which adds up to ten dances ... Whoever wishes to hold board for an evening in the hall or houses and wishes to be entertained on recorders and crumhorns with four double dances, one girl's dance [and] one bride's dance, for this the payment is six farthings.

Finally, there was an annual tradition in the German-speaking areas whereby the civic wind band performed throughout the town on New Year's Day for donations. A civic edict in Delitzach (1599) suggests that in one case this was unpopular with the citizens for here the town council passed a special bonus of one Taler for the civic wind band, if they would not carry out this performance!

'Augsburger Geschlechtertanz' by Abraham Schelhas shows a wind band providing the music for an aristocratic dance in Augsburg, ca. 1600 (See detail on page 106)

Italy

Every sixteenth-century Italian town of almost any size had two civic wind ensembles. First there was an ensemble of trumpets which were used in particular for ceremonial purposes. When great state visitors would arrive, these civic trumpets would often join with the aristocratic visitor's trumpets, and perhaps with borrowed trumpets from other towns, to form large numbers. One reads, for example, of the welcome given Louis XII of France in Milan in 1499 when not only the six *'trombatori del Comune'* played their silver trumpets, but one hundred additional trumpets encircled the king, in front and to the rear. The statutes of Urbine (1559) contain an interesting suggestion that the repertoire of these official trumpeters was not always merely of the fanfare type, for here it specifies 'devout' music.

> … shall be preceded by trumpets … and … with a devout and sonorous sound of trumpeters playing on loud trumpets.

Each town also had a civic wind band, usually called '*musica di piffari,*' or '*compagnia di piffari,*' or simply '*piffari,*' but it is clear that during the sixteenth century some combination of shawms, trombones, and cornetts were intended by this term and not primarily instruments of the flute family. A curious exception was Torino, which called its civic wind band, '*Banda di tromboni.*'

One of the many large towns which had both kinds of ensembles was Bologna. This band, called the '*Concerto Palatino,*' had a regular instrumentation of four cornetts and four trombones and was famous throughout Italy for its concerts.

In Florence the civic wind band traditions seem to have been so deeply rooted that they continued to flourish despite the great political upheavals which began the century. It is said that there was such a close relationship between music and the other arts in Florence, that the father to Benvenuto Cellini began flute lessons for his son at an early age believing that, whatever craft he might wish to follow when he was older, the entry to a craft would be facilitated by his son's having been a musician.

The civic wind band in florence, '*I pifferi della Signoria,*' consisted of three shawms and two sackbuts in 1510, with a sixth player added in about 1520. The leading scholar on the civic band in Florence at this time, Keith Polk, believes that the impression in general history texts that the members of the string instrument family were popular by this time in Florence may be quite in error; indeed, he was unable to find a single reference to a string instrument in the civic archives between 1490 and 1532!

In addition to the wind band, Florence also had civic trumpets, who are called '*trombetti,*' or '*trombatori.*' These two terms represent a distinction in the instrument used, as one can see in a description of a civic procession held during the final years of the Republic (1525–1530). First one saw eight '*trombetti,*' with long, ornate, silver trumpets, 'very heavy,' weighing 3 pounds, 3 ounces. Next came six '*trombadori,*' with equally ornate trumpets, weighing 3 pounds, 3 ounces.

Another town which maintained a relatively large civic wind band during the sixteenth century was Lucca. This band had eleven members by 1517 and at least ten throughout the century. Among the members of this band were the Dorati family, chiefly Nicolao Dorati (d. 1593), who was hired as a trombonist in 1543 and became the leader of the band in 1557. This civic wind band was named the '*Musica di Palazzo*' and we have a very interesting municipal decree of 1557 which provides an excellent picture of their organization and duties.

> Nicolao Dorati is to be the director and head of said musicians, and they must obey him in performing whatever music in whatever manner he may choose. When playing at the city hall, before and after the dinner of the *Signoria*, Messer Bernardino da Padova is to play the first soprano, and Vincenzo di Pasquino Bastini the second soprano; but when playing in the hall or the chambers of the *Signoria*, each one is to play or sing the part assigned to him by said Messer Nicolao, their director. However, outside of the city hall, in church, on the public square, at weddings, feasts, serenades, or other events, where they will number at least six, Messer Giulio is to play the first soprano, Messer Bernardino, his father, the second, and Messer Vincenzo the third, that is, contralto. And if by chance, which God forbid, there should arise among them a quarrel, ill-will, or other trouble, Messer Nicolao is to intervene and restore peace, and if anyone should refuse to listen to reason, he is to be reported to the *Signoria* in office at the time, so that steps can be taken accordingly. And since beautiful music and perfect harmony are the result of constant practice, there should be assigned to them for this purpose a room ... equipped with tables and benches in which they are to meet for practice twice a week for two hours, namely, Wednesdays and Saturdays. From the first of February to the last of September they shall meet in the morning, two hours before dinner, and from the first of October to the last of January, in the afternoon, two hours before supper. In order to enforce these rules, the *maestro di casa* shall take the attendance, and those who are absent, shall be fined one *carlino* for each time, except in case of illness or other legitimate excuse.

This general pattern seems to have been followed in many of the smaller towns in Italy. Udine had five civic wind band members in 1560 and seven by 1575, consisting of '*piffari*' and trombones who played outdoor concerts, processions, for civic guests, and in the church. Perugia during the sixteenth century had six civic *trombetti* and a wind band of four '*pifferi*' and a trombone. Parma's wind band was called the '*compagnia di piffari*,' which at the beginning of the century consisted of four '*pifferi*,' in addition to four civic *trombettieri*. The highest paid of its players were two *trombetti*, called '*trombetti foresi*,' for it was their responsibility to go outside the walls of the town to recruit new players.

The civic wind band in Palermo is called in a document of the sixteenth century, '*musici bifari salariati della citta,*' and are referred to as '*pifferi, trombeti e timpani.*'

Because of the unique government of Venice, it was the Doge's wind band which usually appeared as the official representative at both civic and church festivities. This band also gave an hour-long concert each day in the Piazza St. Mark.

'Basilica Di San Marco' by Carlo Grubacs, 1849

Venice also had at least six independent *piffari* bands which were associated with the religious fraternities of the city and which will be discussed below. Our greatest interest is reserved for a civic wind band which seems to have been created at the end of the sixteenth century, conducted by, and perhaps founded by, Girolamo Dalla Casa. The name of the band is seen in his title, '*Capo de Concerti delli stromenti di fiato della Illustriss. Signoria di Venetia,*' or, 'Leader of the Venetian Civic Wind Band.' While virtually nothing is known of the function of this civic wind band, an extraordinary portion of their actual repertoire is extant in the two volumes of Dalla Casa's *Il Vero Modo di Diminvir* (1584). Dalla Casa was one of the greatest performers of the cornett during the sixteenth century and these volumes represent his solo literature which was accompanied by the wind band. They consist of the solo part fully written out, with identification of the madrigal or motet over which the solo line is to be played. It is, then, the most extensive body of early literature for a solo wind instrument and wind band accompaniment.

Verona had a famous civic institution, the *Accademia Filharmonica*, which sponsored concerts. An inventory of its instrument collection in 1569 lists five sets of viols, keyboards and a large number of wind instruments. Among these are some unusual references to a 'chest of 22 recorders,' 3 'dragonbelled cornetts,' and trombones with 'their crooks and tuning bits.'

7   Church Wind Bands

STUDENTS OF PAST GENERATIONS may have been given a rather incomplete picture of sixteenth-century church music, the professors and textbooks following the concentration of nineteenth-century scholarship on the great Roman Church music of Josquin, Palestrina, etc., left at least one student with the impression that this was an 'a cappella' era. Nothing could be further from the truth. In the English-speaking world, our perspective has been blinded in particular by the fact that the crucial third volume of Praetorius' *Syntagma Musicum* has never been published in a modern translation.

Nothing demonstrates the significance of this misunderstanding of sixteenth-century church practices more than the traditional view of the great wind masterworks of Gabrieli and his school. This body of music, while acknowledged as important, is sometimes presented as something of an isolated phenomenon, as something which somehow just appears at one place and one time, rather than as the logical climax of something which was going on throughout the century.

We can see today that there were much wider traditions of church music during the sixteenth century. This is clear in these pages, above and below, where the reader has seen examples of contracts and payments to civic wind bands throughout Europe and in the examples of personal wind ensembles maintained by the church princes themselves, first and foremost being the wind bands of the popes.

The rich iconography of the sixteenth century stands as an additional testimony to this wider tradition. First, there are icons which clearly picture these wind bands participating in the actual service. The most striking example is the often reproduced engraving by Adrian Collaert, *Mass, with several choirs* (1595), in which one sees not one but two separate wind bands, consisting of cornetts and trombones, performing with the choirs. Another widely reproduced icon which shows a wind band performing during the service is the woodcut appearing in Hermann Finck's *Musica Practica* (1556).

Opposite page: 'The Coronation of Pius III,' a fresco decorating the exterior of the Piccolomini Library in the cathedral of Siena, ca. 1503, by Bernardino Pinturicchio. The wind band accompanying the service can be seen on the right.

Finally, one must mention the new pipes being included in sixteenth-century organ construction, for they are clearly an imitation of the contemporary wind band sounds.

The Low Countries

Extant documentation from the sixteenth century suggests that in the Low Countries, as in Germany, performance in the church may have been a regular duty of the civic wind band; Polk believes that such performances were common by 1550. A typical contract from early in the century is found in Mechelen (1505), where the civic band was required to 'play on cornets and other instruments during the solemn masses celebrated by order of the magistrates.' In Mechelen this tradition seems to have continued for in a civic document of 1550–1551 one again reads of payments to members of the civic band for performing

An engraving by Philippe Galle after a work by Johannes Stradanus, features a wind band performing during a Mass (Antwerp, Belgium, 1595)

during the Mass, as well as in church processions. Similar civic documents are extant from Mons (1588) and Antwerp, where new trombones were purchased in 1541 for use with the choir.

There is also a reference to the actual literature used by the Antwerp wind band in the church in a 'lovely large songbook,' created by Anthony Barbe, chapel master of the Cathedral of Our Lady in 1550. The music was to be used at High Masses, 'to be sung out of by the choir, and to be played out of by the city musicians.'

A similar volume of motets to be used by a civic wind band in the church was commissioned in 1484 of Casin de Brauwer, Master of the Children at St. Donaes, by the town council of Bruges. Following this, the civic wind band apparently did not appear in the church for a few years at the turn of the century for one finds that the choir master, Obrecht, no less, received an order from the city demanding correction. In 1509 the accounts again note the presence of the 'chapel master, singers, organist and wind players.'

The court chapels in the Low Countries seem to have had permanent wind players, rather than resorting to borrowing the local civic wind bands. A list of personnel of the royal chapel in Brussels for 1576 lists three priests, nine singers, two cornett players, one trombonist, an organist, and an organ tuner. Similarily, the court of Margaret of Austria, the Regent of the Low Countries, also maintained wind players for use in the service.

France

A well-known example of French wind players participating in a Mass is the one which occurred on 23 June 1520, quoted above, during the historic meeting between Francis I and Henry VIII. It appears that the English and French royal chapels alternated in singing the movements of a Mass written by a composer named Perino. One account indicates some movements were accompanied by organ and others by sackbuts and fifes (certainly shawms is meant). Another account indicates the entire Mass was accompanied by organ, sackbuts and cornetts.

There is at least one indication that under Francis I the court wind band participated in the Mass while in Paris as well. One of Wolsey's correspondents heard High Mass in the chapel of

Francis I and mentioned that it was accompanied by 'hautbois (shawms) and sackbutts.' Speaking of Wolsey, his counterpart in Paris was John, Cardinal of Lorraine (1498–1550), who also maintained his own personal wind players.

A court document from late in the reign of Francis I gives the personnel of the *schola cantorum*, founded in 1543, as 'two undermasters, six children, two cornett players, twenty-six singers, twelve clerics, and two grammer teachers for the children.'

Finally, there is an indication that in some of the provincial cities the town wind bands also assisted in the church music. In Toulouse, during the sixteenth century, the civic band supplied 'oboes, trumpets and drums for ceremonial motets and masses in the principal churches.'

Spain

According to Walter Salmen, during the sixteenth century it was a normal occurrence for 'ministriles' to participate in the performance of polyphonic music in the great Spanish cathedrals. Thus one reads in a description of the instrumental music of the Granada Cathedral,

> instruments were used at first only to accompany certain processions (when portative organs were also used), but from 1563 six instrumentalists were employed for the daily services; they played flutes, trumpets, trombones and bassoons.

In Seville in particular one finds accounts of the use of the wind band in the cathedral, under the leadership of Francisco Guerrero (1528–1599), a musician second only to Victoria in importance as a composer of Spanish church music and himself a cornett player. According to Salmen, the instruments he used were shawms, sackbuts, and bassoons. Robert Stevenson gives a somewhat broader range of consorts of instruments used in the cathedral.

> Throughout his long tenure at Seville Cathedral, instruments such as families of shawms, cornetts, flutes and bassoons were constantly used to add divisions, embellishing and alternating with his vocal lines.

Francisco Guerrero (1528-1599) by Francisco Pacheco

In another place, Stevenson quotes an actual cathedral document, dated 11 July 1586, which specifies,

> At greater feasts there shall always be a verse played on recorders. At Salves, one of the three verses that are played shall be on shawms, one on cornetts and the other on recorders; because always hearing the same instrument annoys the listener.

With this background, it should come as no surprise that one finds evidence that the New World churches also made extensive use of wind bands in their services. Regarding Mexico, for example, one finds in Geronimo de Mendieta's *Historia Eclesiastica Indiana* (ca. 1571–1596) the interesting observation that,

> nowhere in all of Christendom are there so many recorders, shawms, sackbuts, orlas, trumpets and drums as in the Kingdom of New Spain.

A bronze medallion by Juan Marin and Bautista Vazquez from the Seville Cathedral shows a wind band, 1564

Further south, in Guatemala, there is a document recording the purchase of a case of recorders for the main cathedral already in 1549.

Even in South America, one reads that when Fernandez Hidalgo was in charge of the cathedral music in La Plata (now Sucre, Bolivia), he

> lured a number of other musicians from Cuzco and maintained a rich establishment which included players of cornetts, sackbuts, flutes and shawms as well as singers.

Finally, a few notes about Portugal are appropriate here, especially regarding an important individual player, Andre de Escobar (fl. 1560–1580). This man held the title of 'Master of the Shawms' at both the Evora Cathedral and the University of Coimbra. He also was the author of a method book for the shawm, the *Arte musica para tanger o instrumento da charamelinha*, which unfortunately does not survive. There was also a wind band in residence in the cathedral in Lisbon. We know, for example, that in 1592 the musicians of this cathedral consisted of twenty-four adult and twenty-two boy singers, two bassoons, a cornettist and two organists.

England

References to the use of wind bands in English churches, especially in the performance of Te Deums are fairly frequent in the literature of the sixteenth century. One reads of Henry VIII and Cardinal Wolsey attending Mass at St. Paul's, in 1525, after which 'the quere sang Te Deum, and the mynstrelles plaied on every side.' An eyewitness, writing of Elizabeth I's visit to Oxford in 1566, notes, 'and afterwards ... she entered into the church, and there abode while the quyer sang and played with cornetts, a Te Deum.' Another observer of the same service wrote, 'in the middle of which service was an anthem called Te Deum, sung to cornets.'

Canterbury Cathedral seems to have been an early example of a cathedral which maintained its own small wind band from an early date. As early as 1532, a cathedral statute calls for the employment of '2 sackbutteers and 2 cornetteers.' A visiting Italian heard this wind band in 1589 and was very impressed.

> Seeing him (the Archbishop) upon the next Sabaoth day after in the Cathedrall Church of Canterburie, attended upon by his Gentlemen, and servants ... also by the Deane, Prebendaries, and Preachers in their Surplesses, and scarlet Hoods, and heard the solemne Musicke with the voyces, and Organs, Cornets, and Sagbutts, hee was overtaken with admiration ... that (unlesse it were in the Popes Chappell) he had never saw a more solemne sight, nor heard a more heavenly sound.

Another eyewitness from the period of Elizabeth I makes a similar comparison with the pomp of the Roman Church.

> The service was sung not only with organs, but with the artificial [skillful] music of cornets, sacbuts, etc., on solemn festivals ... That, in short, the service performed in the Queen's Chapel, and in sundry cathedrals, was so splendid and showy, that foreigners could not distinguish it from the Roman, except that it was performed in English.

Similar descriptions of the use of cornetts and sackbuts continue throughout the reign of Elizabeth as in the case of the civic wind band assisting with the actual church service in St. James Church, in Bristol, in 1583; in Norwich for the Christmas Service in 1575; and in Chester in 1591.

Of course, associations with royalty demanded wind music as always. Both visits by the queen to Worcester Cathedral in 1575 included cornetts and sackbuts, the Sunday Service being, 'a great and solemn noise of singing of service in the quire both by note and also playing with cornetts and sackbuts.' During a visit to the queen by Frederick, Duke of Württemberg, in 1592, one finds an account of the use of winds in the more private surroundings of the queen's palace at Windsor, one of his secretaries writing, 'the music, especially the organ, was exquisitely played; for at times you could hear the sound of cornets, flutes, then fifes (shawms?) and other instruments.'

At least one early writer has suggested that on occasion the wind band actually replaced the choir. Roger North (1695–1728), writing of this earlier period, commented, 'wind musick was frequently used in churches, instead of voices, or else to enforce the chorus.'

The German-Speaking Countries

During the sixteenth century in the German-speaking lands, one can see an extraordinary development in the use of wind bands in the church. In the first part of the century one can still see many examples of the aristocratic wind bands continuing the traditions of the fifteenth century, yet by the end of the century one finds the post-Luther, Protestant, multi-choral works for voices and winds which one usually associates with the early German Baroque.

The use of the aristocratic wind band in the private chapels of the noble continues as a strong tradition in sixteenth-century Germany and Austria, following the example set by the Emperor, Maximilian I, who had many 'trumetten, pfeiffen (shawms) und orgeln' in his private church music, '*des kunigs cantarei.*' During the Reichstag meeting he attended in Trier, in 1512, one heard only trombones, cornetts, and trumpets with the church music. His son, Philip the Fair, followed his example, as is suggested by an eyewitness who describes hearing a Mass in Philip's chapel, during which the trombones joined in playing the 'Deo gratias' and the 'Ite messa est.'

Another example of such a private chapel later in the century is that of the Elector Moritz of Saxony, who hired six cornett and sackbut players in 1549 for his church music. One of those hired was the composer Antonio Scandello (1517–1580), who was also a cornettist of such fame that cornett students came from great distances to study with him.

Of course the personal wind bands of the nobles continued to perform in family ceremonies in the church. A typical example is an eyewitness account of the wedding of Duke Ludwig of the Württemberg court in Stuttgart, in 1575, which describes the wedding music as an eight-part work for singers and trombones which was 'so lovely and noble that the heart was refreshed.' Later, in a descriptive poem, the same observer makes a reference to one of the performances by the duke's wind band.

Portrait of Maurice (Moritz), Elector of Saxony (1521–1553) by Lucas Cranach the Younger, 1578

> Zinks and five shawms,
> Held with flying fingers,
> Faster than an eye blink,
> They played the best pieces.

Aristocratic trumpet choirs also participated in church services in Germany and an excellent account of how these trumpet choirs actually functioned in church music is given in a description of the ordination service of Bishop Amsdorf in Naumberg, in 1542. The principal musical performance, a work given as 'Nun bitten wir den heiligen Geist,' consisted of the first verse heard in the organ, the second by a five-part choir, and the third by the five-part trumpet choir.

An even greater number of documents refer to the participation of civic wind bands in the church service. Of these accounts, most are descriptions of music in the Protestant services for it was there that the new multi-part music in the Italian style was first championed. Nevertheless, one does find descriptions of civic wind bands appearing in the Catholic Mass as well. The Zwickau civic wind band was paid in 1559–1560 to perform the Mass and in the same city in 1565 a visiting wind band was paid for performing in the church.

One account from St. Anne's Church in Dresden, in 1578, also gives us the actual repertoire performed. On this occasion the student choir of St. Anne, together with the Dresden civic wind band, performed a six-part motet, 'Jubilato Deo,' by Clemens non Papa and a six-part motet, 'Te Deum Patrem,' by Orlando di Lasso.

There are also a few sixteenth-century accounts of wind music in the Catholic convents and monasteries, in particular at Melk and Kremsmünster in Austria. The convent at Hall (now Solbad Hall, near Innsbruck) had a full wind band of cornett and trombone players for which it was famous at the time.

Traditional accounts of the early Protestant Church sometimes make the assertion that the early church leaders were opposed to the use of instrumental music in the services and celebrations of the church. Numerous accounts of the use of civic wind bands in their services during the sixteenth century, particularly in polyphony, suggest that this idea was short-lived at best. Even as early as 1539 one finds Martin Luther himself praising a church procession which included trombones, harps, timpani, cymbals, and bells.

An account from Halle, of an Easter morning service, speaks of a shawm band playing a 'beautiful motet.' In Linz (Austria) the civic wind band played in the Lutheran Landhauskirche after 1550. Towns which had no civic wind bands would import them, so the Wurzen band appeared in Finsterwalde in 1581 and the Altenburg band in Oschatz in 1598. Two such accounts are more valuable as they hint at the musical function of the civic wind band. In Berne, in 1572, they were used to help accompany the congregational singing and in Zwickau, in 1558, the band was ordered to play with the organ (in *die Orgel pfiffen*), an expression which one scholar takes to mean playing a chorale over an organ cantus firmus.

Additional clues to the role of the civic wind band in the Protestant Service can perhaps be found in the surviving music itself. Ehmann mentions a three-part chorale composed in 1540 by Johann Kugelmann (in this case, a court wind player) and the 'Instrumental Songs' of Martin Agricola, Kantor at Magdeburg. The latter three-part works are unspecified but Ehmann believes that they were for winds, as this was the prevailing practice. One should also mention the 26 *Fugen* (1542) composed by Johann Walther (1496–1570), Luther's musical advisor, composed 'especially for cornetts.'

It was, however, for the performance of polyphony that civic wind bands were most used in the Protestant Service. Jakob Gallus, who was one of the first German composers to write multi-part church music, wrote in his *Opus Musicum* (1587) that where there were small numbers of singers the winds *must* help out.

It is evident that the use of winds with multi-part music in the protestant church increased greatly during the latter part of the sixteenth century. A report by a trumpeter in the service of the protestant Bishop of Halle a. d. Saale says that winds were used all the time for this kind of church music.

This increase in the performance of multi-part music is clear from the numerous examples of new contracts specifically requiring the civic wind band's participation. A new order from the Zwickau civic council in 1569 tells the civic wind band they must serve in the church with their instruments whenever multi-part music is performed. An almost identical regulation is found in Delitzsch in 1580 in the contract for new civic band members. In this same year (1580) the civic wind band in Munich began playing in the cathedral and a payment was made in Weissenfels for the performance of the civic wind band in church. When the Dresden civic wind band was reorganized in 1572, the four members were called upon to 'strengthen and enhance' the Kreuzchor with their playing on feast days, Sundays and at weddings and other occasions when polyphony was performed.' A civic council ordinance of 1571 in Ulm speaks of the civic wind band playing on cornetts and trombones in the Münster Cathedral (in *die Cantorey blasen*). A similar ordinance is found in Torgau in 1596.

Further examples could be given, but the point must be clear by now that during the second-half of the sixteenth century the civic wind bands in Germany were actively engaged to help perform multi-part music in the protestant churches. But how exactly did they function with the choir in performing this music?

The answer to this question is found in a fascinating discussion by Praetorius in the third volume of his *Syntagma Musicum*, the most important contemporary source for information on the instrumental performance of late Renaissance church music. Here one finds an extensive and surprising discussion relative to the impromptu forming of *additional* instrumental choirs from pre-existant multi-part church music. I might add that Praetorius says many times that while he and other German musicians are observing the principles below, the original idea came from Italy and specifically from the generation including Gabrieli. Praetorius begins this discussion of the extraction of material to form new and additional choirs of voices and instruments under his definition of 'capella.'

> In my opinion the Italians originally used it (the term *capella*) only to designate an additional separate choir, extracted from several different choirs with various kinds of instruments and voices, as are employed in the larger Imperial, Austrian, and other Catholic musical establishments. This choir is called *chorus pro capella*, because the whole vocal choir or the whole *capella* performs this as a group, placed entirely apart from the other choirs and chiming in like the full *Werk* on an organ. This produces a glorious richness and splendor in such music ... In every *concerto* [a term Praetorius uses for any large scale musical, 'concerted' composition] one, two, or three such *capallae* can be extracted and set up in different parts of the church, each of them consisting only of four persons, or more if available.

As startling as this may seem to the modern reader, the implication is that a multi-choral vocal or instrumental composition by a composer such as Gabrieli is to be considered only a kind of 'basic source material' from which one may construct larger, spatial configurations.

The basic principles which Praetorius sets forth for the creation of the 'new' choirs or ensembles are rather simple. First, the use of unisons, that is, the performance of material in the new ensemble which is drawn directly from a pre-existant ensemble, 'can be used throughout without hesitation in high, low, and middle parts by voices as well as instruments.' Second, one may create music in the new ensemble which is either an octave higher or lower than the pre-existant music, provided that one part is sung and the other part played on an instrument. Praetorius particularly recommends the addition of lower octave doubling of the bass line, going so far as to say that in multi-choral music the bass lines can be three octaves apart! The justification for this idea is based in part on the tradition of organ coupling. The only real caution which Praetorius adds to this seemingly rather free concept has to do only with the placement of these 'new' ensembles in the church building. When one begins to add new ensembles and as a result has three or four ensembles spread out in the building, one must be careful that the congregation hears, either through doubling or placement, the true bass line.

The choice of which consort to use seems to Praetorius mostly a question of range. He engages in a lengthy discussion of the clefs appropriate to the more common instruments, and in particular (given the sixteenth century's preference for *consorts*) the clefs which must be used to transcribe a vocal work for an ensemble of like instruments. He also discusses the various members of each consort, pointing out which are the most or least effective. For example, he says, 'better to leave the squeaky discant shawm alone' and use only the larger instruments.

Regarding the use of string instruments in the church, which Praetorius calls *capella fidicina*, his remarks suggest that as a consort these instruments were not commonly known.

> But it is up to anyone's pleasure to use this capella, or leave it out. For, as mentioned above, I have only added it [to this discussion] because of the approbation of certain listeners and would not otherwise have deemed it very important. If one would thus want to compose and arrange such a *capella fidicinia* ... one would attract those listeners in Germany who still do not know what to make of [this] new style.

Praetorius sums up this discussion by giving examples of his own compositions for the church which demonstrate this rich instrumental practice, including compositions with up to thirty-four parts in nine choirs!

For variety, Praetorius suggests one may use a different consort for each verse, a practice he found common in secular music. Also, one may place the various vocal and instrumental choirs on opposite sides of the church, which adds to variety from the listener's perspective and helps guard against the possibility of the instrumental forces overpowering the voices. Another interesting source of variety in church music was the insertion of instrumental compositions between the movements of the mass, magnificats, or motets, in the manner of the *intermedii* found in the theater.

In more general terms, Praetorius suggests that in the performance of church music a more moderate concept of both tempo and dynamics are appropriate, as compared to secular music. In particular his comments on dynamics seem to suggest that in his experience he had heard some rather dire results from the natural competition among performers.

> No one must cover up and out shout the other with his instrument or voice, though this happens very frequently, causing much splendid music to be spoiled and ruined. When one thus tries to outdo the other, the instrumentalists, particularly cornett players with their blaring but also singers through their screaming, rise in pitch so much that the organist playing along is forced to stop entirely.

Although the introduction of consorts must have greatly improved ensemble intonation in the sixteenth century, one can see in Praetorius' remarks that musicians, then as now, were constantly checking their pitch. Praetorius could not understand why the responsible instrumentalist could not do this unpleasant task at home before he came to play!

> But it creates great confusion and din if the instrumentalists tune their bassoons, trombones, and cornetts during the organist's prelude and carry on loudly and noisily so that it hurts one's ears and gives one the jitters. For it sounds so dreadful and makes such a commotion that one wonders what kind of mayhem is being committed. Therefore everyone should carefully tune the cornett or trombone in his lodging before presenting himself at the church or elsewhere for a performance, and he should work up a good embouchure with his mouthpiece in order that he may delight the ears and hearts of the listeners rather than offend them with such cacophony.

Finally, Praetorius discussed the handling of the aristocratic trumpeter choirs in the church. His first concern was that care must be taken that their 'powerful sound and reverberation' not 'drown out the entire music.' Especially interesting is the possibility he holds out for a composer to compose a church work in such a way that the trumpet choir could superimpose their (quasi-secret) memorized repertoire pieces, which Praetorius identifies as 'Sonadas, of various kinds, those played at banquets, before and after dances, the *Intrada*, and the *final*.' This was apparently possible due to the simple and predictable harmonic structures of the natural trumpet. But, even if these pieces should co-ordinate harmonically, how, in performance in the church, does one control a group of trumpeters who do not read music and are not accoustomed to having to follow a conductor? The answer, says Praetorius, is to follow them!

Italy

The most convenient source of wind players for use in important church services and celebrations were, of course, the civic wind bands, the '*piffari*.' In some cases this duty was actually part of the civic players contract with the town council, as one can see in a typical contract from Bergamo.

> [The players were instructed] to serve on festivals in the choir with their instruments, and in the morning and evening; and further to play without extra pay either in part or altogether at all feasts, solemnities and other public occasions on request.

Similar contracts can be found for the civic wind bands in Lucca, Florence, Bologna, and Udine. In the case of Udine a civic document addressed to the civic band reads,

> To the shawm and crumhorn (?) players in the service of the city, five in number, serving in the choir of the aforementioned church of Udine.

Another source of wind bands for appearances in the church were the unique Italian religious fraternities, called academies, companies, or sometimes, as in Venice, '*Scuola*.' These lay organizations existed in part to help support the church and they contributed to the celebration of all church festivals as well as the funerals of their members.

The regulations of the '*Compagnia della Serenissima Madonna della Steccata*' of Parma required its musicians to sing and play at all the greater festivals, with all their Vigils. We must assume these musicians were for the most part wind players and singers, as the pay records of this organization do not mention a single string player before 1621!

The '*Scuole*' of Venice are the best known of these religious fraternities today. An English visitor described a musical performance in the luxurious building of the Scuola di San Rocco, in 1608, as,

> so good, so delectable, so rare, so admirable, so super excellent, that it did even ravish and stupifie all those strangers that never heard the like. But how others were affected with it I know not; for mine owne part I can say this, that I was for the time even rapt up with Saint Paul into the third heaven. Sometimes there sung sixteene or twenty men together, having their master or moderator to keepe them in order; and when they sung, the instrumentall musitians played also. Sometimes

sixteene played together upon their instruments, ten Sagbuts, foure Cornets, and two Violdegambaes of an extraordinary greatness; sometimes tenne, sixe Sagbuts and foure Cornets.

This same Scuola di San Rocco, by the way, issued a very interesting document to its wind players, in 1550, which read, 'Those players was cannot play canzoni in procession shall be deprived of their employment.' To American band directors of the twenty-first century this has a familiar ring, 'If you are not in the marching band, you can not be in the concert band!'

A wind band marching in Matteo Pagan's 'Procession in St. Mark's Square on Palm Sunday,' Venice, Italy, 1556–59

Some larger cathedrals employed their own instrumentalists to perform regularly with the choir. One of these was in Treviso, where the '*maestro di cappella*,' Pietr'Antonio Spalenza, once took his choir and wind band of trumpets, trombones, and cornetts to a nearby convent for Augustinian nuns for a performance and was reprimanded as the organ was the only instrument allowed in closed convents.

The best known example of a cathedral which employed winds is, of course, St. Mark's in Venice. The first permanent instrumental music in St. Mark's dates from the employment of a group of musicians in 1568, which included the famous cornettist, Girolamo Dalla Casa (ca. 1543–1601), together with his brothers Zuanne and Nicolo. The music director, Zarlino, specified that the group was to play concerts from the organ lofts, but they probably also accompanied the singers. A pay record from the cathedral, dated 21 April 1568, mentions four mute cornetts, two alto cornetts, and a *fifero* (shawm?). Reports of concerts by as many as twelve players continue during the tenure of Dalla Casa. As Gustave Reese points out, these musicians seem to have been mostly players of cornett and trombone.

Gabrieli shows a decided preference for cornetts and trombones, a choice no doubt influenced by the fact that these instruments were used at St. Mark's, having been commonly included in performance there after Zarlino became *maestro di cappella* in 1565.

Dalla Casa was succeeded as *maestro di concerti* (ensemble conductor) by another cornettist, Giovanni Bassano (d. 1617). It was only under the tenure of the next ensemble director, the violinist, Francesco Bonifante (b. 1576), that string instruments began to equal in number the winds.

The best description of the function of these wind bands in the actual church service is found in the extensive discussion by Praetorius, which has been quoted above, for he clearly states that the German traditions he describes originated in Italy. But what do we know of the music played in the church by these Italian wind bands?

The earliest multi-part music played by wind bands was the direct transcription and the paraphrasing of vocal polyphony, much of it sacred in origin. Just as the original wind dance literature grew out of this tradition, so also, in Italy, an entirely new imitative form begins to develop in the sixteenth century.

The first prototypes of what would become the canzona begin to appear near mid-century and are called *ricercare*, *fantasie*, and *capriccio*. These early prototypes do not seem particularly identifiable, but rather all are synonyms for the same style: three and sometimes four-voice works which begin in imitation, but fail either to continue the imitation or to present clear formal designs. Willaert, Rore, Bassano and Julius de Modena are all represented by such compositions.

This activity led to the body of literature called *canzoni*, extant examples of which date from ca. 1570. For about a fifty-year period hundreds of canzoni were composed and published; those well-known examples by Gabrieli being only the 'tip of the iceberg.'

Where were all these canzoni performed? The evidence is that they were intended to be used during the Mass and are perhaps best thought of as a kind of sacred 'interlude' music, in substitution for the organ. This is consistent with the remarks by Praetorius in his *Syntagma Musicum*, III, and also a catalog kept by the organist, Carlo Milanuzzi, of Venezia, who listed such items as,

Canzon a 5 detta la Zorzi per l'Epistola
Concerto a 5 per l'Offertorio
Canzon a 5 detta la Riatelli per li Post Communio

Near the end of the century another instrumental form appears in contrast to the popular canzona, the *sonata*. The definition of this new form as given by Praetorius seems to correspond with the extant music.

> In my opinion the distinction between sonata and canzona lies in this: The sonatas are made to be grave and imposing in the manner of the motet, whereas the canzonas have many black notes running briskly, gayly, and rapidly through them.

The most distinguished compositions from this vast body of Italian church wind band music are those by Giovanni Gabrieli, of whom his student, Heinrich Schütz, said, 'Ye Immortal God! What a man was that!' What is it which causes us to set his music apart from his contemporaries?

To consider only his canzona contributions, he was the first to write for more than eight parts, the first to assign parts for specific instruments, and the first to treat the canzona as a polychoral (*cori spezzati*) composition. No one else's canzoni were so varied in their alternation of polyphonic and homophonic textures and binary and ternary metric structures. Harmonically, one sees his bass lines beginning to move in fifths, pointing to later concepts of modulation, and his use of unprepared and unresolved dissonances and faster harmonic rhythms gave his music a great deal more harmonic color than that found in the older Roman polyphonic style of his contemporaries.

Giovanni Gabrieli by Annibale Carracci (1560–1609), ca. 1600

But, it is important to think of this music as simply being better than that of his contemporaries and not as a body of literature which was in any way different in instrumentation or in its practice.

We should like to present here a few thoughts, which have not otherwise found a place in this volume, on performance practice of the sixteenth century. In particular we should like to include a few more general suggestions by Praetorius, in the belief that his third volume of his *Syntagma Musicum* has not been generally available to the English reader.

Regarding the performer's approach to the notation, Praetorius first cautions against merely playing the composition 'the way the composer wrote it.' This, he says, is a frequently heard flaw.

> The discrimination of the performer does not go far enough to explore and grasp the artfulness of the written composition.

In a discussion of tempo, Praetorius states that the general practice was to use the common time signature when a slower tempo was needed and the allabreve signature when a faster tempo was desired, that is, it was a characteristic of speed, and not necessarily an indication to conduct in two or in four. He goes on to say that the Italian composers were just beginning (1619) to replace this system with Italian words, such as '*adagio, presto*, etc.,' but that recent Italians, Gabrieli in particular, were not consistent. In summary he suggests that the conductor should decide for himself where the beat is to be slow or fast and cautions that if the conductor conducts too fast he risks

> making the spectators laugh and offend the listener with incessant hand and arm movements and give the crowd an opportunity for raillery and mockery.

Another interesting discussion deals with how to end a composition in performance. Most musicians today understand that a *ritard* as we understand it is not in the style, but Praetorius mentions a practice which seems to be entirely lost in our performance of sixteenth-century music today. It is not very commendable or pleasant, he writes, when singers, organists, and other instrumentalists from habit hasten directly

> from the penultimate note of a composition into the last note without any hesitation. Therefore I believe I should here admonish those who have hitherto not observed this as it is done at princely courts and by other well constituted musical organizations, to linger somewhat on the penultimate note, whatever its time value—whether they have held it for four, five, or six *tactus*—and only then proceed to the last note.

PART III
The Baroque

8 *The Birth of the Hautboisten and Harmoniemusik*

DURING WHAT WE CALL THE BAROQUE PERIOD (1600–1750) in music history there occurs a pivotal moment in the history of the wind band. During the first half of this period the instrumentation of wind bands continued very much in the consort tradition of the late Renaissance. Beginning in the middle of the seventeenth century the woodwind makers in Paris began to make fundamental changes in the old instruments and we can use the date 1675 to represent a date when the old Renaissance instruments were retired and the modern oboes, bassoons and flutes began to replace them.

Under Francois I (1515–1547) the top artistic wind band of the French court was called *Joueurs d'instrumens de haulxbois et sacqueboutes*, and it was a typical late Renaissance mixed consort of shawms and trombones. By the reign of Henry III documents as early as 1580 have given a new name to this ensemble, *Les Grands Hautbois*. But it is under the reign of Louis XIV (1638–1715) that this ensemble, featuring the new modern oboes, changed the history of the wind band in Europe. The *Les Grands Hautbois* using the new modern oboes was imported, together with the French oboe players, to Germany where a new half-French, half-German term was coined, the *Hautboisten*.

The musical forms, the *Overture da camera* and the *Ouverture*, also traveled to Germany and by 1750 these forms became the *Sinfonia/Partita* and *Divertimento* of the Classic Period performed by a wind band whose name changed from *Hautboisten* to *Harmoniemusik*. The *Hautboisten* and its repertoire is the bridge from the Renaissance consorts to the *Harmoniemusik* of Mozart, Haydn, Beethoven and Schubert thus giving the modern wind band a continuous, unbroken line of artistic life from the late Middle Ages to the present day.

On the Development of the *Hautboisten*

The success of the twelve-member oboe–bassoon band, *Les Grands Hautbois*, under Louis XIV in France, together with the development of the new French oboe, was imitated by courts throughout Europe, exactly as the same courts imitated so many other facets of the 'Sun King's' court (one need mention only architecture). Indeed it seems to have been a necessary part of every German aristocrat's cultural education to spend some time in the court of France. 'Everyone in Germany goes there,' wrote Frederick the Great in 1750, 'The French taste rules our food, our furniture, and our clothes.'

Traditional studies treat the *Hautboisten* band only as a military unit (and indeed the name continues to mean military musicians for a long time in Germany), but as the following chapter will document there was a concurrent court *concert* band existing at the same time, under the same name, and with the same instrumentation. It was this concert wind band which would develop into *Harmoniemusik* and not its military counterpart.

In Germany the appearance of the new *Hautboisten* band can be documented widely by the last two decades of the seventeenth century, as for example in Stuttgart (1680), Weissenfels (1695), Dresden and Gotha (1697), and Gottorf (1699). According to Braun, by 1700 almost every great German residence had such a band.

In many cases the arrival of the new French oboe in Germany came in the hands of French players. The impact of the new French oboe was such that even in those cases where some players continued to play the older shawm (even as late as 1749), they were now invariably called '*Hoboisten*.' The actual creation of this new oboe in France, the development of a more cylindrical instrument as opposed to the more conical shawm, remains an important question which has never received definitive study. This writer should like to venture the hypothesis that the factor which may have served as the catalyst was the musette, which became very popular in the French court at about the same time. It shares a bore more similar to the modern oboe and was played by the oboists of the French oboe-band.

The appearance of the other member of the *Hautboisten* bands, the modern bassoon, is more difficult to date, due to the fact that the name (from *bassus* in Latin) was used long before to include other kinds of bass wind instruments. One can see, however, that by the seventeenth century it was clearly associated with the oboe family. Regular bassoon players appear in court records in Germany simultaneously with the *Hautboisten* itself, the final third of the seventeenth century.

The *Hautboisten* band, then, existed from ca. 1680 to ca. 1730 in an instrumentation of oboes and bassoons. The military appearances are in greater documentation, but the existance of such groups performing in a concert environment, in the court itself, is clear from court records and in outstanding examples of extant literature. The most extraordinary example of this literature is a complete library for such a band now in a private library in Germany. Here six original leather bound volumes are labeled in gold printing: Hautbois I, II, III, Taille, Basson I, and Basson II. This collection, dated ca. 1720, contains more than twenty multi-movement works, including Concerti (a form which will be discussed below), Symphonias, and Ouvertures. Two additional important collections are the set of twelve *Sonatas* for oboes in three parts, taille, and bassoon by Johann Müller, printed in Amsterdam, ca. 1709, and the set of three (French) *Overture-suites* by Venturini, composed in 1723 and scored for two oboe parts, hautcontre, taille, and two bassoons.

The next crucial development occurs shortly after the dawn of the eighteenth century when horns began to be added to the *Hautboisten*, for then one has an ensemble with the precise instrumentation of the early *Harmoniemusik*—pairs of oboes, bassoons, and horns.

Horns of one sort or another had been used much earlier in Germany, as elsewhere, for the hunt, but the important fact is that until the eighteenth century these early horns were not accepted in the indoor, 'concert' ensembles. Traditionally, the introduction of the more modern (single-coil) horn into indoor use is credited to a very cultured Bohemian aristocrat and supporter of the arts, Franz Anton, Count von Sporck, Lord of Lissa, Gradlitz, Konoged, etc. Whatever is the case, the idea of using the horns in the indoor ensembles does seem to come to Germany from the East as one can see in one of the earliest references to this expanded *Hautboisten* wind band as the 'Sächsische Variante.' This new wind band, which was *Harmoniemusik* in all but name, seems to have rapidly replaced the short-lived *Hautboisten*.

The extant literature for this new wind band of oboes, horns and bassoons includes both military music, as for example in the oldest extant Saxony military music (for two oboes, two horns, and two bassoons), dated 1729, and non-military music as well. Outstanding examples of the latter include the eight important compositions by Telemann, probably written for the court in Hamburg, and the several works by Handel.

Thus the wind band *medium* which would later be called '*Harmoniemusik*' developed from the addition of horns to the *Hautboisten* band, which in turn had been formed with the new oboes and bassoons after the model of the famous French *Les Grands Hautbois*. But this is only half the story of the origin of *Harmoniemusik* and speaks really only of instruments. Far more important, and more interesting, is the story of the aesthetic function, the metamorphosis of the 'concert' literature of the sixteenth-century Italian church to that of the eighteenth-century German court.

The Development of *Hautboisten* Literature

The key to understanding the origin of *Hautboisten* literature, and a very large part to understanding the function of the pre-*Harmoniemusik* wind band in the courts of the German Baroque, is found in a considerable body of extant German literature for wind band under the name of 'Concerto.' These works are neither solo concerti nor concerto grossi, but are examples of an almost never discussed form, the *concerto da camera*. It is this form which provides proof of a continuous and direct development in wind literature from sixteenth-century Italy to the *Harmoniemusik* of the Classic period.

In order to chart the course of this development, we must first review briefly the use of the word 'concerto,' itself, beginning, of course, in Italy. The word 'concerto' was first used only to mean a group of musicians, as we might today use the word 'ensemble.' 'Concerto' was frequently used as part of the title of an Italian wind band in the late sixteenth and seventeenth centuries, as for example in the famous '*Concerti delli stromenti di fiato della Illustriss. Signoria di Venetia*,' conducted by Girolamo Dalla Casa (ca. 1584); the wind band called '*Concerto di Palazzo*' in Siena (1559); and the '*musici del concerto di Campidoglio*,' an ensemble of shawms, trombones, and cornetts under the Pope's jurisdiction in Rome (1702). The word seems to have had only this meaning in the oldest extant appearance in a musical composition, the *Concerti di Andrea, et Gio. Gabrieli* of 1587.

By the time of Gabrieli, and certainly evident in the music of Gabrieli, the term seems to designate music in which there is some nature of contrast, either of instrumental textures or of dynamics. This is confirmed both by Bottrigari in 1594, who wrote that 'If you inquire into the word Concerto you will find that it signifies "contention" or "contrast",' and by Praetorius, who pointed out in 1619 that 'concerto' derived from *concertare*, to compete, and not from *conserere*, to consort.

The word 'concerto' at this time did not seem to refer at all to form, as we understand it, which has contributed to some misleading scholarly commentary on the music of this period. In particular, sonata, sinfonia, and concerto are all synonyms between ca. 1580 and the early part of the seventeenth century and all tend to have fugal first movements. Indeed, as Manfred Bukofzer reminds us canzonas appeared frequently under the title Sinfonia or Sonata and that 'Sonata,' is in fact nothing but an abbreviation of 'canzon da sonar.' According to Arthur Hutchings the word 'concerto' did imply what we might call today 'concert' music.

With regard to Italian music under the name 'concerto,' one can identify four basic types: the large and small church concerti and the large and small chamber concerti. The large Italian church concerti, often called *Missa concertata*, *Motetti concertati*, or most often, *Concerti ecclesiastici* are very familiar to musicians in the compositions by Gabrieli and in the extensive discussion by Praetorius in *Syntagma Musicum*, III.

During the early years of the seventeenth century there also appeared church concerti for smaller ensembles, of both voices and instruments. An example of a small church concerto for voice and winds is the 'Concerto a cinque,' for four trombones and tenor in Franzoni's *Appartato Musicale de Messa* (1613). One should add, of course, that the entire body of Italian instrumental canzonas are actually small church concerti.

The chamber concerti, *concerto da camera*, also existed in considerable numbers during the Italian Baroque, in vocal, string, and wind versions. An example of the latter is the Albinoni *Concerto* for three oboes, bassoon, trumpet, and bass. The fact that nearly all the surviving examples of music using this title are prints from late in the seventeenth or early eighteenth century does not, it seems to me, preclude the existence of this form much earlier during the seventeenth century.

In the case of the Italian wind instrument *concerto da camera* I believe the use of this word as a synonym for the wind band itself during the sixteenth and seventeenth centuries implies a continuity of the literature as well. Evidence of this continuity can be seen in Cerone's *El Melopeo y Maestro* of 1613 (Naples), which gives a list of wind instruments which he says were used in the *concertos* ('*que entran en los Conciertos*'):

Sackbuts, curtals or bassoons, doppioni, recorders, dulcaymas, cornetts, cornamuse and crumhorns.

It also seems quite obvious that both wind ensembles and string ensembles co-existed as completely separate mediums at this time. The co-existence of these different kinds of ensembles was one of the characteristics of the new concerto grosso late in the seventeenth century. This new form differed with the earlier instrumental music first as a distinction in size of ensemble. Second, as Arnold Schering points out, while the new concerto grosso symbolizes the transformation of the 'up to now predominate wind orchestra to the homogeneously organized and technically dependable string orchestra,' the essential characteristic was the 'contrast of bodies of sounds, as strings against winds, as opposed to early forms, such as the sonata, where they might be mixed.' Bukofzer adds that the original idea was not only a contrast of mediums, but the spatial factor was fundamental to it.

Given this characteristic of the contrast of bodies of sound, one should not be surprised to find many Italian concerti grossi with real wind bands in the concertino, including works by Torelli and Vivaldi.

As is commonly known, all of these Italian forms traveled to the North during the seventeenth century. Not only did the various representatives of these forms for wind bands also travel north, but they found a very receptive atmosphere in

Germany, for as Schering points out, 'In general, Germany cultivated in the first place "Blaserkonzerts."' Bukofzer adds that not only did the Germans prefer winds to strings for the ensemble canzona, but winds were considered more noble than strings.

Thus church works for voices and wind instruments, both the large and small *concerto da chiesa*, appear in Germany as is documented in Praetorius and so gloriously represented in the works of Andreas Hammerschmidt and Heinrich Schütz (who was, let us not forget, Gabrieli's student).

Of greatest interest, with regard to the birth of *Harmoniemusik*, is the appearance in Germany of the *concerto da camera* for winds, nearly all of which seem to have been composed for the *Hautboisten* band with no horns. One of the few concerti with horns is one of several wind band concerti, each accompanied by strings, by Handel, for they stand at the very point in time when the new ensemble with horns was beginning to appear in Germany. Handel acknowledges this transformation by composing several concerti for double *Hautboisten* bands (oboes and bassoons), but at least one for double '*Harmoniemusik*' bands (oboes, bassoons, *and* horns). In general, however, one can say that the *concerto da camera* for winds in Germany are identified with the *Hautboisten* period and are completely indebted to the Italian models.

Toward the end of the seventeenth century a new instrumental form appears briefly in Germany called the 'Overture' (usually referred to today as the 'French Overture-suite'). The wind band music which appeared under this title is, I believe, of considerable historical value. First, this literature documents the continued presence of the 'concert' *Hautboisten* through the end of the Baroque, for even a cursory glance at this music reveals that it had nothing to do with the functions in society of the concurrent military *Hautboisten*. Second, and more important, the transformations which occur in this body of wind band literature reveal clearly the emergence of the classical *Harmoniemusik* and the relationship of that literature to earlier forms.

The earliest generation of wind band overtures seem to have been written for the *Hautboisten* band (without horns) and typically have a very long imitative first movement called 'Overture' (often with concertato technique), followed by several short movements with dance titles. The second generation of these works add the horns. Examples of this repertoire include four outstanding examples by Telemann and the original version of the Handel 'Fireworks Music,' which in the original autograph is called 'Overture.'

In the following generation one finds that cross currents of style which we call the 'Pre-Classic' Period, as is clearly evident in the wind band works by Wagenseil. Wagenseil (1715–1777) has left wind band works with older sounding titles (Suites) and wind band works with the new titles we associate with the *Harmoniemusik* of the Classic Period (Divertimenti and Partitas). It is the works with the new titles which interests us more, as they reflect the very moment when the new *Harmoniemusik* begins to emerge. The form of both a *Divertimento in F* and the *Partita in C* seem at first glance to be nothing more than the old Overture-suite under a new title, for they consist of eight and seven movements, respectively. Closer examination reveals important new formal characteristics: the dance titles have given way completely to Italian tempo markings and the first movements are clearly the early, two-part sonata form. Here are compositions which are truly half-baroque and half-classical, with the multi-movement form and the very heavily ornamented slow movements pointing toward the Baroque and with the new titles and sonata first movements pointing toward the Classic Period. Another *Divertimento in F*, in four movements (Allegro, Minuetto, Andantino, and Chase), seems much closer to the classic style, but retains the baroque slow movement (in spite of the title, it is actually an 'Adagio,' performed in a sub-divided common time).

These 'half-way' *Harmoniemusik* compositions can be found in great numbers throughout Bohemia, in particular. Often they appear with the new title, 'Partita,' while retaining the old pair of taille instruments (English horns). It is interesting to note, parenthetically, that in this first generation of music under the new Classic titles works were composed for both the indoor wind band ('*a la Camera*') and the military counterpart ('*di Campagna*'), but examples of the latter soon die out.

If some works during this transition period seem more old fashioned, there were, of course, some which had an entirely new sound and breathed a new spirit. Let me only note that it was still during the lifetime of both Telemann and Wagenseil that Haydn composed his Divertimenti for two oboes, two horns, and two bassoons in 1759–1761. These compositions belong in every respect to the Classic Period and announce that the metamorphosis of the *concerto da camera* has ended and a new kind of music had arrived: *Harmoniemusik*!

9 *Court Wind Bands*

France

History treats Louis XIII poorly because he was king in name only; the real power was the famous Cardinal Richelieu. Nevertheless he had a large musical establishment, including the usual aristocratic trumpets. There seems to be sufficient evidence to suggest that the *Les Grands Hautbois*, a twelve-member royal wind band established at least as early as 1580, under Henry III, continued throughout the reign of Louis XIII, although an engraving of his coronation (17 October 1610) pictures only an eight-member wind band. Shortly after the coronation, in any case, the twelve-member band can again be documented, consisting of two shawms and two cornetts playing treble parts, four alto or tenor shawms playing *haute-contre* and *taille* parts, two trombones playing *basse-taille*, and two bass shawms playing a *basse* part.

Everyone has read of the almost incredible opulence of the court of Louis XIV. Like its symbol, the buildings at Versailles, everything about this court was bigger and richer than any court in Europe during modern history. So too was his musical establishment larger and better, including numerous wind players organized into several distinct ensembles. These musicians were organized under four broad administrative divisions: the *Écurie*, the *Chapelle*, the *Chambre*, and the *Maison Militaire*.

The musicians under the *Écurie* enjoyed high prestige: they possessed the right of *commensaux* (meal companions of the king), they were exempt from many taxes and obligations to church-wardens and civic officials, and they were not required to quarter soldiers in wartime. They received gifts of food and clothing, in addition to regular income and bonuses for special ceremonies. During their time off they could live and work in Paris and were free to accept private students. A surviving contract between one of the oboists of the *Les Grands Hautbois*, Jean Desjardins, and a prospective student, Francois Gillotot, is very interesting. Not many teachers today would sign a legal

Opposite page: The Coronation of Louis XIII showing the wind band in the upper left corner

document promising not only to provide the student with an instrument but guaranteeing eventually obtaining for the student a good job!

> Today it has appeared in front of the notary of Paris that the undersigned Jean B. Desjardins ... is obligated to Francois Gillotot, servant of M. the Abbey Bouchart ... to show him how to play the oboe, flute and instrumental music which this entails. Gillotot may be free to obtain this goal and do his profession without being obligated. Mr. Desjardins will furnish him with instruments. This contract entails the sum of 185 livres [about $1200 in 1983 dollars] ... [the final payment] is made when Mr. Desjardins succeeds in placing Gillotot in a quality position as an oboist. Desjardins must try to place Gillotot ... Gillotot must go precisely all the days to take his lessons with Desjardins.

Detail from Jean Le Pautre's engraving of the coronation of Louis XIV at the cathedral of Riems, 'La Pompeuse et Magnifique Cérémonie du sacre de Louis XIV,' 1654, shows a wind band of twelve players

The band which interests us the most, among those of the *Écurie*, is the *Les Grands Hautbois*, which was one of the most important wind bands in the history of music. This ensemble of twelve winds continues as a pure wind band into the seventeenth century, although under the reign of Louis XIV several records list each member as playing a specific secondary string instrument. As one will see among the civic musicians in seventeenth-century Germany, it was not uncommon for players to play several instruments. Marcelle Benoit, the leading scholar on the music of this court, and who has considered this question in depth, concludes that the band was basically a twelve-member wind band. Its members probably did in fact have a doubling ability on strings (before 1715), but Benoit believes the evidence is that if they played strings to augment the already large group of string players, it must have been only very occasionally, for they were clearly primarily wind players.

The *Les Grands Hautbois* consisted of three sizes of oboes: *dessus* (the modern size instrument), two larger forms, *haute-contre* and *taille* (two players played each of these instruments), and two more who performed on '*basse de hautbois*,' which most scholars take to mean bassoon. To these eight double-reeds were added two cornetts and two trombones.

Les Grand Hautbois, unknown artist

This wind band made numerous appearances, both private and public, in the chamber, the chapel, and outdoors. The rather large gifts of food they received (bread, wine, meat, poultry, and lard) six times a year alone suggests they were a busy ensemble.

One contemporary (ca. 1665) description of the performance of this wind band seems to suggest fine musicians struggling with less than perfect (or perhaps newly developed) instruments.

> The oboes, whom one can now hear at the king's palace and in Paris, have stately repertoire and style. Their cadences are correct, their vibrato is sweet, their ornaments are just as correct as the more edu-

cated vocal ones and those of the most perfect instruments. We have seen their success in the theater, especially in certain entrees. They had a marvelous effect in one Pastorale. But one can never be confident of the air; the shortness of breathe, the thickening of the lungs, the fatigue of the stomach and finally, one is conscious of a notable difference in beginnings and endings; here one could discover more exactness.

When these players joined the 'Twenty-Four Violins' of the king, they played their wind instruments, yet doubled the string parts.

Another, separate, wind band of six players, the *Musettes et Hautbois du Poitou*, is one of the strangest and most enigmatic in character. Both the *musette* and *hautbois de Poitou* were pastoral, folk instruments and their popularity in the court of Louis XIV reflects the pretense by members of that court that they had a natural sympathy with the peasant.

The *musette* was a small, highly decorated, bagpipe, which played the treble in this ensemble, according to Mersenne. The *hautbois de Poitou* was used in three sizes (alto, tenor, and bass) and differed in construction with the chanter of the bagpipe only in size and with its windcap. Since no examples of this instrument are known to be extant, our only insight into it comes from references in contemporary literature, the most revealing of which is an observation by Pierre Trichet.

> But without getting involved in detailed discussions concerning the names of shawms, suffice it is to say that there are two types used nowadays in France: some are simply called *haubois*, others *haubois de Poitou*; the difference between them is that the former look more like recorders.

Suffice to say, all these instruments were performed by regular oboists in the Écurie and in 1661 they were described in court records as two players on '*dessus de haulbois,*' one '*dessus de muzette,*' one '*basseconte de muzette,*' and two players on '*taille de hautbois.*'

Another wind band in the *Écurie* is somewhat enigmatic, in this case because there is some question regarding what the *Cromorne* itself was. Until recently scholars have assumed this was an ensemble of crumhorns, even though in the rest of Europe the period of the crumhorn was very near its end. One has to take note that a present day authority on the crumhorn, Barra Boydell, rejects this idea in favor of an unknown instrument of the bassoon family. Whatever the instrument was, the band usually appeared in the court records of Louis XIV as an ensemble of five players, consisting of two *dessus*, one *quinte*, one *taille*, and a *basse*. In a few records it appears with a sixth player, but was permanently set at five in 1689.

Two small ensembles of wind players were maintained under the *Écurie* solely for ceremonial needs, which of course were almost without pause. The fifes and drums had consisted of only four members during the sixteenth century, but under Louis XIV they grew to eight players, four of each. Although this organization had little musical significance, it was an indispensible part of court life during the seventeenth century. Virtually every moment of the king's day was defined in elaborate ritual and each ritual was carefully spelled out in court organizational documents. Twelve royal trumpets are usually found in the *Écurie*, of which four were nearly always near the king and thus more honored than their colleagues.

Aside from all these wind bands under the administrative accounts of the *Écurie*, there were still more wind players employed in the court of Louis XIV. In the *Chambre*, another administrative wing, there were musette and flute players and in the *Chapelle*, serpent and cornett players, all of whom seem to have been independent of those in the *Écurie*.

Finally, under still another administrative section, the *Maison Militaire*, one finds numerous additional wind players who played, from time to time, at court. These included trumpets and timpani of the regiments of the king's guards, fifes and drums of the *Cent-Suisses*, and the musicians of the troops known as *Les Mousquetaires*. Among the latter, '*8 hautbois des Mousquetaires*' appear frequently in the court pay records for both Versailles and Fontainebleau. As above, these eight oboes, four from each company, should be thought of as oboes in several sizes, including no doubt bassoons. Of these various entries relative to the performance of the eight oboes of the *Mousquetaires*, one is very striking. We know oboes, in general, doubled the violins when the court ballets and comedies were performed. On one occasion, in 1698, these oboes were with the court at Fontainebleau, performing with the 'twenty-four violins' in the comedy, '*Bourgeois gentilhomme*.' For some reason the 'Violins of the King' had to return early to Versailles and the oboes alone apparently played the final production of the comedy.

It appears that many of the above components were drawn together for the great state celebrations, as well as for the entertainments of Louis XIV and his court. Judging by the frequency and scale of his entertainments, one concludes that a considerable staff must have been necessary just to see that not a single moment of Louis's life went unfilled. Even so simple a thing as a walk, was planned as it if were a state voyage. As Louis would leave the building trumpets would play their fanfares and then as he made his way through those extraordinary gardens at Versailles he heard constant background music, for hidden among the trees, carefully out of sight, would be an oboe ensemble here and a violin ensemble there. The ensembles would play until the king had passed and then run ahead to be in position a bit further in the route to play again!

Because of the size of the court, entertainments for the entire court had, of necessity, to be on vast scales. Among these were the carrousels, relics of the age of armed tournaments. By this time these were in part state processions, horse ballets, tilting matches, and allegorical pageants. It was for one of these horse ballets, called 'Carrousels,' that we have an extant four-movement composition by Lully for three oboes, bassoon, four trumpets and timpani, composed for a carrousel in 1686—one of a large number of surviving works written for the wind bands of this court by this composer.

The largest of the court entertainments were called *divertissements* and three of these were of such a magnitude that they are known today as the *grands divertissements*. The first of the *grands divertissements* was given in 1664 ostensibly to honor two queens, Anne of Austria and Marie-Therese, but actually as a vehicle for Louis to announce to the aristocratic world that he intended to lay claim to the Spanish crown, as the lawful inheritance of his wife (Louis himself was half-Spanish and only a quarter-French).

This divertissement was called, '*Les plaisisrs de l'ile enchantee,*' taken from Ariosto's tale of the imprisonment of the knight, Roger, by the sorceress, Alcine. The *divertissement* began with a carrousel on the first day, with the king, dressed as Roger, participating. Other members of the court appeared as Apollo, the Centuries, the Twelve Hours, and the Signs of the Zodiac. Lully marched into the carrousel stadium dressed as Orpheus, followed by thirty-four musicians. I assume these were all wind instruments for following a dance by the Four Seasons (who entered riding four different animals: a horse, an elephant, a camel, and a bear!), Lully conducted a concert of 'oboes and flutes' (which probably meant a full consort of recorders and several sizes of oboes and bassoons). Next a machine-operated forest of artificial trees lifted dancers into the air. Finally a ballet was performed by the twenty-four dancers of The Hours and the Zodiac. The allegorical figures of Abundance, Joy, Propriety, and Good Cheer carried in a table of food for the hungry royal observers.

The second day featured a play by Molière, '*La princesse d'Élide*,' with musical intermezzi by Lully. A sextet at the end sang the theme, 'A heart begins to live only on the day that it knows love.' During this song, another machine-operated tree lifted sixteen 'fauns' into the air, each faun playing a flute.

On the final day the royal audience saw a palace, which had been constructed near the small lake behind Versailles, illuminated, while Lully conducted a concert. Trumpets then announced the entrance of Alcine and her nymphs, who were riding mechanical sea monsters. Next was a ballet battle between dwarfs, giants, and Moors against the monsters and knights. In the end Roger conquers Alcine, breaking her spell of sorcery with his magic ring. In the background, the palace disappears in a blaze of fireworks!

All the separate wind bands discussed above, under Louis XIV, continued throughout the reign of Louis XV, although a document of 1724 suggests that the financial support for this music was not as forthcoming as it had been in the past.

> The oboes, musettes, cromornes, drums and fifes request the Prince to pay them their wages in clothing as in the previous year, and should the Prince decide not to grant them this grace, they beseech him to fix their clothing at 120 lt, like those of other officers, instead of only 90 lt or 100 lt, which the tailors allow each one for their clothes.

The German-Speaking Countries

The appearance of the new *Hautboisten* band dates from the final two decades of the seventeenth century, as can be seen in documents from Stuttgart (1680), Weissenfels (1695), Dresden and Gotha (1697), and Gottorf (1699). In the case of Weissenfels, it is quite interesting to note that the Elector was apparently dissatisfied with the *Hautboisten* he hired in 1695 and was able to replace them by engaging an entire band (*Kammerpfeifer*) in Vienna in 1697. Courts which did not yet have one of the new *Hautboisten* bands could hire visiting bands for important court events. Thus we see the twelve-member *Hautboisten* band from Jena performing for the Weissenfels court (1676) and the twelve-member band from Eisenberg performing in Zeitz (1686–1689). In any case, according to Werner Braun, by 1700 virtually every major court possessed one of the new bands. By the way, regarding why the number twelve was selected as the standard number of players, perhaps we have a clue in the *Hautboisten* ensemble in Eisenberg who called themselves, 'the Apostles.' In any case, one cannot help noticing that this number seems to continue to be influential in later scores, such as the original manuscript for Handel's *Fireworks music* and the Mozart *Gran partita* of 1784 for twelve winds and string bass.

Once again it should be stressed that while almost every mention of the *Hautboisten* bands in current literature has been with respect to military functions, it is clear that there were either separate *chamber Hautboisten* or, in some cases, these bands worked in both spheres. The indoor 'concert' existance is clear first and foremost, it seems to me, from the extant literature which is nearly always 'concert' and not military in nature, and from the use of such terms as '*Kammerpfeifer*' (as in the case in Weissenfels, above) or '*Hofkunstpfeifer*' (as in the case of Berlin, below).

It may be true that the wind players in some courts were considered rather lowly as musicians, on the other hand, there were also *Hautboisten* bands which were highly esteemed and even made concert tours. One of these *Hautboisten* bands which gave concert tours was from the Brandenburg court in Berlin. These tours can be documented both between 1693 and 1700, under an oboist-director called '*Lubuissière*,' '*La puisier*,' or '*La Bassire*,' and under his successor, Gottfried Pepusch, who with a wind band of seven players even made a tour to London in

1704. Another outstanding *Hautboisten* band was found in Hannover, where Johann Mattheson, visiting in 1706, was astonished by the '*Virtuosen*,' especially the '*exquisite Bande Hoboisten.*'

While there was a concert facet to the existence of these *Hautboisten* bands in Germany, one does have to acknowledge that the broader range of their duties must have been quite wide, as it had been for court wind bands since the fifteenth century. Even the fine '*Hofkunstpfeifers*' of Berlin were required to help out with the church music on great festival days and to perform from the palace tower at ten o' clock in the morning and five o'clock in the evening during the Summer (four o'clock in the evening during the Winter). But even in this case, we note the seven-member band was instructed to perform 'not only artistic and good works, but Psalms.' Not only did these *Hautboisten* bands have to perform in a wide variety of situations, but also on whatever instrument was required at the moment and, furthermore, had to always be ready to travel with their prince. No wonder the *Konzertmeister* of the Weissenfels court, Johann Beer, wearily expressed,

> With the court you've got to be in one place today, tomorrow in another. Day and night, unfortunately, makes no difference. Tempest, rain, sunshine—it's all the same. Today you've got to go into church,—tomorrow to the dining hall, the day after tomorrow to the theatre. Compared to all this disturbance, life is somewhat more peaceful in the towns.

During the Baroque there were two musical emperors in Vienna, first Ferdinand III (1637–1657), a composer whose works include a *Hymnus de Nativitate* (ca. 1649) for SATB and ten wind instruments. It was Ferdinand III, by the way, who imported from Italy the horse ballets, which became an important fixture in Viennese life. For the celebration of the marriage of Ferdinand III with Maria Anna of Spain the riders spelled out the names of Ferdinand and his bride on the floor of the stadium.

Leopold I (1658–1705) was also a composer and has left a *Beatus vir* for voices and wind instruments. In 1700 Leopold I had a *Hautboisten* band of five oboes and four bassoons, together with six trombones and two cornetts for use in church music. According to Köchel, strings begin to appear in larger numbers in the extant records only in ca. 1707–1708.

In January 1667, Leopold sponsored a great horse ballet to celebrate his wedding to Margareta Theresa of Spain, for which published descriptions and engravings were sent all over Europe. Here is also a rare case where some of the actual music is extant, consisting of a few movements for trumpets and timpani by Johann Heinrich Schmelzer. An idea of the seriousness of purpose which these horse ballets entailed can be seen in the fact that the first rehearsal for the one given in January 1667 occurred in August 1666!

Under Karl VI (1711–1740) the large *Hautboisten* band appears to remain and in 1725 consisted of eight oboes and seven bassoons. Beginning with Maria Theresia, however, there is apparently somewhat of a retrenchment of the wind bands in favor of the instruments of the new classical orchestra. In 1741 one finds only three oboes, four bassoons, five trombones, one cornett, together with a corps of six trumpets.

Finally, the Baroque in Germany was 'The Golden Age of the Trumpet,' with a dramatic increase in the numbers of these instruments in almost every court in the German-speaking nations. In Berlin, Friedrich Wilhelm I had twenty-four trumpets and two timpani divided into two choirs in order that they could alternate performing the announcement of the meal and for the entertainment of the guests. One scholar suggests that on such occasions these '*Kammer-*' or '*Concerttrompeter*' played '*Bicinium, Tricinium* or *Quadricinium.*'

This great preference for the trumpet during the Baroque is of course also reflected in literature. Looking back on this proud chapter in the long history of the trumpet, Altenburg observed in 1795,

> A sovereign may have ever so good an orchestra, venery, royal stables, and other such ministrations, but if he does not retain at least one choir of trumpeters and timpani, there is, in my opinion, something lacking in the perfection of his household.

These aristocratic trumpeters formed their own guilds, called *Kameradschaft*, and these guilds became much more vocal during the seventeenth century in attempting to guarentee their 'rights' and to protect their domain from infringement by other musicians. During this century they frequently called upon the aristocracy itself to help set down these rights in legal definitions. Indeed, in the first important example of such a document, by Ferdinand II, in 1623, it seems as if the aristocracy genuinely shared in these concerns.

> No honourable trumpeter or timpanist shall allow himself to be employed with his instrument in any way other than for religious services, Emperors, Kings, Electors and Princes, Counts, Lords and Knights and nobility, or other persons of high quality: It shall also be forbidden altogether to use a trumpet or a timpani at despicable occasions; likewise the excessive nocturnal improper carousing in the streets and alleys, in wine- and beer-houses. He who transgresses in this way shall be punished.

In 1653, Ferdinand III issued another imperial edict, which deals with the apprentice system in considerable detail. One may not take a student without first obtaining adequate information about the student's 'honorable ancestry and birth.' The apprentice pays a fee at the beginning of a two-year period of study, at the end of which an examination is given.

> Each master shall instruct his apprentice very diligently in his art, and shall not send him into the field [a reference to a period of service in the army] until he knows his field pieces [Feldstucke] perfectly. In order to test this, the apprentice must present himself beforehand to the highest and oldest trumpeter and play his test piece for him. If this is not done, then as a bungler he will not be allowed to go into the field.

Very specific obligations are defined in the case that either student or teacher should quit during the two-year period of instruction. It is also very interesting that strict limitations were placed on how many students one could teach and how often—an obvious attempt at guarding against over-crowding the profession. If a trumpeter gives up his art for a higher position, he also gives up the right to teach. If, however, he retires to become a farmer, he may continue to teach—so long as he is not caught 'making the boy work in the fields or the wine cellar and not at his music.'

Since only a student who could demonstrate an honorable birth, as mentioned above, could be an apprentice, the trumpeter is warned that if he 'behaves dishonorably toward a widow or an honest man's daughter and makes her pregnant,' even though it is his own acknowledged child, he may not instruct him in trumpet playing. A strong hint is given that if one marries 'a person of public ill repute' he will no longer be permitted to be a trumpeter. Further, he would be immediately thrown out of the profession, should he,

> lose his skill at the trumpet, play in the company of jugglers, court mutes, town watches or at lotteries and the like ... (or) give up his art to become a watchman on a tower, or join the jugglers or comedians.

A particular fear of the trumpet guilds was that their positions might be taken over by the civic musicians, who read music and, judging by the extant music, were better musicians. The trumpet guilds tried to protect their domain first by attempting to define the kinds of playing which belonged to them, as opposed to that which belonged to the civic musician. There were so many restatements of this one must conclude that the idea was never accepted outside the trumpet guild.

Next, the trumpet guilds tried, and largely succeeded for a time, to restrict to themselves the trumpet, leaving to the civic musicians the old S-trumpet and the cornett. As a reflection of the importance this issue held for the trumpet guilds, one finds several documents during the seventeenth century which suggest that they were even concerned that another instrument, especially the trombone, might try to *sound* like a trumpet!

There is a very interesting discussion of the seventeenth-century trumpet in Daniel Speer's *Instruction in the Musical Art* (1687), where he gives five indispensible qualities for good trumpet playing: healthy physical strength; strong, long continuing breath; a quickly moving tongue; a willing industry in constant practice, whereby the embouchere is conquered and preserved; and good, long trills, that are made with the chin, which must therefore be accustomed to trembling or shivering. In addition, Speer gives an interesting discussion on the embouchure.

> There are but few private persons who learn this instrument. Cause: it requires great bodily exertion, difficult for an incipient to perform. With a view to learn more easily how to blow the trumpet, he should at once accustom himself to apply the mouthpiece most accurately to the upper large or hanging lip, and not so as to touch the nose; for then the flesh of the large lip is apt to gather, and fill the cup of the mouthpiece, leaving no room for tonguing; yea, it even prevents the air from getting in; and though physical strength may not be lacking, it will gradually

become exhausted, as the aperture for the breath is stopped up, and the breath cannot proceed. The correct embouchere, therefore, is the chief feature of trumpet blowing.

...

Above all, an incipient shall accustom himself to draw in his cheeks, not blow them out, for this is not only unseemly, but hinders the breath from having it due outlet and causes a man pains at the temples, so that true teachers are accustomed to box the ears of their pupils to cure them of this bad habit.

Italy

The Italian nobles also had their private trumpet players and a few of their names are known today, in particular Girolamo Fantini who served under the Grand Duke Ferdinando II of Florence. Fantini's famous trumpet treatise was no doubt taken from his eight years' experience in this court.

The popes continued their personal trumpet choirs, called *'concerto de' 4 trombetti dell'Inclito Popolo Romano.'* The Statutes of 1717 for this ensemble states that their first obligation, of course, was always to the pope. Their pay included additional funds for the persons who cared for their horses, their clothes and their barbers. There was a standard payment of six giulii per day (a 'day' is defined here as dawn to the 'Ave Marias' in the evening) for appearances in university or diplomatic ceremonies. On great public occasions, such as horse parades, fireworks, funeral processions, the celebration of cardinals, etc., the trumpets had to be content with the gifts of money offered by the sponsor; if they complained in this regard they were subject to a fine. The Statutes of 1734 deal in addition with problems of discipline: abusiveness, fighting among themselves, etc.

Girolamo Fantini

Another separate papal ensemble was the '*Tamburini del Popolo Romano.*' The constitution of 1715 indicates this ensemble consisted of fourteen players, but a lack of funds resulted in only eight principal players together with official alternates. The oldest member became the leader, '*Capo tamburo*,' and he carried the flag of the arms of the pope and was responsible for the regulations of the ensemble and the quality of their performance.

There was also a wind band under the juristiction of the pope. Housed in the *Castel Sant'Angelo*, they are called in documents of ca. 1702, '*musici del concerto di Campidoglio*,' in 1702, '*Concerto de tromboni e cornetti del Senato et inclito Popolo Romano*,' and apparently '*Concerto Capitolino*' in 1705. The constitution of this year calls the leader the '*Priore*,' who was elected for a month by the players and was responsible for the selection of the repertoire, their performance, and their pay. Members are cautioned against blasphemy and urged to show the necessary respect toward their colleagues. This ensemble consisted of six trombones and two cornetti.

It is in Italy that one finds the origins of the popular court horse ballets, known as 'Ross Ballet' in the German-speaking countries and as 'Carrousel' in France. These were in part a replacement of the medieval and renaissance tournaments, which no longer made sense after the introduction of firearms, but in Italy they were also the last stage of development of popular horse festivals which can be dated to the fourth century.

Finally, the extant examples of early opera also include some music which must reflect the participation of courtly wind ensembles. The examples of fanfares in *Orfeo* (Monteverde) and *Il Pomo d'oro* (Cesti) immediately come to mind, but also the five-part instrumental '*Chiamata alla caccia*,' in *Le nozze di Teti e di Peleo* (Cavalli, 1639), for '*Chiamata*' was a seventeenth-century Italian term for military fanfare. The *Euridice* by Peri contains a ritornello for flute consort entitled, '*Zinfonia con un riflauto*.'

No doubt there were also occasions when all the available court wind players appeared on stage in great processions, etc. An example perhaps is the opera, *Berenice* (1680), by Giovanni Freschi which included a procession of a chorus of a hundred virgins, several hundred soldiers, two elephants, six trumpeters on horse, six drummers, six trombones, six 'great' (regular?) flutes, six minstrels with 'Turkish' instruments, six with 'octave' flutes, and finally six 'cymbalists.'

Spain

In terms of land, Spain was still the greatest empire of the seventeenth century, but economically she was in trouble. She had lost her naval power, which had controlled her commerce, and she had experienced two important defeats early in the century.

The consequent retrenchments which were necessary can be seen in the organization of the court wind band at Madrid between 1652 and 1655. Spain, which had often hired players from the West, could no longer afford such a luxury. An extant document orders the head of the court minstrels, Francesco de Baldes (or, Valdes) to begin a school for minstrels so the court could create its own musicians instead of hiring them abroad. He is ordered to form a band of twelve winds, which as we have seen in Germany, seems an obvious imitation of the *Les Grands Hautbois* of Louis XIV in Paris.

- 4 soprano shawms
- 2 tenor shawms
- 2 'contra altos de shawm'
- 4 trombones

England

James I was inclined toward books, young men, and extravagance in dress. He considered his ideas as divine imperatives, informing Parliament in 1609,

> For kings are not only God's lieutenants on earth, and sit upon God's throne, but even by God Himself are called gods.

This attitude began the flow of events which would mark that century in England with so much civil unrest and regicide. Still, the Western world remembers two great events from his reign: the flow of his subjects to America, symbolized by the Pilgrims of 1620 who landed in Plymouth, and the 1611 translation of the bible which bears his name.

The musical establishment of James I included some forty instrumentalists, of whom at least half represented independent wind bands. Three groups appear consistently: a consort of six recorders, a consort of six flutes, and a consort of nine oboes (the name 'shawm' is now rarely used in England) and trombones, two of which were bass trombones. In addition, there were regular payments to a consort of cornetts, but these players' names appear among those of the previous players—they were, as the English say, 'Double-handed.'

Among the duties of these wind bands was performance in the English Masque, which we associate with this period. A typical masque usually began with a prologue in verse, with songs and changes of scenery, followed by a dance, actors, and then a main dance in which the maskers invited the royal spectators to dance with them.

Among those masques which are known to have included wind band music are several by Ben Johnson, including *Masque of Beauty* [1607–1608]; *Masque of Queens* [1608–1609], ('In the heat of their dance, on the sudden was heard a sound of loud music [the English synonym for wind band], as if many instruments had made one blast.'); *Oberon* [1610-1611], ('loud triumphant music'); *Pan's Anniversary* [1624], ('loud music'); and *The Fortunate Isles* [1624-1625], ('loud music,' and later, 'the three cornets play').

Often these masques began with music by the independent wind band, as in the case of the *Masque of Beauty*, with music composed by Ferrabosco, as well as between the scenes, while the scenery was being changed.

Under Charles I, the basic wind band seems to have consisted of eighteen players, divided into two rather identical bands of five trombones (one a bass trombone) and four woodwinds (oboes, cornetts, flutes or recorders). After 1630, when the court spent a considerable amount of money on new cornetts, these bands seem to have found a rather stable instrumentation of three cornetts (SST) and three trombones (TTB).

Under the restoration of Charles II one finds the climax of the baroque wind band in England. In 1661 one first finds the wind band, called, 'consort, being his Majesty's wind musick,' consisting of thirteen players, and by 1668 it reached its largest size with nineteen players. A document dated 18 June 1669, announced the 'retrenchment of his Majesty's musick' and here one can see the wind band reduced from nineteen to ten; by 1679 there will be only five members.

Another important document announces, 'Mathew Lock in the place of Alphonso Ferabosco (II), composer for the wind music.' Among the repertoire of this band were the various compositions by Locke, called 'ffor his Majesty's Sagbutts & Cornetts.'

The leader of the wind band was Nicholas Lanier, who, as head of the entire musical establishment, had the specific duty of controlling rehearsals.

> Nicholas Lanier ... hath power to order and convocate (his Majesty's musick) at fitt time of practize and service ... if any of them refuse to wayte at such convenient tymes of practize and service ... I shall punish them either in their persons or their wages.

After the above mentioned retrenchment the royal wind band remained an ensemble of approximately eight musicians, usually referred to as oboists, until the end of the Baroque. Nevertheless, some remarkable repertoire survives this period, namely that by Purcell and Handel.

Purcell's *March* and *Canzona*, written for the funeral of Queen Mary, are beautiful compositions, an opinion shared by one who heard their first performance.

> I appeal to all that were present, as well such as understand Music, as those that did not, whither they ever heard any thing so rapturously fine and solemn & So Heavenly in the Operation, which drew tears from all; & yet a plain, Naturall Composition; which shows the pow'r of Music, when 'tis rightly fitted & Adapted to devotional purposes.

From the pen of Handel we have a dozen or so compositions for small *Hautboisten* band, although better known is his 'Fireworks Music.' It was composed for three oboes, two bassoons with contrabassoon, three horns, three trumpets, and percussion, although notes in the score indicate the first performance was given by a band of some sixty players as part of a celebration held in Green Park, London, on 27 April, commemorating the peace of Aix-la-Chapelle. The music received a public reading at Vauxhall on Friday 21 April 1749, attended by twelve thousand people, causing a tremendous traffic jam on London Bridge. The composition gained the name known today from the fact that the celebration included a fireworks 'machine' (which misfired causing a moment of concern), designed by Chevalier Servandoni.

Portrait of Henry Purcell by John Closterman, 1695

*Military version of the Hautboisten,
Band of the First Foot Guards, 1753*

10 *Military Bands*

THE REPEATED BATTLES WITH THE OTTOMAN EMPIRE between 1526 and 1699 made the Turkish nation for a time the primary fear of Western civilization. This empire was a particular source of anxiety for the Viennese for their city lay on the border between East and West and more than once the Turkish armies were at the very gates of the city. There was, of course, a great curiosity about these 'heathen' neighbors and the museums in Vienna today are filled with objects collected outside the city walls after the Turkish troops had left. Every visitor today is told of the discovery, in this manner, of a bag of coffee beans which led to the craze for drinking coffee in Vienna.

This curiosity was shared by musicians, in Vienna in particular, for a long time. Mozart's first real success in Vienna, for example, was his opera *The Abduction from the Seraglio*, which was the 'hit' of the 1782 season. Similar examples of music '*alla Turca*' in works by Haydn, Gluck, and even the Ninth Symphony by Beethoven, are familiar to all musicians.

The basic Turkish military band unit was a five-member ensemble called the *Mehter* band, which was doubled and redoubled according to the rank of the person by whom they were employed. The Sultan's band, called *Mehterhane*, was usually the largest and consisted of a nine-fold version of the same basic instruments. For great battles even larger proportions were assembled. The Sultan Selim (1512–1520) took more than two hundred players to the battle of Mercidabik, as did Suleiman the Great (1520–1566) to Vienna.

The instruments included an oboe, conical and wild-sounding like the medieval shawm. Made of plum or apricot wood, it was decorated with precious stones and silver bracelets and called by the Turks, the '*zurna*.' There was a primitive trumpet, which seems to have been used more as a rhythmic than a melodic instrument, called the '*boruzen*.'

It was the percussion instruments, however, which were the most influential in the West. There were cymbals ('*Zil*,' the player being called '*Zilzen*') very much like the modern ones. These were prototype small timpani, called '*Nekkare*,' with leather stretched over twin copper bowls, played in a sitting position on the ground. The final member of the normal *Mehter* band was a large bass drum, played with a large stick in the right hand and a smaller one, sometimes a branch of a tree, with the left hand.

In larger bands the '*Cevgen*' was added, played by a musician who also sang. In English we call this instrument the 'Jingling Jonnie,' or 'Turkish crescent.' It was a high pole surmounted by one or more metal crescents ('*Mehter*,' itself, is derived from the Persian '*Mahi-ter*,' for 'moon'), from which hung many small bells and on each end, horsehair plumes. The contemporary Western bell-lyre is nothing but a surrogate for this instrument.

Engraving of an Ottoman Mehter band from 1839

A seventeenth-century visitor from the West reports that of twenty-four compositions he heard one of these band play, six were of a melancholy nature, six were *allegro* and light-spirited, six furious, and six mellifluous or even amorous.

These bands played at regular times during the day, beginning early in the morning. A Prussian soldier, sent to Constantinople early in the eighteenth century, recalled that the band which marched before his quarters every morning, 'split the ears with its incredible charivari.' On fortresses, these bands also performed a watch duty.

It was in battle that the *Mehter* band was considered most valuable. Their playing thrilled and excited the soldiers, lifting their morale and driving them into action. Many accounts also remark on the effect of this thundering noise in diminishing the morale and dissipating the enemy. One of the band leaders during the Kara Mustafa Pasha's attack on Vienna, remembered,

> Toward the middle of the afternoon the grand Vizier's mehter band started to play first. Then the bands of the governors of provinces and the bands on the right started to play all together. Thus, after the evening prayer and at dawn, the sound of drums, oboes, kettle-drums, and cymbals joined from every corner the rumble of cannon and gunfire, and the whole countryside echoed with these sounds.

The sultan's band performed concerts each afternoon in the palace during peace time as well as during coronations and other ceremonies. During battle, concerts were performed in front of the royal tent. One such concert performed before a guest, Osman Gazi, began a tradition somewhat similar to the curious tradition in the West of audiences standing during the famous chorus in the *Messiah* by Handel. Gazi, out of respect for the Selijuk Sultan, stood during the concert by the *Mehter* band and for the following two hundred years, until Mohammed II (1451–1481), sultans stood when these bands performed concerts.

The adoption of these instruments became wide spread near the beginning of the eighteenth century, following a visit to the King of Prussia in Berlin by the Turkish Ambassador, Achmet Effendi, and soon became an instant 'status symbol' among Europe's leading aristocracy.

The vital contribution these new percussion instruments made to Western armies must be understood in context with a fundamental change in the nature of these armies during the seventeenth century. It was at this time that the concept of a standing army began to be employed in Western Europe, whereas for centuries earlier when battles were necessary they were conducted by troops hired for that purpose, mercenaries. With a standing army, who could practice marching, the generals could at last successfully introduce co-ordinated marching. The louder 'Turkish' style bands provided the music which made this possible.

In Germany, most military music at the beginning of the seventeenth century was provided by the aristocratic trumpeters. The famous book (1795) by Ernst Altenburg, one of the last of these men, is filled with detailed descriptions of this music and advice for young followers. Regarding the envoy duty often given trumpeters he warned, 'conduct oneself soberly, moderately, and carefully, since one can otherwise easily run the risk of being shot dead.'

The first true military bands in Germany appear to be found under the Prussian Elector, Friedrich Wilhelm (1640–1688), called 'the Great Elector.' In 1646 the elector founded his Dragoon Life Guards ('*Charbrandenburgische Liebguardie*'), which consisted of two hundred troops and a band of four '*Schalmeyer*' (two discant and an alto shawm with a Dulcian) and four drums which 'concertized' for the troops.

It was during the reign of the Elector Frederick I (1688–1713) that the new *Hautboisten* band begins to replace the older shawm band and by the end of the seventeenth century such military bands were found throughout Germany.

Frederick William I (1713–1740) added the trumpet to the *Hautboisten* band, although this player marched in front of the band and alternated his music with that of the band. Frederick William's interest in the military and its music is clearly documented in his founding of the Prussian Army Music School in 1724. Unfortunately little is known of the details of this school, especially from its earliest years. It was housed in the Military Orphans Home in Potsdam, a building dating from 1722. The first director of the school was Gottfried Pepusch, who was also the director of the king's (indoor) *Hautboisten*.

An interesting military treatise, published in 1726 by Hans von Fleming, offers a description of the new oboe, as compared to the old shawm.

Portrait of Frederick William I of Prussia by Antoine Pesne (1683–1757), ca. 1733

> During the time of the shawm there were four players: two discant, an alto, and a Dulcian. After the oboe took their place, one finds six oboes as the oboes were not so strong but had a softer sound. The harmonie was now completed with two discant, two taille, and two bassoons.

The most frequently quoted passage from Fleming's work is a passage in which he describes performances by one of the *Hautboisten* bands which were more in the nature of 'concert' music.

In the morning, in front of the commander's quarters, the *Hautboisten* playa Morning Song, a newly composed march, an Intrada, and a pair of minuets, which the commander likes; these are often repeated in the evening.

The most important extant example of original military band music from this period is the *lustige Feld-Music* (1704) by Johann Philipp Krieger (1649–1725). The composer specified

Die Feldmusik (Hautboisten) Regiment, 1720, Nürnberg

the work for 'four wind instruments,' which in the parts are labeled *Premier Dessus* (three players), *Second Dessus* (two players), *Taille* (one player), and *Basson* (three players). The composer says these (six Overture-suites) may be played by *Hautboisten* in either the court or in the field and, in the latter case, he hopes that if they are played during a lull in battle, they will be 'like a ray of sun on a stormy day.'

During the seventeenth century in France, as in Germany, one finds the prevalence of the military trumpet, especially with the mounted cavalry. Documents from this period indicate that most companies maintained only two trumpets, with companies of two hundred men having three. Each regiment maintained a Trumpet-Major, who trained new members and was the keeper of the repertoire during this age when the music was still memorized.

During parades the trumpets rode three or four paces in front of the commander, in front of the troops. In battle, however, both the trumpets and the commander stood safely at the rear, with the trumpets conveying the various orders for movement. In addition to this purely practical function, these military signals had a psychological value as well, as pointed out by Mersenne in 1636.

> As to the usage of the trumpets, they serve in time of peace and war for all sorts of public celebrations and solemnities, as is seen in marriages, banquets, tragedies, and carrousels. But its principal usage is destined for war ... it is easy to conclude ... how they would prepare the heart and mind of the soldier for going to war, for attacking, and engaging in combat.

Mersenne gives a summary of the seventeenth-century French military trumpet signals:

> The first is called the *cavalcade*, used when the army or one of its regiments approaches towns, through which it passes going to a siege or places of combat, to warn the inhabitants and make them participants in the cheerfulness and expectation of winning the victory. The second is named *to the saddle*, used for breaking up camp, and then follows the *call to saddle*. In the third place is sounded *on horseback*; and then *to the standard*, and *the charge*. Further is sounded the *watch*; but all these ways of sounding are most often distinct only through the interval of meter, for the fourth is performed almost always ... Thus two or more trumpets are easily heard a quarter league away and make many discourses which can take the place of speech. Still there is nothing particular in that, except that they can be heard from further away than the other instruments, which can be similarly used to hold some desired discourse.

To this list of signals, Kastner adds '*la sourdine*,' which he says was an order to march 'with little noise.'

These trumpeters, if few in number, were in a position of responsibility in the cavalry and no doubt were carefully chosen for this position. A famous French military treatise of 1691 describes the character of the man needed for this role.

> The trumpet must be a man of patience and vigilance, to be ready at all hours to excute the orders of the calls (military signals) ... the trumpet must be a discreet man, primarily when he is used in the negotiations, where he must never use other terms than those he is instructed with, never interfere by giving counsel, in order that in conferences and treaties there will be no ambiguity or statements contrary to those proposed.

In spite of such testimonials to the importance of the cavalry trumpeter, a contemporary officer testifies that he often had the experience of finding, in an army of twelve or fifteen thousand men, ten trumpets who did not know their signals.

French cavalry units began to use the timpani at about the time of the reign of Louis XIV. The timpanist improvised together with the trumpets in their signals, forming the harmonic bass. A contemporary treatise says of this player:

> The timpanist must be a man of heart, preferring to perish in combat rather than surrendering his timpani. He must have good arm movement and an accurate ear, and be able to divert his master with agreeable tunes (in peace time).

The new oboes arrived in the French military in approximately 1665 and according to one source these bands now included four 'oboes,' two treble, a tenor (*taille des hautbois*), and a bassoon.

From the period of Louis XIV we have an interesting account of a military band concert held during the Siege of Namur, and given in the field under a tent before the king, his officers, and a number of ladies invited for the occasion. The music was taken from the works of Lully.

> The king having invited the ladies to dinner the next day treated them to a war-like concert, composed of 120 tambours of the Gardes, 40 tambours of the Swiss Guards, with trumpets and timpani of the Gardes du Corps, the Light-Guard, to the number of 36; and all the oboes of the Mousquetaires and the Regiment of the king. Altogether they played a French march, and then the Swiss march. The trumpets and timpani gave separately the pleasure of a march on horseback. Mr. Philidor, whom the king had put in charge of the concert, had arranged a great finale for the entire ensemble. The oboes played airs from La Grotte de Versailles and Mr. Philidor played with them. The trumpets and timpani then gave a divertimento of the old airs de guerre, which they did in two choirs, interspersed with menuets played by the oboes. All the tambours, timpani and trumpets then played 'la charge' at the same time and the king had them repeat it three times. After that one heard the three last arias from Psiche. One then played 'la Generale, l'Assemblee, la Retraite Francaise, et les Dianes.' All of these airs were well played, nicely orchestrated, and played by all of these excellent men, each (of whom was) outstanding in his profession.

In England, by 1610, there was concern that the traditional military signals were being lost (Altenburg blamed this on the new concept of notating signals, rather than passing them down by ear),

> through the negligence and carelessness of drummers, and by long discontinuance so altered and changed from the ancient gravity and majestie thereof, as it was in danger utterly to have been lost and forgotten.

The new *Hautboisten* band appears in England first in 1678, with the creation of the new Horse Grenadiers, the first English troops who served both mounted and dismounted. Six 'hoboys,' which is to say, four oboes and two bassoons, were added at this time and were clearly a reflection of the influence of the French court on Charles II. In 1731 it was ordered that the music of the Grenadier Company of the Honourable Artillery Company of London should have 'one curtail three hautboys and no more!'

The first military 'oboe bands' in Rome appear in 1708 as '*piccoli concerti*,' consisting of oboes, bassoons, and sometimes timpani. These seem at first to have been organized privately, independent of the civic government. The military bands in Piemonte during the second half of the seventeenth century are more interesting, due to more international influence. One influence was French, as Vittorio Amadeo II had married a niece to Louis XIV in 1684, as one can see in the change of his court band's name from '*banda di tromboni*' to '*banda di hautbois*.'

The development of truly Western military bands in Russia began with Peter the Great (1682–1725) who made extensive travels throughout the West for the purpose of learning first-hand everything he could to bring Russia up-to-date. Peter imported German players of oboe, bassoon, trumpet, horn and timpani and established additional military music schools in the garrisons themselves in order to train the children of the soldiers.

MILITARY BANDS 185

Zurich infantry and Hautboisten, 1758

11 *Civic Wind Bands*

Germany

Civic wind bands in Germany attained their greatest stature, before the modern era, during the seventeenth century and their importance in German culture can be seen in the fact that they were the training ground for virtually every career in music. Centuries of increasing demands on the individual civic wind player, both in the numbers of instruments he must play and in quality of performance, resulted in a very high standard at this time. This can perhaps be appreciated in a letter by a *Stadtpfeifer* in Stralsund recommending his son for consideration for a similar position in Stettin in 1607.

> My son has arrived at a point in his art where he has studied and learned diligently all the musical instruments. First he is a good trumpeter and secondly a good cornett player and plays well the discant violin, Querpfiefe, Dulcian, quart-, tenor-, and alto-trombone. In summary: all perfect instruments, although without proclaiming his fame—for as one says, 'Self praise stinks.' But he can prove himself where it matters, in what the ear hears and the eye sees. To cover the subject, he doesn't quarrel or critize, has good friends, takes care of things quickly, and can use the instruments I have given him in praise of God: trombones, cornetts, a good quart-trombone; a Dulcian consort; a large and small bombard consort; a large cornett consort; a crumhorn consort; a Querpfeiffen consort; a flute consort; and a violin consort. He can play all parts and use the fifth, sixth, or eighth voices (read all the various clefs), comes from a good home … and is twenty-six years old.

Ordinarily, the one instrument the *Stadtpfeifers* were not supposed to use was the trumpet, which, as the reader has seen above, the strong aristocratic trumpet guilds attempted to reserve for themselves. One finds, for example, that the city council in Leipzig had to make a formal report to the elector explaining why their music director, J. H. Schein, used trumpets in a performance in St. Thomas Church (Schein was directed to use the cornett in the future!). Perhaps one famous incident can speak for the seriousness of this issue.

The civic wind band of Brussells featured in Denis van Alsloot's 'Procession en l'honneur de Notre-Dame du Sablon a Bruxelles le 31 mai', 1615–16

> At the end of the seventeenth century in Hannover, the Elector's trumpeters once broke into the house of the chief Stadtpfeifer, with whom they were at loggerheads, took his trumpet on which he was practicing and knocked out several of his front teeth with it. And what is more, these worthy Kameraden contended that they had only asserted their just right—and escaped all punishment.

The best known of the many services of the seventeenth-century German *Stadtpfeifers* was, of course, the *Abblasen*, the performance of chorales and hymns from civic or church towers. The spiritual and psychological impact of this music on the citizen on the street should not be underestimated. The trombones, on which the *Abblasen* were most frequently performed, had themselves become symbols of God and Christian music, as the fiddle had become the symbol of the Beer hall. Kuhnau, Bach's predecessor in Leipzig reflected, 'When our civic musicians at Festival time blow a spiritual song on the loud trombones, every measure stirs the image of angels singing.' No other instruments, but wind instruments, he says are played in Heaven by the angels! One can imagine the effect of this spiritual music, floating down several times a day from on high, played by instruments which were themselves symbols of God, on the ordinary man.

This tradition is referred to by one of the most famous of these men, the senior *Stadtpfeifer* in Leipzig, Gottfried Reiche, in the preface to his collection of original music for the civic wind band, his *Vier und zwantzig Neue Quatricinia*.

> Nothing in all art can claim finer qualities than Noble Music. My pen is much too weak either to repeat here, or to say better what professional and highly-learned men have affirmed so competently. As this matchless art spreads its charms in many ways, we find in most cities the praise-worthy custom of having the so-called 'Abblasen' sounded from churches and town halls. This is always a sign of joy and peace; because, wherever such music must be discontinued there must be national mourning, war, or other misfortune.

Gottfried Reiche, copperplate engraving by C. F. Rosbach after a portrait by E. G. Haussmann

A similar collection, composed for use during the performances given daily during the ten o'clock pause, is the *Hora decima* (1670) by another Leipzig *Stadtpfeifer*, Johann Pezel.

Of course the civic wind bands continued to perform for all civic festivities. Reiche, in fact, died after playing for a procession honoring Friedrich Augustus II in 1734!

On October 6th the skilled and experienced musician and stadtpfeifer, Gottfried Reiche, ... and senior member of the local musician's guild suffered a stroke not far from his lodging in the Stadtpfeifergasschen, as he was on his way home, so that he collapsed and was brought dead into the house. And this is said to have occurred because on the previous day he had been greatly fatigued by playing in the royal music and had suffered severely from the smoke of the torches.

The title page of Johann Hermann Schein's 'Fontana d'Israel' features a wind band performing with a conductor, 1623, Leipzig, Germany

One also reads of their performances in the church, for university ceremonies, and for the celebrations of the craft guilds. A typical example of the latter was the 1731 procession of the Nürnberg carpenters, which included three wind bands, each of three oboes, two horns, and bassoon.

But, as busy as they must have been, these civic wind band players were probably better off than most musicians of this time. The *Kapellemeister* of the Weissenfel court, Johann Beer, writes of his envy of the civic musician.

> Many princely musicians long for the city, because the service in the court is so insecure and he must be ready to move if the support for music by the noble fails or if he decides to cut back. What good are riches without stability? I say continued poverty could be called better luck than irregular riches, where one may go from a horse to an ass and from the ass even to sit in the dust.
>
> ...
>
> [In the city one can hope for quicker advancement] ... this has the civic musician, but at court even if he had a doctorate in all three faculties he waits without hope. The more excellent he is, the more he will remain in his station which he once accepted, to remain used, all feathers plucked from his wings so he can not hope to soar higher.

The civic musician guilds remained very strong during the seventeenth century. Indeed, in the years immediately after the Thirty Years War, one sees an extraordinary gathering of forty such guilds from upper and lower Saxony, in an instrumental music 'Collegium,' through which they hoped to strengthen these rights. In Leipzig, the civic band guild also controlled the rights of the regular *Stadtpfeifers* as opposed to their adjunct, and lesser esteemed, colleagues, the *Kunstgeigers*. Even so famous a player as Reiche had to wait in Leipzig for eighteen years before being admitted as a *Stadtpfeifer*. Once admitted, the *Stadtpfeifer* seems to have held his position for life, as the average tenure in the eighteenth century was thirty-three years!

England

While Germany reached a great climax in civic wind band performance during the seventeenth century, this ancient tradition was now in decline in most of the other countries. In England one sees the pure wind band tradition diluted by the demands for the players to learn the new string instruments and even to be proficient in singing. Thus a famous description of the Norwich Waits, in 1600:

> Passing the gate ... where ... stood the Citty Waytes ... such Waytes (under *Benedicite* be it spoken) fewe Cities in our Realme have the like, none better; who beside their excellency in wind instruments, their rare cunning on the Vyoll and Violin, theyr voices be admirable, everie one of them able to serve in any Cathedral Church in Christendoome for Quiristers.

The gradual breakdown of these old traditions also resulted in a breakdown of the normal professional disciplines, as one can see in numerous examples of various civic wait bands being reprimanded or even discharged by their civic governments. Pepys, in his famous diary, said of the Cambridge Waits, 'But Lord! What sad music they made.'

Even the proud London waits seem to have experienced the general decline in the fortunes of the seventeenth-century waits, or so it would seem in the evident loss of spirit-de-corps reflected in the following 1625 edict by the civic government:

Through the contentions and ill dispositions of some particular persons of this society (of waits) the whole company suffereth often in their credits and reputations by uncivil and retorting of bitter and unsavory jests and calumnious aspersions upon one or other of them; which only nourish the discord and confusion amongst them with continual quarreling and heart burning yea especially in the times of their service to his honorable city.

By the beginning of the eighteenth century the decline of the London Waits was such that now they were the object of cruel humor in contemporary literature, a sad contrast with their earlier role as representatives of civic pride.

Main picture and detail below: the City of London Waits playing just below the Royal Box for a civic procession, 16 November 1761

The old watch duty was now only a ceremony and in some cases no longer appreciated at all by the citizens. In Aberdeen, where this role was performed by a bagpiper, one reads the magistrates decided to discharge

> the common piper of all going through the town at nycht, or in the morning, in tyme coming, with his pype—it being an incivill forme to be usit within sic a famous burghe, and being often found fault with, als weill by sundrie nichtbouris of the toune as by strangers.

The appearances one would wish to know more about today are the ones for which the least information is extant: the concerts. We know that both the Norwich and London wait bands, at least, gave regular performances of a concert nature.

One now finds some accounts of student wind bands. A ceremony at Oxford in 1634, for the laying of the cornerstone of what is now the Bodleian Library, included music by what was apparently a wind band in residence at the university itself. An eyewitness wrote that after all the officials were seated, 'the University Musicians who stood upon the leads at the west end of the Library sounded a lesson [composition] on their wind music.' At the conclusion of this particular ceremony, a scaffold broke and a hundred or so people, 'namely the Proctors, Principals of Hall, Masters, and some Bachelaurs fell down all together one upon another into the foundation.'

There is also an eyewitness account of a student wind band, consisting perhaps of younger students, who performed before the queen when she visited in 1613. Returning from Bath, her route took her

> over the downes at Wenskyke within the parish of Bishop's Cannings; of which Ferebe having timely notice, he composed a song in four parts, and instructed his scholars to sing it very perfectly, as also to playa lesson or two (which he had composed) on their wind instruments.

As during the sixteenth century, the civic wait bands were hired to supply music for the theaters in London. An extraordinary testimonial to one of these performances comes to us from Samuel Pepys. The play, *The Virgin Martyr*, was pleasant, but not worth much, he wrote.

But that which did please me beyond any thing in the whole world was the wind-musique when the angel comes down, which is so sweet that it ravished me, and indeed, in a word, did wrap up my soul so that it made me really sick, just as I have formerly been when in love with my wife; that neither then, nor all the evening going home, and at home, I was able to think of any thing, but remained all night transported, so as I could not believe that ever any musick hath that real command over the soul of a man as this did upon me: and makes me resolve to practice wind-musique, and to make my wife do the like.

The Low Countries

A painting by Sallaert, of a celebration in Brussels in 1615, pictures the Brussels civic band as a six-member band with cornett, trombone, curtal, and three shawms of at least two sizes. The trombonist appears to be holding a piece of music in his hand, which has led to the suggestion that perhaps he played the cantus firmus above which the other musicians improvised.

Both functional and concert appearances continued during the seventeenth century and sometimes, as in the case of a concert in Audenarde, in 1700, the accounts speak of the new *Hautboisten* instrumentation.

Archduchess Isabelle and Archduke Albert at the procession of the maids of the Sablon, Antoon Sallaert, 1615

Concerts by the civic wind bands of the Low Countries continued during the seventeenth century. A civic edict from Mechlin (1606) describes very carefully several characteristics of these concerts. They were to occur every Sunday and feast day, for one half-hour, from eleven to eleven thirty o'clock in the morning. The musicians were to play the concert, 'for the honor of the city,' on *'schalmayen, trompet tes et autres instruments.'* To prepare these concerts the band was ordered to rehearse at least twice per week.

France

Some documents indicate that in France many ancient duties of the civic musician remained unchanged, as for example in the case of a Bordeaux edict (1631) relative to the town crier.

> The same officers are employed with their trumpets to make public proclamations and are obliged to be present at executions of criminals condemned to undergo some punishment for their crimes as an example to their fellow men.

Aside from the descriptions of typical civic duties there are also accounts of continued performances for the weddings of even the most humble citizens. Extraordinary is the account by Evelyn of hearing a band in Marseilles consisting of captives of a slave ship.

> The Captaine of the Gally royal gave us most courteous entertainment in his Cabine, the Slaves in the interim playing both on loud & soft musique very rarely: Then he shew'd us how he commanded their motions with a nod, & his Wistle, making them row out; which was to me the newest spectacle I could imagine, beholding so many hundreds of miserably naked Persons, having their heads shaven cloose, ... a payre of Course canvas drawers, their whole backs & leggs starke naked, doubly chayned about their middle, & leggs, in Cupples, & made fast to their seates: and all Commanded ... by an Imperious & cruell sea-man ... Their rising forwards, & falling back at their Oare, is a miserable spectacle, and the noyse of their Chaines with the roaring of the beaten Waters has something of strange & fearfull in it, to one unaccostom'd. They are ruld, & chastiz'd with a bullspizle dry's upon their backs & soles of their feete upon the least dissorder, & without the least humanity ... after we had bestow'd something amongst the Slaves, the Cap: sent a band of them to give us musique at dinner where we lodged.

Italy

References to the instrumentation of civic wind bands in Italy during the seventeenth century vary with the location. In Modena, one reads of the performance of three cornetti and five trombones, in Siena of trombones, and in Palermo of '*trombe et pifari.*' In Bologna, another city with a rich wind band tradition, an eyewitness in 1602 describes the two civic ensembles of the ruling city council.

> [The city officials] are accompanied by a very respectable household of eight trumpeters, with a drummer, or player of the nakers, who with these trumpets play certain Morish drums. To both the drums and trumpets are attached banners with the arms of liberty; also eight excellent musicians with trombones and cornettos.

Another reference speaks of concerts played by the last mentioned civic wind band.

> And after the trumpets have finished, very pleasant music is played on trombones and cornettos at the same Piazza as well as the great building of the church of St. Petronio.

Extant musical literature suggests such bands existed in both Rome and Venice, for there is a manuscript in Berlin composed in ca. 1700 for the '*Sonatori di fiato*' by Francesso Magini, a professor at the conservatory of Rome and the sonatas of Gussaghi (1608) are dedicated to the 'Excellent Virtuosi' of Venice, specifically the cornettist, Lodouico Cornale.

One must also mention the *Sonate/Symphonie* (1626) and *Sonate e sinfonie* (1629) of Biagio Marini, although neither is extant in a complete form. The latter was for two cornetti and three trombones, with one composition for four cornetts and four trombones.

12 Church Wind Bands

England

FOR MOST OF THE SEVENTEENTH CENTURY, until after the restoration of Charles II, whenever instrumental music, other than the organ, was used in English cathedrals it seems to have been almost exclusively wind bands (undoubtedly civic wind bands). Numerous accounts of performances can be documented in the major cathedrals of London, York, Norwich, Exeter, Winchester, Worcester, Salisbury, Durham, and Lincoln. Indeed the leading scholar on this subject, Andrew Parrott, maintains that only one unquestionable reference can be found for this entire period which even mentions string instruments in the church.

Why, then, was there an almost exclusive preference for wind bands? One reason was the historic association of these instruments with the church, but a contemporary also offered the opinion that it was felt that wind instruments, and not strings, could play in tune!

> ... becaus *Entata* [stringed instruments] ar often out of tun; (Which soomtime happeneth in the mids of the Musik, when it is neither good to continue, nor to correct the fault) therefore, to avoid all offence (where the least shoolde not bee givn) in our Chyrch-solemnities onely the Winde-instruments (whose Notes ar constant) bee in use.

The seventeenth century in England was a period of great religious upheaval and there were some opposed to any instrumental music in the church. The organ especially was held by many to be unsuitable, a view already long held by some. A large part of this concern was a puritanical desire to rid the service of everything extraneous to the simple presentation of the Anglican tenets. A typical expression of this concern can be seen in a sermon by a preacher in Durham in 1629.

> Why then are set before us so many objects of vanity, so many allurements of our outward senses, our eyes & eares, & consequently our minds from the meditation of Christs death & passion, and our sins which were the only cause of all our miseries & his lamentable sufferings. Can such paltry toyes bring to our memory Christ and his

Opposite page: Grazzi Chapel of Santissima Annunziata, 1644, Florence, Italy, fresco by Il Volterrano blood-shedding? Crosses, Crucifixes, Tapers, Candlesticks, gilded Angels, sumptous Organs, with Sackbuts & Cornets piping so loud at the Communion table, that they may be heard halfe a mile from the Church? No … Such glorious spectacles, draw away from God the minds of them that pray, they further not, but hinder entire affections, and godly meditations.

Those in favor of instrumental music based their views, as always, on the bible. To some degree, the puritans had their say, for in ca. 1660 the organs were in fact suppressed and did not reappear generally until 1860! During this period the music in many smaller churches was provided by church bands, consisting of a half-dozen or so wind instruments, with an occasional cello.

The royal wind band continued to perform in the king's chapel during the seventeenth century, but Charles II, who had lived part of his exile in Paris, introduced upon his restoration a group of strings into court life, modeled after Louis XIV's famous 'Twenty-four Violins.' This brings the first real tradition of using strings to accompany the English service, as can be accurately dated by the eyewitness, John Evelyn, in 1662.

> (One) of his Majesties Chaplains preachd: after which, instead of the antient grave and solemn wind musique accompanying the Organ was introduced a Consort of 24 Violins betweene every pause, after the French fantastical light way, better suited a Tavern or Play-house than a Church: This was the first time of change, & now we no more heard the Cornet, which gave life to the organ, that instrument quite left off in which the English were so skilfull.

The German-Speaking Countries

The polychoral performances by winds and voices described by Praetorius continued throughout the seventeenth century in Germany and further accounts of it can be found by Mattheson and Marpurg. This music was performed, of course, by the local *Stadtpfeifers*, the civic wind bands, and numerous contracts of the seventeenth century specify this obligation. A typical example, from Rothenburg, reads,

> The Stadtpfiefer should appear with their instruments as early as Vesper prayer time, on Sundays and Festival days, but also during the week as the Kantor requires, to help rehearse the music to be used the following Sunday.

This practice of using the local civic wind band was so popular with the congregation that in those cases where the choir music director preferred the old 'a cappella' music he was sometimes replaced, as happened in Wittenberg in 1628.

One also finds many examples at this time of individual churches purchasing their own wind instruments for the civic musicians to use. The church music director in Schweinfurt, in 1606, for example, acquired 'two new cornetts, two trombones, two pair of crumhorns, and two *Zezstück*.' The arrival of the string tradition, familiar to the reader in the music of Bach and his contemporaries at the end of the Baroque, can be seen in a similar purchase of two 'new' violins in 1701 by St. Thomas Church in Leipzig.

Extant documents for the purchase of wind instruments by the monasteries and cloisters indicate that some of them also used wind bands in their private celebrations. Perhaps the most interesting of these is a document, relative to a negotiation between the Gottweig Abbey in Austria with an instrument maker, dated ca. 1720. Mentioned here is the possible purchase of consorts of oboes, clarinets, and flutes. There are numerous accounts of wind band performances at the Melk monastery in Austria as well, the most extraordinary among these being the music for a public 'bleeding' ceremony!

Finally there is a very large extant repertoire of publications for use by wind bands in the German church services. One of these collectons, the *Geistliche Harmonien* by Johann Horn (ca. 1630–1685), published in Dresden in 1681, carries an interesting note.

> If shawms are not available use flutes, and if there are no trumpets use cornetti, etc., letting the musical director make the most agreeable arrangements.

The smaller *concerti d chiesa*, including compositions for solo voices and smaller numbers of winds, were also carried on in the Italian tradition. The nine compositions for voices and winds among Schutz's *Symphoniae sacrae* (1629) are a perfect example, scored sometimes for consorts of trombones or bassoons and sometimes for hetergenious collections of flutes, cornetti, trombone or bassoon. Similar works exist by Able (with Sinfonias for four bassoons!), Grandi, Hintze, Krieger, Christoph Peter, and Christian Sartorius.

A few church works include parts for 'horns, reflecting the approach of the *Harmoniemusik* tradition of the Classic period. These include works by Giovanni Hasse, Rahtgeber (1736), and Jungbauer. A wedding composition by Georg Riedel, composed in 1715, is scored for 2 *'Cors de Chasse,'* 2 oboes, trombone, and timpani.

There are also many examples of short wind band movements within larger church compositions. Buxtehude's *Ihr lieben Christen*, for example, contains a Sinfonia for three cornetts and three trombones.

An Oratorio by Bollius contains sinfonias for flute consort and for two cornetts and bassoon.

France

The conservative clergy of Paris issued the *Ceremoniale parisiense* in 1662, a document based on the discussions of the Council of Trent, which warned against using any instrument but the organ in the church. This seems, indeed, to have retarded the introduction of string instruments in French church music, as one does not see violins introduced at Notre Dame in Paris until the end of the seventeenth century or in the case of Chartres and Nantes, the early years of the eighteenth century.

Wind instruments, on the other hand, seem to have been continued to some degree, either as a necessity for choral support or for special ceremony. During the seventeenth century the clergy themselves in Nantes played the serpent, cornet, and crumhorns. The music master at the Chartres Cathedral, taught the dozen or so boys not only singing and composition, but also bassoon and serpent.

The immediate court of Louis XIV probably placed themselves above the rulings of the clergy, as the use of instruments continued in all forms. Not only did the numerous Te Deums of a military or political nature demand trumpets and drums, but more aesthetic efforts also enjoyed wide experimentation with instruments. In the *Messe pour plusieurs instruments au lieu des orgues* by Marc-Antoine Charpentier, for example, one finds a 'Kyrie,' 'Domine Deus Agnus,' and 'Quoniam' for four-part woodwind ensembles and two other movements for two oboes and continuo. The 'Offerte' is for two ensembles, one of strings and the other a wind band (*Choeur des instruments á vent*).

Italy

At the end of the sixteenth century, the use of wind bands in the church reached a tremendous artistic climax in the distinguished music composed for the musicians of St. Mark's Cathedral in Venice. This rich tonal splendor continues in the church ceremonies of the first several generations of the seventeenth century.

An eyewitness to some of these celebrations, Jean-Baptiste Duval, French ambassador to the Republic of Venice in 1607–1609, reported a procession on the eve of Ascension, 1608, with 'eight standards, six silver trumpets and oboes'; and for the procession of Corpus Christi in 1609, he reports 'six oboe players dressed in long robes with wide sleeves of dark blue or of rosy silk.' Duval also reported the use of winds during the actual Mass, in one case 'different wind instruments were sounded, such as clarions, trumpets, oboes, and drums.'

Another visitor to Venice, the Englishman, Thomas Coryat, wrote of the music he heard inside St. Mark's at about the same time.

> At that time I heard much good Musicke in Saint Markes Church, but especially that of a treble violl which was so excellent, that I thinke no man could surpasse it. Also there were sagbuts and cornets as at St. Laurence feast which yeelded passing good musicke.

Finally, canzoni in the style of Gabrieli continued to be composed and published in great numbers until about 1630, in addition to other sacred music in all forms for voices and winds.

The Spanish-Speaking Countries

The renaissance tradition of using wind bands in churches can be documented in both Spain and Portugal, where during the seventeenth-century wind bands of cornetts, sackbuts, and bassoons were the principal accompanying ensembles in the Badajoz Cathedral.

This seventeenth century preference for wind bands in Spanish cathedrals can be seen reflected in the export of this style to the New World. In Puebla, the second largest city in seventeenth-century Mexico, the cathedral used recorders, shawms, cornetts, sackbuts, and bassoons to double or even replace the voices; violins do not appear until the eighteenth century. Surviving documents indicate that one of the leading composers, Juan Gutierrez de Padilla, maintained a shop in his home in which salaried workers produced 'ecclesiastical instruments,' bassoons, shawms, and recorders.

Similarily, in Mexico City, a poem of 1691 by the celebrated Juana Ines de la Cruz, which was set to music by a leading composer, Antonio de Salazar (ca. 1650–1715), gives a typical ensemble as being 'clarino, trumpet, cornett, trombone, bassoon, and organ.'

Detail from 'God the Father and the nine angelic choirs' by Joan Gascó, 1503–1529

PART IV
The Classic Period

13 Court Wind Bands

UNTIL THE ENLIGHTENMENT, wind bands enjoyed an almost unrivaled position of importance in society, from the fundamental role they played in Greek and Roman societies to the enviable positions they held as regularly employed bands in the cities, courts, and churches of Western Europe during the period of 1400–1700. Where an instrumental ensemble was held in high esteem it was nearly always a wind band. The trumpet, which was played only by high priests among the ancient Hebrews, continued its association with the highest level of society in Western Europe by becoming a symbol of the aristocracy, a virtual aural coat-of-arms.

During the Baroque the wind band also acquired a strong spiritual association. The use of wind instruments for spiritual purposes had strong roots in the 'natural' sources of the instruments themselves, having their origin in bones, reeds, shells, animal horns, etc. In addition, performance on a wind instrument was viewed as the closest relation to the voice ('the God given instrument') for one used, if not the body itself, as in the case of singing, at least breath from within the body. Thus it was only natural that during the first two-thirds of the Baroque the common man was surrounded by spiritual music played by the wind band, both by the Abblasen from the civic towers and in the performance of multi-part church music.

The music of the Classic Period continued the great interest in expressing the emotions which one finds in nearly all commentary during the Baroque Period. Now, however, a new vehicle for the expression of emotion arrives in the form of Italian Opera, which swept Europe. With Italian Opera (a medium much like daytime TV) it is the soprano who cries on the stage and so music becomes much more melodic oriented than in the previous period, and the melody is concentrated in the upper part ('No mother raises her child to play second violin!'). The arrival at the same time of the new string instruments from Italy presented a natural surrogate for the soprano, the violin.

Opposite page: Court Harmoniemusik, 1751

These changes, together with the financial aftermath of the civil unrest during the seventeenth century led to cities cutting back on spending for many of their traditional expenditures on music. Independent civic wind bands all but disappear from notice during the Classic Period (although a new, stronger tradition will appear during the nineteenth century), and with them the ancient wind instrument guilds. It is particularly interesting that Kaiser Joseph II closed the office of the leader of the wind guild (*Oberspielgrafenamtes*) in Vienna in the very year (1782) that he formed his personal new *Harmoniemusik*!

Even though the Classic period is one in which the old traditions died, the very important new wind band, *Harmoniemusik*, finds a place for itself at the very highest levels of Western European society. Its musicological importance lies, in part, in this fact (a position the wind medium has not held since that time), and because its repertoire reveals, as the symphonic repertoire does not, that many wind players were the equal of any musicians of that era.

Geographically, *Harmoniemusik* shares the central European locale which one associates with the great masterworks of the Classic period. The greatest activity is found in the Austrian-Bohemian-Hungarian 'triangle' formed by Vienna, Prague, and Budapest. There was considerable *Harmoniemusik* in a few courts in Southern Germany, but comparatively little in Northern Germany. Similarly, as one moves west, there are relatively few important works from the Low Countries and surprisingly few original, significant compositions from England.

France presents a curious enigma, for while the medium (the instrumentation) of *Harmoniemusik* begins in France, and Paris was a center for publication of *Harmoniemusik*, there is very little in the way of original compositions by French composers in French libraries today.

In Italy *Harmoniemusik* seems to have been concentrated in areas under the influence of the Austrian Empire.

Some *Harmoniemusik* even found its way to America, via the Moravian settlements in North Carolina and Pennsylvania. The presence of such European traditions, of course, characterizes nearly all the early instrumental music of the United States. One wonders if it were even the case that some American 'aristocrats' may for a time have wished to emulate their

European contemporaries in having a personal *Harmoniemusik*. The knowledge of this special 'status symbol' seems at least suggested in a letter written by Thomas Jefferson during the American Revolution to a friend in Europe.

> I retain for instance among my domestic servants a gardner … , weaver … , a cabinet maker … and a stone-cutter … to which I would add a vigneron. In a country where, like yours, music is cultivated and practised by every class of men, I suppose there might be found persons of those trades who could perform on the French horn, clarinet or hautboy and bassoon, so that one might have a band of two French horns, two clarinets and hautboys and a bassoon, without enlarging their domest[ic] expences … Without meaning to give you trouble, perhaps it mig[ht] be practicable for you in your ordinary intercouse with your pe[ople] to find out such men disposed to come to America. Sobriety and good nature would be desirable parts of their characters.

The repertoire of *Harmoniemusik* grew out of the forms composed for the baroque *Hautboisten* band, the divertimento developing from the overture-suite and the partita developing from the concerto da camera. The partita is identical in form with the classical symphony and indeed, as the most famous scholar of this period, Robbins Landon, points out the two terms were interchangeable as late as 1830. By the late eighteenth century it does appear that a tradition evolved for using one term for the string–wind ensemble and the other for the pure wind ensemble. Accordingly, Mozart was as unlikely to write a 'Partita' for strings as he was a 'Symphony' for winds. It was the publishers, by the way, who labeled his wind ensemble masterworks, K.370a and K.384a, 'Serenade'; his autographs clearly say 'Partita.'

But to speak of 'Symphonies' for winds is to suggest a role for the classical wind band which is almost completely unrecognized by traditional musicology. Even though we speak of a period when most composers were 'craftsmen,' and not yet 'artists,' and of a period during which much music was to some degree functional and true concerts in the modern sense were comparatively rare, traditional musicology has tended to lend the impression that string ensemble music was 'art' music, while wind music was only functional.

The primary explanation for this perspective is that previous scholars did not have the opportunity to know of the vast amounts of wind ensemble and wind band music which have only been rediscovered during the past twenty years, nor have access to the many studies which have appeared in recent years regarding the musical practice in individual central European courts.

Today, however, we can see that the wind band performed both functional and 'concert' music, as did all other mediums—and probably in about the same ratio as other mediums.

Bohemia

Various eighteenth and early nineteenth-century observers have left hints of the high development of wind instrument music in Bohemia and Moravia, but it was only with the opening of the private palaces of this region after World War II that the full appreciation of this practice became evident. It is now clear that a period of considerable growth in all aristocratic musical ensembles in this area began about the middle of the eighteenth century. Wind bands were a fundamental part of this environment and when the larger organizations began to be reduced, ca. 1760–1780, it was often only the wind band which remained.

One of the princely seats which seems to have especially developed wind bands was that of the Bishops of Olmütz (Olomouc) who resided in Kroměříž, where a very large collection of original partitas is still housed. The most extraordinary collection of aristocratic *Harmoniemusik* from eighteenth-century Bohemia, however, is that which belonged to the wind band of Johann Joseph Philipp Graf Pachta, of Prague. Although a large part of this collection is now lost, no fewer than two hundred and fifty works survive in the National Library in Prague.

Several references in contemporary literature seem to suggest that this *Harmoniemusik* was the best and most artistic of the Bohemian representatives. Johann Ferdinand von Schönfeld, writing in 1796, observed:

> Herr Graf Johann Pachta maintains a special wind Harmonie and very often during the year gives musical entertainment.

Graf von Pachta by Franz Fahrenschön, 1765

These views are shared in several notices in the *Allgemeine Musikalische Zeitung*. One reads in the issue for 9 April 1800,

> Many nobles have Kapelles of artists, mostly of wind instruments, and foremost among them is the one of Graf Joh. Pachta.

An article later the same month mentions that many of the noble ensembles were no longer in existence, but that Johann Pachta had a very good *Harmoniemusik* consisting of the best artists on wind instruments. Another contemporary, writing in 1815, mentions the 'musical Harmonie' still existed and that Pachta himself was a good musician and had in fact composed a symphony for two oboes, two horns, and bassoon in 1780.

Since at least one of the manuscripts of this collection is dated 1762, one can account for the continued existence of this *Harmoniemusik* for a period of more than fifty years! It is particularly interesting that one finds in this collection partitas with parts for pairs of the old tenor oboe, the taille, one of the hallmarks of the baroque *Hautboisten* band. I believe the appearance of these *Hautboisten* relics during the first generation of classical *Harmoniemusik* strengthens the hypothesis that the *Harmoniemusik* was not in fact a *new* medium, but rather an evolution from the baroque *Hautboisten* band which also played music in the 'chamber.' The appearance of two English horns in other manuscripts of this collection must be taken as only a new, but concurrent, name for the old instrument, for their function as tenor oboes remains musically unchanged.

Another aristocrat in Prague who maintained an important *Harmoniemusik* and who was himself, like Pachta, a musician, was Christian Philipp Graf Clam-Gallas. His extant wind band collection is characterized by unusual instruments, such as basset horns and an occasional flute.

Given the interest in *Harmoniemusik* among these important aristocrats in Bohemia and Moravia, there must also have been many minor aristocrats who, to some degree or other, also supported wind bands. One of these was a man whose name would have long ago been forgotten, had he not hired in 1759, as '*Musikdirektor*' and '*Kammer compositor*,' a twenty-seven year old musician named Josef Haydn! He was Count Ferdinand Maximilian Morzin, who maintained an estate at Lucaveč near Plzeň.

While very little is presently known of the musical traditions at the Court of Count Morzin, judging by the extant music of Haydn he seems to have had a typical six-member *Harmoniemusik* of oboes, horns, and bassoons during the period of the composer's residence. If we can again judge by the music Haydn wrote for this ensemble, these players were outstanding. In the opinion of Robbins Landon, the horns 'were among the greatest of their age, and indeed among the greatest, perhaps, of all time.'

Haydn's tenure at this court was brief for apparently Count Morzin dissipated his fortune in a short time and had to disband his musical establishment. It was in any case for this Count's *Harmoniemusik* that Haydn composed at least eight extant divertimenti for pairs of oboes, horns, and bassoons. These compositions are all in brief five-movement forms, but are by no means minor works. Robbins Landon gives the following summary of their style:

Joseph Haydn by Thomas Hardy, 1791

> Haydn is extremely adept with the scoring, and the pieces sound magnificent. One feature which must have struck the contemporary listener is the curious sense of poignancy engendered by the adagios … One is also intrigued by the many unusual dynamic marks in these slow movements, including crescendi and many contrasts of f–p … Altogether, one cannot escape the strong feeling that Haydn deliberately experimented far beyond that which the form usually contained, both in formal scope and in particular regarding the actual sound.

One of the special Haydn compositions for his wind band at this time, the Divertimento, Hoboken II:23 in F, contains a minuet based on the Gregorian chant for Holy Week, the 'Lamentations of Jeremiah.' Robbins Landon enjoyed wondering what those aristocratic guests sitting at Count Morzin's dinner table thought when,

> from the wind band at the end of the room, floated over the dining table at Lukavec Castle the ghostly sounds of Good Friday or Maundy Thursday, recalling penitent processions and monkish prayers?

Hungary

The reader has seen in this volume much evidence of the strong influence the East had on Western wind music. During the eighteenth century, ironically, the courts of Hungary began to imitate the West. Thus there were several important aristocrats in Hungary who formed *Harmoniemusik* ensembles during the Classic Period.

Because of its proximity to Vienna, the Esterházy court in Eisenstadt was one of those Hungarian residences in which one would have found a strong Western influence, not only in music, but language, dress, architecture, and literature. It was here, sometime before May 1761, that Haydn joined the musical establishment of Prince Paul Anton Esterházy.

Such evidence as there is seems to suggest that it may have been Haydn himself who introduced the *Harmoniemusik* concept to this court. We know a catalog of the court's archives dated 1759 includes no such music and that the document which formalized Haydn's appointment also announced the appointment of two oboists and two bassoonists. During the same month there was a payment to two horn players in the service of Paul Anton's brother. A document for the 'Table and Chamber' musicians dated 15 June 1761, gives the entire musical establishment as a *Harmoniemusik* of pairs of oboes, horns, and bassoons; five strings (including Haydn), and a flute.

After the death of Paul Anton, in March 1762, a number of documents appear by his brother and successor, Nicolaus, with regard to the organization of the court. One of these is an interesting order relative to the continuation of the wind band, which outlines the duties and expectations for the behaviour of its members.

Prince Nicolaus Esterházy by Martin Knoller, 1790

> Apart from the salaries indicated, the *Feld Musique*, consisting of 6 persons, namely 2 oboists, 2 bassoon players and 2 horn players, are to receive a daily payment of 17xr. when and only when they are in Eisenstadt. And to all this the above-listed musicians should receive a uniform every year or every two years two uniforms but with the expressed proviso: that they should be satisfied with such a salary and not bother us further.
>
> (1) They are to appear, not only in Eisenstadt, at the Chamber and Choir *Musique* diligently and as long as the *Herrschaft* orders, whether early or late, also in Vienna and in other places whereto they may be ordered to perform their duties.

(2) They are subordinate to the *Vice-Capel-Meister* and to follow his orders without contradiction.

(3) Each shall comport himself honestly, quietly and peacefully, as is expected of any honest man in a princely court.

(4) They are not to absent themselves without our permission from Eisenstadt, Vienna or wherever the court happens to be, nor to be absent from the Chamber or Choir *Musique*, but to make such a request to the *Capel-Meister* and according to the circumstances our Resolution shall be made.

The considerable number of *Harmoniemusik* compositions by Haydn which apparently date between 1761–1766 are evidence for his responsibility for this kind of music. His greatly expanded duties after 1766 seems to have precluded much further composition for this medium. The wind band itself, however, continued as an identifiable ensemble in the Esterházy court for most of the rest of the eighteenth century. Indeed one may assume that, whatever its function, it was an important part of court life for when Prince Anton dismissed the entire orchestra in 1790 (two days after the death of his father, Nicholas), he nevertheless retained the *Harmoniemusik*.

One should assume this wind band's duties included all kinds of functional obligations, but most of the surviving music is clearly of a concert nature. Among the more unusual manuscripts are the massive arrangements by Druschetzky of the *Seasons* and *Creation* of Haydn (the first oboe part of the latter runs to forty-five pages!).

Austria

In view of the *Harmoniemusik* activity in Bohemia and Hungary, outlined above, it should come as no surprise that it is from the capital, Vienna, that we should find some of the most interesting accounts of aristocratic wind bands. Indeed, it appears that after the Emperor formed his *Harmoniemusik* every major Viennese prince soon adopted this new 'status symbol.' A measure of the wide interest in this form of music can be seen in the fact that Johann Traeg, who was in the business of selling manuscript copies, offered in his catalog of 1799 more than two hundred separate compositions for *Harmoniemusik*, in five to nine parts!

The evidence is that the Emperor's *Harmoniemusik* first began to function as an independent ensemble in 1782. In that year the players were all members of the court opera orchestra, but received extra pay for their appearance as a *Harmoniemusik*. One of the first eyewitness accounts of this new ensemble dates from 1783.

> Among all kinds of musical news which has been related to me, one piece that was to me especially remarkable concerned a group of musicians organized by the Kaiser, the sound of whose wind instruments has achieved a new high level of perfection. It is known in Vienna as the Kaiserlich-Koniglich Harmonie. This group consists of eight persons, it performs by itself as a complete and full ensemble. In it they even perform pieces which are in fact intended only for voices, such as choruses, duos, trios, and even arias from the best operas; the places of the vocal parts are taken by the oboe and clarinet.

Another very early eyewitness, Reichardt, heard this ensemble and that of the emperor's brother as well.

> The discussion finally turned to harmoniemusik, consisting of genuine wind instruments, which was beginning at the time (1783) in Vienna with great perfection. The Kaiser and his brother each had his own full harmonie and as they heard that Reichardt was particularly taken by these, they promised that he should one morning hear both groups playing together in the Kleine Redoutensaale. This duly took place and afforded a wholly delightful pleasure. The atmosphere and the performance were alike pure and harmonious; some movements by Mozart were also exquisite.

It does seem to have been this *Harmoniemusik* that popularized the idea of including opera and ballet arrangements in their repertoire. The nineteenth-century Viennese court music catalog lists more than one hundred such arrangements, many of extraordinary length (some containing twenty or more arias). The evidence is that such music was used as all music at this time, that is sometimes for concerts and sometimes for functional purposes.

The leader of this *Harmoniemusik* was Johann Wendt, who was both a distinguished oboist and composer.

Another very important Viennese *Harmoniemusik* belonged to the influential and powerful Prince Liechtenstein. The earliest mention of such an ensemble is found in an extraordinary letter by Mozart, dated 23 Janury 1782, shortly after his arrival in Vienna. Writing to his father, relative to the employment opportunities he was exploring, he revealed,

> I have my eye here on three sources (of permanent income). The first is not certain, and, even if it were, would probably not be much ... (he) is young Prince Liechtenstein, who would like to collect a *Harmoniemusik* (though he does not yet want it to be known), for which I should write the music. This would not bring in much, it is true, but it would at least be something certain, and I should not sign the contract unless it were to be for life.

It is interesting to observe that in this letter Mozart gives no indication that the *Harmoniemusik* medium was new to him, nor that he considered it in any way beneath his talents. His only concern seems to be that it might not pay enough to live on. The implied secrecy on Liechtenstein's part should perhaps be viewed as his not wanting to preempt the emperor, who was also forming such an ensemble at the same time. Most startling of all, of course, is to contemplate on what might have happened if it had all worked out—if Liechtenstein had formed his *Harmoniemusik* at this time and if he had employed Mozart. How would the subsequent development of the wind band have changed, if Mozart had composed primarily wind band music during the final decade of his life? What would we have had instead of the Requiem, and the final symphonies and how would that music have changed the nineteenth-century perception of the wind band medium?

The evidence is that the Prince did not follow through with this idea until the Fall of 1789, when he hired eight wind players to form a *Harmoniemusik* under the leadership of Joseph Triebensee. The contracts for the members of the Liechtenstein *Harmoniemusik* carry the traditional language relative to the expected standards of behaviour. In the case of one extant order by the Prince, given in Vienna in 1798, the members were warned that they risked dismissal if they failed to heed Triebensee's orders.

As was not unusual, the members of the *Harmoniemusik*, Triebensee included, even had to have the permission of the Prince to marry. Court records indicate the *Harmoniemusik* played all kinds of functional music, but also regular concerts three evenings a week during the summer.

Among the other important princes in Vienna who maintained *Harmoniemusik* ensembles were Prince Schwarzenberg (whose ensemble used English horns, rather than clarinets), Prince Grassalkovics (whose conductor was Georg Druschetzky), Prince Lobkowitz (whose *Harmoniemusik* had to play the extraordinary partitas of Cartellierei), and perhaps Count Palm.

It was because the *Harmoniemusik* was a leading aristocratic activity in Vienna that Mozart contributed his partitas during his residence there. Among these is the so-called 'Grand Partita,' a title correctly reflecting its larger than usual instrumentation. This masterpiece was composed in February 1784, and we read the announcement of its first performance in the *Wienerblättchen* (23 March 1784).

> [Today] Herr Stadler, the elder, in actual service of His Majesty the Emperor, will hold a musical concert for his benefit at the Court Theater, at which will be given, among other well-chosen pieces, a great wind piece of a very special kind composed by Herr Mozart.

A chance reference by one who heard this very concert confirms that the musical impact of this work has never varied.

> Musical concert held by Stadler, Clarinet Virtuoso
>
> My thanks to thee, brave Virtuoso! I have never heard the like of what thou contrivest with thy instrument. Never should I have thought that a clarinet could be capable of imitating a human voice so deceptively as it was imitated by thee. Verily, thy instrument has so soft and so lovely a tone that nobody can resist it who has a heart, and I have one, dear Virtuoso; let me thank thee!
> I heard music for wind instruments today, too, by Herr Mozart, in four movements—glorious and sublime! It consisted of thirteen instruments, 4 horns, 2 oboes, 2 bassoons, 2 clarinets, 2 basset horns, and string bass, and at each instrument sat a master—Oh, what an effect it made—glorious and grand, excellent and sublime!

Germany

Considering the degree to which the emperor's *Harmoniemusik* was considered a status symbol and was emulated by the major princes in Vienna, it comes as no surprise to read that the emperor's brother, Maximilian Franz (1756-1801), the Elector of Bonn, formed his own *Harmoniemusik* almost immediately after his brother. It was for this *Harmoniemusik* that Beethoven composed his various compositions for this medium. This *Harmoniemusik* may have even been recruited in Vienna, in any case an eyewitness found them to be outstanding performers.

Archduke Maximilian Franz of Austria (1756-1801), eighteenth century

> These eight players can be called complete masters of their art. It is rare to find music played with their artistry, with ensemble as good as theirs, with understanding as good, and especially music that had reached so high a standard of truth and perfection in the production of tone.

It is in the geographical area in Germany which lies south of Bonn, that one finds today the largest collections of extant *Harmoniemusik*. Certainly the best known of these German aristocratic *Harmoniemusik* bands was the one maintained by Prince Kraft Ernst von Ottingen-Wallerstein (1748–1802) at Schloss Harburg. His interest in *Harmoniemusik* can be seen in the palace collection which today has more than eighty extant partitas, by Rosetti, Joseph Reicha, Feldmayr, Wineberger, and others.

Another German court in the South which apparently had a very active *Harmoniemusik* was that of Prince Karl Egon von Fürstenberg at Donaueschingen. Two early catalogs of this library list more than one hundred and fifty partitas and a great number of opera transcriptions which were located there before 1804. Among these are twenty-two compositions by Fiala, one of the few composers admired by Mozart.

There are also large collections of partitas, reflecting strong court traditions, in Regensburg and in Rudolstadt.

Due to the destruction of Dresden during World War II it is impossible to judge the extent of *Harmoniemusik* activity in Dresden, but there are two fascinating reviews of public concerts in 1789 by such an ensemble.

At a private concert here Mozart's excellent opera *Il Don Giovanni* was performed in an arrangement for 8 wind instruments; the effect it had on the listeners is not to be described.

...

On 30 March, at the instigation of a music-lover, a concert of wind instruments was given in the large music-room of the Hotel de Pologne, namely, in the first part the sinfonie and the finest arias from Mozart's Don Juan, and in the second, the sinfonie and the finest pieces from Un Cosa rara by Martin; the extraordinarily numerous audience, which included almost all the high nobility and many other music lovers, departed in unanimous satisfaction.

France

The reader will recall the impact which the *Les Grands Hautbois* of Louis XIV had on the adoption of *Hautboisten* bands in Germany during the late seventeenth century and the subsequent development from them of the new *Harmoniemusik* medium. This same sequence of events occurred again during the beginning years of the Classic Period when France produced a new wind band instrumentation, which would define the direction for all later European bands and indeed the bands of today! The distinguishing characteristic of the new French instrumentation was the replacement of the oboes, as the primary melodic vehicle, by clarinets.

The initial enthusiasm in France for this new instrumentation may have been related to the anti-monarchial political environment which was already present by mid-century, for in France the oboe and the wind band named for it, *Les Grands Hautbois*, was first and foremost associated with the monarchy. This hypothesis seems to me confirmed, as the reader shall see below, by the second generation of these new French 'clarinet bands,' the bands of the French Revolution. These new, larger bands with many clarinets, were intended to stand in sharp contrast, both in instrumentation and musical style, to the previous aristocratic wind bands, one of the familiar status symbols of that class.

All of the royal wind ensembles of the French Baroque, discussed above, continued during the Classic Period, but these ensembles were now relics and dramatic new changes were taking place in French society. Not only had the *philosophes* challenged the traditional role in society of religion and stimulated freer thought on all subjects (represented by the famous *Encyclopédie* of Diderot), but a basic economic change was also occurring: the pre-eminent wealth was moving to those who controlled industry, commerce, and finance from those who owned land. As Voltaire wrote in 1755,

> Owing to the increasing profits of trade ... there is less wealth than formerly among the great, and more among the middle classes. The result has been to lessen the distance between classes.

These economic changes also made the middle class a significant factor in the arts, as Will Durant describes,

> Businessmen like La Popeliniere could build palaces that were the envy of nobles, and adorn their tables with the best poets and philosophers in the realm; it was the bourgeoisie that now gave patronage to literature and art. The aristocracy consoled itself by hugging its privileges and displaying its style.

The individual example Durant provides, Alexandre-Jean-Joseph Le Riche de La Pouplinière (1693–1762), is in fact a man central to our story. He was perhaps the most influential and wealthy financier in Paris and through his palace and country estate at Passy passed virtually every important figure in literature and art; he can be linked with Voltaire, Rousseau, Van Loos, La Tours, and even such characters as Casanova. He was also an amateur musician and maintained his own orchestra, led by three extraordinary music directors: Rameau, J. W. A. Stamitz, and Gossec.

Portrait of Pouplinière, engraved by J.J. Bachelou after Louis Vigée, ca. 1750

Although La Pouplinière's style may often have only been in imitation of the aristocrats, credit must be given to his 'court' for significant musical developments. It was here that the first use of both horns and clarinets can be documented in French orchestras and here that these instruments combined to initiate the French enthusiasm for wind ensembles with clarinets. Indeed, before the performances of La Pouplinière's musicians, information on the concert usage of both these instruments is very difficult to find.

La Pouplinière had a small *Harmoniemusik* of at least clarinets and horns. When his household was dispersed in 1762, Gossec and nearly all the wind players went immediately into the service of Louis-Joseph de Bourbon, Prince de Condé, for whom Gossec wrote his extant works for pairs of clarinets, horns, and bassoons.

Other French aristocrats followed the example of La Pouplinière, and not the king, in forming *Harmoniemusik*s with clarinets. Among these were the Prince de Condé, as mentioned, the Duke d'Orléans, the Duke de Villeroy, Prince Louis de Rohan, and the Prince of Monaco. A review has survived from a concert by the Duke d'Orléans's ensemble of pairs of clarinets, horns and bassoons performing '*morceaux de symphonie*' in 1767. The newspaper, *La Mercure*, reported they were

> a happy and rather unusual ensemble (who played) a most agreeable choice of melodies with a certainty of execution and in a well-organized and most economic way—that is what characterizes the artists that we mention and the music that they played. Also that they received great applause, the first reward of men of talent.

By about 1770 this new French 'clarinet band' also began to use the name '*Harmonie*,' but was never called, nor ever confused with, '*Hautboisten*.' It is therefore very ironic that while the *Harmoniemusik* of Central Europe developed from the *Hautboisten* band, the French *Harmonie* developed apart from and in distinction with the king's *Les Grands Hautbois*—the *original Hautboisten* band! It is because of this distinction that we can understand today why the French *Harmonie*, even though it was clearly associated with the French aristocracy, continued to flourish during and after the French Revolution, while the *Les Grands Hautbois* passed out of existence with the execution of Louis XVI.

Therefore, while French *Harmonie* publications with oboe parts are virtually non-existant between 1785–1800, publications for the *Harmonie* with pairs of *clarinets*, horns, and bassoons flourished. While there were a number of official publications of original revolutionary music for this instrumentation, under the title *Collection Épogues*, nearly all of the remaining publications were arrangements. The person most identified with these arrangements was Georg Friedrich Fuchs (1752–1821), a German military clarinetist who moved to Paris in 1784. An enormous number of his arrangements for pairs of clarinets, horns, and bassoons were published during the final decade of the eighteenth century by J. J. Imbault and Jean Sieber, père, of Paris.

There is nothing whatever to suggest that any of this music was intended primarily for the military, as has often been assumed. On the other hand, the Parisian firm of Nadermann began a series of publications at the turn of the century which were indeed intended for the military These arrangements, also by Fuchs, are all scored for *four* clarinets, two bassoons, trumpet, and two horns and are a synthesis of both the preference for multiple clarinets developed by the larger revolutionary bands of the previous decade and the instrumentation of the popular French *Harmonie*. It is in this synthesis that most modern military bands have their origin: they remain clarinet-oriented and to this very day some countries still call their bands, '*Harmonie*.'

England

Due to the retrenchment of court music during the Baroque Period, together with the development of the general public taste for military music, there seems to have been very little genuine court wind band music in England during the Classic Period. I have read of only two such ensembles, neither of which has received any attention by English scholars.

Cramer's *Magazin der Musik* (1784) mentions one.

> The Prince of Wales has a Hauskapelle whose members are musical servants; every evening they play Tafelmusik with two clarinets, two horns, and a bassoon.

It was Haydn, however, who provided the only other reference to what may have been a court wind band in the continental tradition. In his second 'London Notebook' Haydn wrote,

> Lord Claremont once gave a large *Soupé*, and when the King's health was drunk, he ordered the wind band to play the well-known song 'God Save the King' in the street during a wild snowstorm. This occurred on 19th Feby 1792, so madly do they drink in England.

The surprisingly small number of original partitas which appear to have been composed in England, and the almost total absence of the word '*Harmoniemusik*' in English literature, seem to confirm the disappearance of this tradition.

Russian Horn Bands

Perhaps the most unusual wind bands of the modern era were the Russian horn bands, large bands of players who individually could play but a single note! This incredible movement began in the court of the Empress Elizabeth during the first years of the Classic Period as the direct result of some particularly poor performance in 1751 by the court Jagdhörner. Offended by the terrible intonation of these natural instruments when played together, the court Master of the Hunt, Prince Kirilovich Narishkin, had a local copper-smith make a set of sixteen instruments all tuned to D. As a result, on their next performance these players, no matter what note of the triad they happened to blow, sounded well.

The Prince was so taken by this improvement that he assigned to a court musician, Johann Maresch (Jan Mares, 1719–1794), the responsibility of organizing a formal concert in which these sixteen natural horn players would be combined with an ensemble of court horn, trumpet, and posthorn players. Maresch found it quite impossible on such short notice to teach the sixteen hunting horn players, who had previously played only memorized signals, to learn to read music. Therefore he arrived at the idea of writing their parts in such a way that each player was responsible for a single pitch, which he played whenever that pitch occurred in the music; in this manner the sixteen hunting horns accompanied the court ensemble.

Next the Prince ordered that the sixteen hunting horn players become a regular ensemble of their own. Maresch now found that by using horns in several different keys he was able to write simple three-part compositions, still performed with each player responsible for only a single pitch. By 1753 he had increased the ensemble to thirty-six players, who spanned a range of three octaves. When the music director, Sarti was asked to prepare a horn band of one hundred players to accompany a Te Deum he was unable to build bass instruments of sufficient volume so he substituted small cannons selected for the specific pitches needed.

Maresch devised an original notation system which showed for each player his pitch, together with a unique system of symbols for rests. This was copied into a small notebook which each player held in his free hand. According to one who heard the group the players were able, in spite of performing only a single pitch, to learn complex dynamic and articulation skills, which made the results musically effective—especially outstanding in 'pathetic movements.'

The usual repertoire of the band consisted of transcriptions of orchestral music, as well as organ fugues. In one extraordinary case the band performed the music for an opera, in this instance using instruments constructed from wood so as not to drown out the singers!

The band also made frequent international tours and some reviews indicate a high degree of musicianship. One who heard this band in 1802 was the famous German composer, Ludwig Spohr.

> Between the first and second part of this concert, the Imperial hornists executed an overture by Gluck, and with a rapidity and exactness which would have been difficult for stringed instruments, how much the more so then for hornists, each of whom blew only one tone! It is hardly to be believed that they performed the most rapid passages with the greatest precision, and I could not have conceived it possible, had I not heard it with my own ears. But as may be imagined, the Adagio of the overture made a greater effect than the Allegro; for it always remains somewhat unnatural to execute such quick passages with these living organ pipes, and one could not help thinking of the thrasings which must have been inflicted (to create such a performance).

On the other hand many reviewers were quite hostile to the entire concept of this band. One humorous letter, supposedly by a member of the Russian Horn Band, to the editor of the English *Harmonicon*, is representative of these views.

To the editor of *The Harmonicon*
From the *F-sharp* of the Russian Imperial Horn Music

Sir,
Can you figure to yourself a man reduced to the condition of an organ pipe? Will you believe, sir, that the person who now addresses you, has, during thirty years of his life, been the F-sharp of the music of the Emperor of all the Russias? I was called, at least I am willing so to believe, to more brilliant destinies; but a cruel event has changed my fate. My fortune having been destroyed in a single day, I was reduced to the necessity of soliciting the favour of the Court; I hoped for an employment worthy of a thinking being, and they have conferred upon me that of a piece of mechanism. I became *mono-musical* at the rate of a hundred roubles per annum.

One day I took it into my head to play an entire melody upon a flute, which had been sent me from France. As a return for my presumption, I received a dozen lashes of the knout, which were unsparingly applied and my appointment stopped. After this I *blew* for six months for the King of Prussia, but wearied out at length by the rigorous treatment I was doomed to endure, I deserted from a body where no encouragement is held out to emulation, and from a country, where intelligent beings are converted into wind instruments, incapable of any farther degree of advancement. My comrades, G, Bb, and A, have followed by example. We have lately arrived in London and wish to give some concerts. We propose playing a melody in four notes, and solemnly assure you that we will not cheat the public by being pleasing; we will scrupulously adhere to the prevailing fashion, and be only surprising.

Your humble servant,
Kouloff
Formerly F sharp to H.I.M. the Emperor of all the Russias

14 Military Bands

Germany

THE MODERN HISTORY OF GERMAN MILITARY MUSIC, not to mention Germany herself, begins with Frederick the Great. He was of course a great military and government leader, historian and scholar, but also a musician, perhaps the most famous amateur flute player in history. The indefatigable Burney heard him and has left a valuable, if perhaps exaggerated, account of the great man's flute playing.

> The concert began by a German flute concerto, in which his majesty executed the solo parts with great precision; his *embouchure* [articulation?] was clear and even, his finger[ing] brilliant, and his taste pure and simple. I was much pleased, and even surprised with the neatness of his execution in the *allegros*, as well as by his expression and feeling in the *adagio*; in short, his performance surpassed, in many particulars, any thing I had ever heard among *Dillettanti*, or even professors. His majesty played three long and difficult concertos successively, and all with equal perfection.

Frederick II (the Great) by Anton Graff

Regarding the instrumentation of his military bands, virtually every book in the English language which discusses military music of this period states, without source, that in 1763 Frederick the Great established a new band instrumentation of pairs of oboes, clarinets, horns, and bassoons. It appears to be untrue. There is no record of such a military order on the part of the king, no move toward such a standardization of instrumentation in Prussia, and nothing in his personal music library to suggest such a repertoire.

How then does one characterize the Prussian military bands during the period of Frederick the Great? Although there is evidence of the arrival of horns in some Saxony military units early in the eighteenth century, two important German scholars on Prussian military music agree that the horns can not be documented generally in the Prussian military bands until the final years of Frederick's reign, about 1775—a date for which Peter Panoff gives the standard instrumentation as two clarinets, two horns, a bassoon and trumpet. The essential question is the arrival date of the clarinet, which made a basic change in

Opposite page: 'Das Flötenkonzert Friedrich des Großen in Sanssouci', A flute concert for Frederick the Great by Adolph Menzel, 1852

the sound of the traditional oboe–bassoon band. Based on the manuscripts in Frederick's library, Panoff defines this period as 'the last quarter of the eighteenth century.' Ludwig Degele, on the other hand, believes that after a reorganization of the infantry bands in 1760 a typical *Hautboisten* instrumentation would have been two oboes, two clarinets, two bassoons, and trumpet. Such an instrumentation is representative of the extant music for the Prussian military bands during the period of Frederick.

The Prussian cavalry regiments apparently used only trumpets and by 1788 one can document ten trumpets and a leader for each *Kurassier* regiment and fifteen trumpets and a leader for each dragoon regiment.

Although Prussia dominates the German scene during this period, there are some interesting notes regarding military band music in some of the other principalities. In particular there is the extraordinary person of Ludwig IX, Landgraf von Hessen-Darmstadt (1719–1790), another aristocratic amateur composer, who composed more military marches than anyone who has ever lived! In his personal diary one encounters such astounding entries as,

> Today I composed 130 marches. (December 27, 1764)
>
> …
>
> Today I have finished (altogether) 70,000 military marches, not to mention Reveillen, Zapfenstreich, Fahnen-Troops, Figatter, Menuetts and Grenadier- marches. (March 3, 1784)

Ludwig IX von Hessen-Darmstadt, unknown painter, ca. 1790

The grand total of his marches, according to Panoff, was 92,176! How could anyone compose that many marches? The answer is given by an eyewitness to this activity in 1780.

> Two Kapellmeisters work from eight o'clock in the morning until four o'clock in the afternoon setting to music the marches composed by the Landgrave. He plays them with one finger on the clavier and they must notate them … He has composed as many as 300 in a day and to date has composed 52,365 works.

When Ludwig IX inherited the throne from his father, Ludwig VIII, in 1768, he established a wind band of oboes and bassoons, together with trumpets, drums and fifes. An anonymous painting, now in Darmstadt, *Landgräfliche Musikkapelle im oberen Schlosshof zu Pirmassens*, pictures an eighteen-member band of ten oboes and clarinets, four bassoons, and four trumpets. Burney heard this large band on parade during his tour of Germany.

> I never heard military music that pleased me more … The whole had an admirable effect, it was extremely animating.

Austria

The normal Austrian infantry band, as in Germany, seems to have remained a rather small ensemble during almost all of the eighteenth century. In two examples of iconography from 1790, one sees Austrian 'Turkische Musik' of four and six winds with percussion. Just as the cornetto is found in Austrian music later than almost anywhere else, a peculiarity of Austrian military music is the apparent presence of the shawm well into the eighteenth century. The clarinet seems to arrive in the Austrian military shortly after 1760.

Brixel dates the addition of the *Hautboisten* band to the Austrian artillery from 1772. An account in 1796 mentions one of these artillery bands in Vienna as being a fine band—so fine, the author says, it might be compared to the artistic court *Harmoniemusik* bands in Vienna.

> The local Artillery band consists of very skilled musicians and the director Herr Gromann plays the oboe admirably. This company plays every evening during the summer by the Limonade-hutte on the Bastion and could very well be employed in Privatakademien [concerts].

As this observation suggests the Austrian bands, in addition to their military functions, helping out in church and in many civic occasions, also performed real concerts. A striking example is reported in the *Presburger Zeitung* (December 31, 1774), describes a concert in the Stadt-theater.

> The concluding work was a new symphony by Herr Glanz, Kapellmeister of the I. R. Karol's Regiment. The symphony is composed exclusively for Turkish wind instruments, most of them obligato. There are no strings, but the piece still has all the merits of a symphony for full orchestra, obligato movements for all instruments, alternation of Forte and Piano, etc.

The cavalry continued with only the customary trumpets and timpani. The signals these instruments played had become extensive multi-sectional calls by the beginning of the Classic Period. This being the case, the Trumpet Ordinances of 1777 seem particularly concerned that new players be held accountable for the level of performance necessary to the performance of such complex signals.

France

During the first years of the reign of Louis XV military music in France seems to have deteriorated, both in quality and in the variety of instruments used. J. J. Rousseau, writing of the period ca. 1750, was dismayed with French military music as it compared to the rest of Europe.

Portrait of Louis XV

> It is remarkable that in the kingdom of France there is not a single trumpet in tune and the most bellocose nation of Europe has the most dissonant instruments. During the last wars [ca. 1756], the countrymen of Bohemia, Austria, and Bavaria, all musicians, could not believe that our regular troops used instruments that were so faulty and detestable, taken from these old corps as new recruits, and they knew not how to say how many brave men lost their lives to these awful sounds; as much as it is true that in the art of war that nothing neglects from affecting the senses.

The first attempts in improvement was the substitution of the piccolo for the ancient fife, which Rousseau opposed as he felt the piccolo made military music sound too light-hearted—it was excellent for foreign troops, but detestable in his own!

The first real modernization of French military bands occurs at the end of the reign of Louis XV with the addition to the French Guards of bands consisting of clarinets and horns, an influence not of the Prussians but of the Parisian fashion discussed above. George Kastner dates the arrival of these instruments from an official ordinance permitting them published in 1764.

Italy

Military bands with the new clarinets and horns seem to have appeared in Italy only late in the eighteenth century. According to Hosto it was only then that one found both the 'band proper,' consisting of oboes, clarinets, horns, bassoons, and trumpets, and the '*Bande Turche*,' with oboes, clarinets, trombones, serpents, and percussion in the civic militia of Rome.

In the Piedmont region the bands changed their names to '*di bande turche*' in 1791 and increased the size to fifteen members. After the fall of this area to Napoleon in 1798, the bands were organized after the French model.

Vessella adds that by the Classic Period it was common in cities, such as Bologna, Milan, Torino, Florence, and Siena, which had regular troops on salary to find the bands giving evening concerts.

England

Again, it is the arrival of the clarinet which defines the Classic Period of English military music. The clarinet as a solo instrument can be documented in London during the 1740s and 1750s, but common military references seem to occur in the 1760s as was the case in France. A very interesting example of the earliest references is found in an 'Article of Agreement,' dated 1762, for the employment of an entire band of German musicians to serve in an English artillery regiment. In England, this employment of German musicians was by no means a singular example, neither was it rare that they were all civilians.

BAND OF MUSICK, ROYAL REGIMENT OF ARTILLERY
1762

II. The regiment's musick must consist of two trumpets, two French horns, two bassoons and four hautbois or clarinetts, these instruments to be provided by the regiment, but kept in repair by the head musician.

VI. The musicians shall be obliged to wait upon the commanding officer so often as he shall desire to have musick, without any hope of gratification, but if they shall be desired to attend upon any other officer, they are to have a ducat per night, but in England half a guinea.

IX. Provided the musicians are not found to be good performers at their arrival they will be discharged, and at their own expense. This is meant to make the person who engages the musicians careful in his choice.

In spite of documents such as this, one finds evidence to suggest that even during the 1770s the clarinet was still not generally familiar. An account from 1778, for example, reads,

> Half a dozen lads of the militia were sent up to London to be taught various instruments to form a military band. The German master Baumgarten put into their hands a new instrument called a 'clarionet' which, with its firery tone, was better adapted to lead armies into the field of battle than the meek and feeble oboe.

For the troops called the Guards, Panoff documents a 'Band of Music,' in the Coldstream Guards from 1768. A very interesting account of this band in 1783 is found in the autobiography of W. T. Parke, one of London's leading oboists during the eighteenth century, who describes it as also being composed of civilians. This band apparently objected to having to leave London with the Guard, as it conflicted with their other playing opportunities, and this led to the hiring of another German band to take their place.

> The duke being at that time in Hanover, consented to the wish of his officers, and, with the approval of the king, a band of a much larger number than hitherto employed, and entirely composed of Germans, was sent over. It consisted of twenty-four members, and included clarinets, horns, oboes, bassoons, trumpets, trombones and serpents, whilst three black men were employed to beat the tambourine and carry a crescent.

This German band, led by the 'music-major,' Christopher Frederick Eley, was certainly the most influential military band of the period in England. The rest of the regular army bands were unofficial ensembles paid for by the officers themselves, which was a frequent practice at this time both on the continent and in America as well. One may imagine they were an important status symbol for the regiment. An anonymous, 'Advice to the Officers of the British Army,' gives a humorous view of these 'private' ensembles in 1782.

> If your regiment should not be provided with a band of music, you should immediately persuade the captains to raise one. This, you know, is kept at their expense, whilst you reap the principal benefit; for besides keeping them always with your own company, and treating them as your private band, they will, if properly managed, as by lending them to private parties, assemblies, etc., serve to raise you a considerable interest among the gentlemen of the country, and, what is more, among the ladies.

There is a nice story of an earlier general who had enough personal prestige as to enable him to forego the expense of these private bands. The Duke of Marlborough, during an important review, was asked by the king,

> what had become of his 'hautboys?' The general struck his hand on his breeches' pocket so as to make his money rattle, and answered: 'Here they are please Your Majesty, don't you hear them?'

If one can judge by a famous anecdote involving Haydn's visit to London, it may be that by the end of the century one would have also found these privately supported bands in the navy as well. Dies tells of the visit to Haydn by a British naval officer, who explained,

> He wanted Haydn to compose two military marches for him. Haydn excused himself, saying that the opera *Orfeo* did not allow him time for anything else, and that he only wrote when he was in good humour, and therefore couldn't tell when the *estro musicale* would visit him, early or late; but if allowed to do so, he would get a clever composer to do the marches, and would supervise the work personally.
>   'The Marches have to be by you. If I had wanted what you suggest, I wouldn't have come to you.' While the officer said that, he played with the guineas in his change purse, several times he lifted a handful and let them roll back into the purse.
>   'The sound of the gold,' remembered Haydn, 'reminded me that England could be the harvest land for me: so I asked him how much time he would allow for the estro to descend on me.'
>   'Fortnight. And the Price?'
>   'Fifty guineas.'
>   'My hand on it. I shall come on that day.'
>   Haydn finished the Marches. The officer came. Haydn sat down at the piano and played the first March in Eb with the greatest expression and emotion. The officer, still as a statue, listened. He doesn't like it, thought Haydn. He finished. The officer said, frigidly, 'ancor una volta!'

Haydn had no idea what this all meant, but he played the March a second time and doubled all his efforts thereby. He sneaked a look now and then at the officer, to see if his expression showed whether he liked it. Not a trace! Haydn thought, he doesn't even want to hear the second March. Meanwhile the officer stood up, took out a roll of fifty guineas from his pocket, gave it to the astounded Haydn, took the march, all in dead silence, and wanted to leave.

'Don't you want to hear the second March?'

'No!' answered the officer. 'Can't be better than the first. Goodbye. I sail for America tomorrow.'

An insight into the character traits desired in the directors of these bands is given in *The Military Medley* (1768) by Thomas Simes.

> [The music directors] should be men whose regularity, sobriety, good conduct and honesty can most strictly be depended upon; that are most remarkably clean and neat in their dress; that have an approved ear and taste for music, and a good method of teaching; without speaking harshly to the youths, or hurrying them on too fast.

Oddly enough, the most important body of extant English military band music survives not the bands supported by the professional officer corps, but those of the civic militia. These were local, part-time civic volunteers, which seem to have also maintained their own (part-time) bands—even in the smallest of villages. These militia bands appear throughout the Classic Period and included the participation of leading citizens.

A great number of English and Scottish towns and villages are thus memorialized by the music which was composed for their bands and published for their citizens. A typical title reads 'March, dedicated to the Colonel, Officers, and other Gentlemen of the Oxford University Volunteers.' And let us not forget that the Derbyshire militia was honored by two original marches composed by Haydn, dating from his visit to England in 1794!

There is evidence that military bands in England also performed outdoor public concerts and there is considerable extant repertoire to confirm this, not the least of which are the symphonies by Johann Christian Bach for clarinets, horns, and bassoons.

Johann Christian Bach by Thomas Gainsborough

15 Civic Wind Bands

FROM THE FIFTEENTH THROUGH THE SEVENTEENTH CENTURIES, the civic wind band was an elite institution and its members were the finest professional musicians of their era. They performed the necessary functional music, of course, but also public concerts—the first in modern history. As artistically indispensable as they were, the civic wind bands began to fade away during the eighteenth century because two new organizations appeared who filled these roles better: the rising new civic string–wind ensembles had more artistic potential and the newly formed military bands were a more attractive and less costly form of functional and entertainment music.

For only a few places in Europe can one find references to civic wind bands during the Classic Period which seem to have continued in the old tradition. More common are indications of the decline of this ancient institution, such as a contemporary reference from England which mentions that the Shrewsbury Waits now could not even read music. The general decline in the fortunes of civic wind bands on the continent can be seen in their smaller numbers of members or in the lowering of their pay.

Needless to say the quality of their performance must also have diminished. An eyewitness in Schwerin, reporting during the final decade of the eighteenth century, speaks of the popular garden concerts sponsored by various 'Friends of Music' societies which had been recently formed and then mentions that the civic wind band alone 'because of their indolence, and their too few and too poor players, could not once bring decent music to be listened to.' In Berlin one reads of the town resorting to the use of students to perform the traditional watch duty of the civic musicians. An account of 1756 reports on the failure of this experiment and perhaps reflects as well on the general decline in the discipline of the profession. The young people, it says, ran away when they should have been doing their watch duty; the apprentices fell asleep during watch, and even rebukes and beatings proved only mildly

'The Syren of the Stage,' from a mid-eighteenth century edition of two hundred pieces, published in 'The Musical Entertainer,' London

useful; and finally the city fathers decided that perhaps it was better if the young not be used as watchmen, but rather be encouraged to be music students!

But if these noble old institutions, the proud representatives of the civic government, were in full decline, a new kind of civic expectation was already taking root in the demand for entertainment by the newly prosperous middle-class. The new, and larger, civic bands of the nineteenth century would be made up of adult amateurs and would serve primarily in an entertainment role.

One can see an early example of this new popular entertainment role in the small bands which performed in the public amusement parks in London during the Classic Period. The most famous of these was called Vauxhall Gardens and there the best of enlightened society gathered. Among the entertainments to be found there were small wind bands placed at intervals to perform for the public. One who heard them in 1797 was the famous oboist, W. T. Parke.

Band performing at Vauxhall Gardens

> Vauxhall Gardens opened on the 15th of May, with a grand concert of vocal and instrumental music … The gardens had been greatly improved and beautified; and, for the first time, bands of horns and clarionets were stationed in various parts of them after the concert, to play whilst the company supped.
>
> …
>
> Vauxhall Gardens opened on the 19th of May … the gardens on this occasion were splendidly illuminated; at the end of (the concert) bands of wind instruments played in different parts of the Gardens, and a large temporary Saloon was erected for dancing.

Only an occasional account mentions such bands playing actual concerts for the public.

One can take no greater measure of the decline in the old civic wind band institutions than to compare their employment in German churches in the year 1650 with the year 1750. In 1650 virtually every German church was using the *Stadtpfeifers* on a regular basis for multi-part instrumental and choral compositions ('figural' music), as so brilliantly outlined by Praetorius, and almost every *Stadtpfeifer* contract specified his obligation to help with church music. By 1750 hardly a reference to civic wind musicians in the church service itself can be found.

When one finds wind bands and wind ensembles in the church during the Classic Period, it is usually an appearance by either an aristocratic ensemble or one supported by the church itself. In England, for example, the old 'gallery bands' still existed in place of the organ which had been banned. These were bands made up of citizen volunteers, not regularly employed civic musicians.

On the continent when regular wind players were employed by the church during the Classic Period it seems to have been only for choral support. Burney reported hearing two bassoons and a serpent participating in High Mass in Antwerp, but was not pleased by the effect.

> A considerable part of the service was chanted in *Canto Fermo*, with only a *serpent* and two bassoons in accompaniment ... The bassoon players in common use, are worse than those nocturnal performers, who, in London, walk the streets during winter, under the denomination of *Waits*; and for the *serpent*, it is not only over-blown, and detestably out of tune, but exactly resembling in tone, that of a great hungry, or rather, angry, Essex calf. Before the service in the choir began with the organ, the canons and boys marched in procession round the church, with each a lighted taper in his hand, chanting the psalms, in four parts, with the two bassoons, and serpent above-mentioned; but all was so dissonant and false, that notwithstanding the building is immense, and very favourable to sound, which it not only augments, but meliorates, and in spite of two or three sweet and powerful voices among the boys, the whole was intolerable to me.

Later, during his visit to the same town, he mentions a procession, now with two horns and serpents.

> At six o'clock this evening a splendid procession passed through the streets, in honour of some legendary saint; consisting of a prodigious number of priests, who sung psalms in *Canto Fermo*, and sometimes in counter-point, all the way to the church, with wax tapers in their hands accompanied by French horns, and *Serpents*.

There are several accounts of the occasional appearance of aristocratic wind ensembles in the church during the Classic Period. Those courts who maintained the old baroque aristocratic trumpet choirs must have continued to require them to follow the nobles into the church for important celebrations. An eyewitness describes such a performance during a Te Deum in the great cathedral in Vienna in 1767.

(The Te Deum was performed) in the most magnificent fashion and with various choirs, trumpets and timpani at 10 o'clock, and also the same at court in the small chapel at the particular order of the Emperor, who attended together with all the highest family and also the most distinguished families at the court. It was repeated by the court chaplain after 11 o'clock also with trumpet and drum flourishes. This *bruyante Musique* was at the instigation of the late Cardinal Trautsohn *edictaliter* forbidden some years ago; but the present, so joyous occasion suggested to those in high station, and the idea was approved by the court, that during the Te Deum and similar solemn occasions—otherwise not— the trumpets and timpani would be allowed to be heard again; which order was received by the people, who always like to see such demonstrations, with the greatest enthusiasm.

A similar performance by three trumpet choirs in church in 1777 is reported in the *Pressburg Zeitung*. No doubt it was for the performance of music of this nature that the 'monster' timpani found by Farmer were used. A catalog note accompanying these great instruments, of a circumference of more than ten feet in one case, speaks of their being employed in 'accompaniment to the organ of the Cathedral of Strasbourg in pieces of military music before the [French] Revolution.'

The most important of the aristocratic wind bands of the Classic Period was of course *Harmoniemusik*. Some of these wind bands also must have made occasional appearances during the church service, if one can judge by a Mass (missing the vocal parts), a Miserere, a Motetto, and a Offertorium de St. Stephan found among the extant compositions of Georg Druschetzky. In some courts such duty may have been on a more regular basis. The surviving 1762 contract for the *Harmoniemusik* of Prince Esterházy, for example, clearly includes service with the church choir as among the duties of the wind band.

One will find extensive documentation for the private wind bands of the church bishops during the fifteenth century. The bishop's palace resounded with the same sounds as the secular palace: tower-watch signals, music for entertainment, and especially for ceremonial purposes.

The monastery at Melk employed musicians for these same purposes during the Classic Period and the very title of the leader of these musicians, '*Thurnermeister*,' or 'Tower Master,' reminds us how ancient this practice was. An extant contract for the appointment of a new *Thurnermeister* in 1779, one Anton Gintscher, offers a fascinating view of both his duties and life within the eighteenth-century monastery.

> Firstly, the aforementioned Thurnermeister shall conduct a respectable and God-fearing mode of life not only for himself, but shall also appropriately maintain his apprentices and subordinates in all respectability.
>
> Secondly, as far as the cloister church services and choir are concerned, he shall take instructions with complete submissiveness and obedience from His Reverence and Grace, from Father Prior and the Regens chori, in addition, however, from the treasurer.
>
> Thirdly, he shall be bound to maintain, in addition to his own person, yet two assistants well skilled in trumpet and clarini and also experienced in other instruments, then two, or at least one good youths, and with these five or at least four persons (including himself) he shall assiduously, diligently and piously tend all church services as these always fall or are arranged in the year; he shall not be absent without the expressed permission of Father Prior, who is to be informed of such conditions, otherwise punishment is expected. Besides these church services the Thurnermeister shall also,
>
> Fourthly, permit himself to be employed with his assistants and music outside the church as His Reverence and Grace or in his absence Father Prior might desire, particularly, however, when music is to be produced at Carnival time and, according to ancient custom, at [the] bleeding [ceremony].
>
> Fifthly, he and his people shall not make themselves too familiar with the monks, much less engage in intimacy, also not set foot in the cell of a priest without important reason, but shall encounter them with all respectfulness. Likewise he is to earnestly forbid his people from loitering inside the clausura or in the kitchen, refectory and similar places outside the period of duty.

The instruments these musicians played, other than the trumpet types mentioned in the above contract, are identified in records of instrument purchases by the monastery and included strings, oboes, English horns, bassoons, and flute.

Given the reference in the contract to regular church duty, one may suppose that these musicians were particularly active on the days of special celebration. One of these, at Melk, was called the '*Marktrichtersfest*,' which was at once a New Year's observation and the Feast of the Town Mayor. The day began with a seven o'clock Mass, followed by fanfares by the monastery trumpets. The next event was a procession, which is described in the prior's diary for 1768.

'The Monastery of Melk on the Danube,' 1845, by Jakob Alt

> At 7:30 the signal is given by the mayor's secretary from the abbot's rooms, and near the prior's apartments the trumpets are blown and the drums are played. A procession is formed. With the aforementioned secretary at the head the drummers proceed to the house of the *Richter* and in front of the doors ... again the strenuous blowing of trumpets and beating of drums. For this ingenious and hastily contrived music, which sounded evanescently unusual, or rather audacious, to the ears, the mayor had to give the musicians an Imperial, that is two Imperial florins.

The procession was followed by lunch, where again the 'trumpets and drums among flutes and cymbals' performed. This part of the day's activities was cancelled the following year, as one reads in a note by the prior.

> January 1 ... No music was allowed in the refectory because the abbot forbade this three [sic] years ago. The Thurnermeister had demanded as his right ten gulden for this music which lasted about five minutes. The abbot refused this unreasonable demand and sudden greed and did away with this usually appropriate and skillful music. The custom will not easily be resumed. The whole affair can only make an intelligent person laugh.

The musicians also performed as a wind band for the noon meal in the abbey. Contemporary references mention 'musica minor with wind instruments only, performed by the four Thurner-musicians' (1760) and 'the usual music, namely two Waldhorns and trumpets' (1763). Some felt this was perhaps a bit noisy, as one reads that the Prior Boratsky complained in 1762, 'at lunch music was produced by clangorous flutes and trumpets which sounded entirely absurd and offensive rather than pleasing to the ears.' An even more interesting objection was rendered by the Prior Rusko in 1781.

> At lunch there was a little music performed solely by so-called wind instruments. The wine tankards, however, were not present, because they would be unhealthy with that unsuitable blaring of trumpets. I have considered abrogating and abolishing this (tradition) which is certainly most ill-matched to our times, a deed, however, which would offend some (of the monks) or ignite ill will among us.

For the funeral services of the high officials of the monastery one heard music by trombones, trumpets, and timpani muted with black cloth.

It appears that the Augustian monastery in Brno also maintained some sort of *Harmoniemusik* during the Classic Period, although few records of its activity or its music seem to be extant. There is an extant library inventory for 1749, which contains a thematic group for *Parthiae et Symphoniae* containing seventy-two items. During the following two decades the number of titles in this category increased to three hundred and fifty-four! In this case the *Harmoniemusik* seems to have been six players on pairs of oboes, horns, and bassoons.

Such wind music must have been part of the daily life of many of the larger monasteries in the German speaking areas of Europe. I would point, in particular, to the large extant bodies of wind music in the archives of the Kloster Einsiedeln and Stift Engelberg in Switzerland.

In general the extant music suggests that the use of wind instruments, at least in some towns, was not as rare as traditional literature would imply. In Prague the surviving church music for voices and winds by Huber, Vaněřovsky, and others, suggests that the popularity of wind bands continued throughout the century. Classic Period German composers of major works for voices and winds include Ernst Häusler, Christian Tag, and Abbé Vogler; in Austria one must mention the four Masses by Johann Michael Haydn. Also many small church libraries, such as those at Weyarn, Augustusburg, and Goldbach bei Gotha, contains many interesting examples of such literature.

But it is especially in Italy that one finds a number of church manuscripts for voices and wind instruments. These include a wide variety of individual works, such as motets, as well as music composed for the actual Mass. Foremost among the latter is the *Messa di Requiem solenne* by Jommelli.

16 Music of the French Revolution in Paris

It is tempting to suggest that the birth of the modern band instrumentation can be directly linked with the activities of the National Guard Band in Paris between 1790 and 1800. But that can not be quite accurate, for no matter how closely the modern band resembles this French model, there remained an entire nineteenth century of experimentation with new instruments, with new combinations of these and the more traditional instruments, and the development of regional preferences, before the arrival of anything which might be called the modern band.

There were, nevertheless, some entirely new concepts associated with this Parisian band which would fundamentally change all wind bands. It was first of all a large band, having at least forty-five members early in a decade when military bands elsewhere were generally about twelve members or so in size. The choice of this new large instrumentation was perhaps not an aesthetic one, but probably a functional one related to the outdoor performances before vast numbers of listeners. From our perspective today, the nature of the choice is not so important as the result: thereafter all concert bands would aspire to be large.

A second new concept of lasting importance was the full acceptance of the clarinet as the fundamental melodic vehicle; the oboe was no longer king. Closely related, but of independent significance, was the idea of doubling several times over the clarinet parts. This idea was probably nothing more than an imitation of the same doubling of the melodic vehicle occurring in the young orchestra at this time, but its influence on all later bands is nevertheless unmistakable.

Probably there were political overtones in these new concepts as well. Surely the size of this large civic band was appreciated in its contrast with the familiar aristocratic wind bands of eight to twelve members. The contrast of a band sound centered on many clarinets with the royal *Les Grands Hautbois* must have been even more evident. When one considers that the *Les Grands Hautbois* were themselves a symbol of the king, perhaps one can view the replacement of the aristocratic oboe by the numerous clarinets as a symbol of the deposition of Louis XVI and his replacement by a body of citizens.

Opposite page: Antoine Vestier's portrait of François Joseph Gossec with his scores for the 'March Lugubre' and the 'Te Deum'.

The Festival of the Federation, 14 July 1790

To say the French Revolution had many authors, would not be a mere figure of speech, for indeed the writings of the entire French Enlightenment prepared men for the roles they would play at the end of the eighteenth century. A famous quotation regarding the influence of these writers, is a contemporary comment on J. J. Rosseau: 'He had a great influence over the minds of the young and made madmen of those who would otherwise only have been fools.'

But also the model of the American Revolution was an influence, as was the general deterioration of government finances and a catastrophic harvest in 1788—causing the price of bread to double and thus making the national financial crisis understood on a personal level.

As an attempt to solve the complicated economic crisis, Louis XVI created an even more serious political crisis by calling for a meeting of an 'Estates General,' the first to have been held since 1614. Foremost among the many dramatic events which followed, the citizens (the 'Third Estate') met separately on 17 June 1789, calling themselves a 'National Assembly.' The King, now in full alarm, began to raise large numbers of troops, many of foreign extraction, to support his position.

Due to genuine concern for protection against such foreign troops, not to mention the general atmosphere of anarchy and potential for riot, the elected Parisian participants in the Estates General decided to take local government into their own hands and to form their own militia. This civic militia, called the National Guard, needed arms and in storming the Bastille in search of them—on that date memorized by every school child ever since, 14 July 1789—provided the revolution with a perfect symbol.

During the first year following this historic event, extraordinary changes were made in French society. The National Assembly had abolished feudal privileges, secularized the Church, reorganized the domestic bureaucracy, and passed a Declaration of the Rights of Man which began, 'Men are born and remain free and equal in rights.'

In fact, these changes were so extensive that many people felt the revolution was over. This notion, which was later to prove so tragically premature, together with a general feeling of patriotic solidarity, caused the National Assembly to plan a great public celebration on the first anniversary of the fall of the Bastille.

The site selected for this celebration was the Champ de Mars, a parade field in front of the old aristocratic military school. The almost unbelievable plan called for the construction of an amphitheater capable of holding four hundred thousand people!

The climax of this great festival was supposed to have been a mass taking of the oath to the new constitution, led by Lafayette. The principal musical portion planned for the program was a Te Deum, an idea which brought cries of protest in letters to newspapers, as the Te Deum had for so long been associated with the aristocracy. Nevertheless a Te Deum was retained in the ceremony and the planners of this ceremony called upon Gossec for this important task. Gossec, whom the reader has encountered above, was then fifty-six, a dependable and respected composer at the peak of his profession. During the following decade he would compose more revolutionary band music than anyone else (the other major composers included Catel, the two Jadin brothers, Méhul, and Cherubini).

The size of the musical forces for whom Gossec was to compose were unprecedented in modern music history, one account reporting a military band of three hundred wind instruments, three hundred drums, and fifty serpents and another speaking of twelve hundred musicians (which must have included the chorus). No French composer had ever composed for so many different wind parts, not to mention the numerous doublings by the hundreds of wind players reportedly present.

In view of these vast numbers of performers, Gossec wrote a work which is essentially a setting of plain chant, with the huge wind band taking the place of an organ. It is an effective work, simple yet very noble. The trombones play only in the 'Judex Crederis,' the most exciting moment in the composition, a *Larghetto-Allegro*, firey in spirit, with thundering drums. Twice the somber choral style is interrupted by quasi-baroque dance movements (with both realized and unrealized ornaments) performed by the band alone, the second with a great deal of percussion.

While this is a work which would have little meaning for an audience today, one has to admire Gossec's accomplishment. He was composing for a medium no one had ever heard and for an environment charged with emotion.

His success may be measured in part by the fact that this composition gave birth to a hundred more and helped transform the military band into a key instrument of the government's efforts at political indoctrination.

The following September another festival was held in honor of the victims of the so-called 'Nancy Affair.' Again a large band performed, one newspaper describing it as,

> twelve hundred wind instruments, accompanied, by interval, by twelve tam-tams. One will have no idea the effect this had on us, and which will probably not be heard again.

Gossec was again called upon to compose the music and for this ceremony he produced, as he could when inspired, a truly great and most unusual work, his *March lugubre*. This extraordinary composition is filled with inspiration and emotion. Contrary to all march tradition, this march is fragmented, interspersed with haunting silences, usually filled with the ominous sound of the gong an instrument never heard in France before this performance. Strange and dramatic harmonic happenings add both great mystery and power to this composition. Few of his works inspired so much comment from the listeners. A typical example is the review of the first performance.

> The sharp noise of the tam tam (instrument arabe) combined with cymbals and brass and interrupted by intervals of silence gives to the soul the most sorrowful sensations and inspires a contemplative mood.

The Development of the Musical Institutions

The impact of the military band on the public during the first great festival of 1790 must have taken the planners of this festival quite by surprise. In any case, one of the immediate developments was the politicalization of the band's music—the use of the band to communicate to the masses the political ideas of the government. Nearly all the following music had such a political origin.

Discussion within the government of this concept must have begun quite soon after this ceremony, for by 1 October 1790, the Commune of the City of Paris had established a paid music corps of the Guards, under the leadership of Bernard Sarrette.

During the first years of the new republic the subsequent ebb and flow of political and economic forces were such, that the members of the band were shocked to read in early October 1791, in a publication regarding the reorganization of the National Guards, that there was no provision for the continued support of the band.

Foreseeing that they must move immediately to establish a need for the financial support of the band beyond the irregular festivals, the band members had a memorandum presented to the town council calling for the establishment of a conservatory, a 'military music academy,' to train musicians for the military. A strong statement of support was contributed by the *Chronique de Paris*.

A miniature portrait of Bernard Sarrette by Jean-Baptiste Isabey

> The music of the National Guard deserves to be distinguished by the influence it has had over the Revolution. We would refuse to see what is obvious if we contested this influence and we wouldn't know the consequence of this powerful art if we had not believed that the sums of money for its progress were well used. If we weren't certain of the fact, we would just notice the impressive words of La Fayette who repeated several times that he owed more to the music of the National Guard than he did to its bayonets.

On 8 June 1792, the General Council prepared the order for the creation of a free music school of the Parisian National Guard. This wind instrument school of music was the very first chapter in the history of an institution we know today as the famous National Conservatory of Music in Paris. The original by-laws included the following,

I. When the pupils arrive ... they will be tested by the Major to determine the kind of instrument in which they will major ...
II. The pupils will receive two courses of solfeggio weekly, each lasting one hour; they will receive one hour each week in the course of study in their instrument and when ready will be admitted to the general rehearsals.
III. The schedule shall contain study hours.
IV. Students will take their lessons only at the time indicated, except if they are [changed] for an extraordinary service.

V. The pupils will perform with their teachers in the National and public fêtes.

VI. The pupil will be responsible for the complete uniform, instrument, and music paper.

VII. A copy class will be established in which the pupils, after their lessons, shall be held for an hour to copy the music necessary for their studies.

VIII. Students who escape from the established discipline will be suspended from school for eight days, two weeks, or a month, depending on the gravity of the offence. In the case of repeated fault, they may be dismissed according to the decision made by a committee composed of the Commandant, five teachers, and four students.

IX. There will be an annual public concert in the presence of the Municipal Corps.

X. Finally, it is essential that every pupil admitted possess the physical qualities necessary for their profession, especially for wind instruments.

By 1793 Sarrette had apparently decided that the fortunes of his band lay in an association with the national government, rather than the civic establishment. Accordingly, in a dramatic gesture, Sarrette took the entire band into the Convention Hall itself on 8 November 1793, to appeal for the establishment of a National Institute of Music. The band played and Sarrette spoke, saying in part,

> In a newly created national institute, we will not only participate in the festivities of the public holidays, but we will also perform magnificent public concerts.
>
> ...
>
> Our [former] despot did not know enough to employ French talent; he looked for artists in Germany. Under the reign of Liberty, we must find most talent among French people.

During a public concert by the band, and their students of the new National Institute of Music, Sarrette again spoke to the public, giving an interesting insight into the relationship of the band's music to the great political festivals.

> Everyone knows the effects of music and the power over the spirit ... Instruction is very necessary because not all music prompts the result we expect for the festivals and battles, and further, all the instruments must not be used indifferently. The composers discuss their works in the Institute, and they adopt or reject the different characters which can

be given to their compositions according to the expected result. In the same Institute we train the students for performance in our festivals. Others are trained who must be sent to the departments for their festivals or to the armies to entertain the warlike spirit in the garrison and in battle.

Because the public spectacles must be guided in order to excite and keep the republican spirit in the souls of the spectators, music has an important role, and education will help us to place well-trained musicians in these various public festivals …

Because the national holidays can only be held in the open air, stringed instruments cannot be used. The quality of their sound does not allow them to be heard. We must then prefer the wind instruments only, over which the atmosphere does not have the same influence; their volume of sound is eight times greater than the volume of stringed instruments.

The *Paris News* reviewed this concert and observed that Sarrette and his men gave evidence of being happier than most of their contemporaries at this time, an observation the paper apparently took to be evidence of their good work. This paper also expressed its appreciation for Gossec and for 'the young Catel, who escaped our applause because of his modesty.'

From about 1791 the so-called National Festivals in Paris began to take on a different character and purpose. In addition to being celebrations, they now became a political arm of the government, organized by a group called 'The Committee of Public Instruction' as vehicles for discriminating propaganda to the masses.

The idea for using the festivals for this purpose was directly related to government members having observed the impact of the band and choral music in the 1790 Federation festival. Seeing this reminded government officials that music had been used to some degree for this purpose in ages past; as later French Revolutionists would often point out, the Hebrews, Greeks, and Romans had all used music to inculcate religious dogma or civic duty.

French intellectuals during the eighteenth century had also prepared the way for this idea to some degree. Montesquieu, in *L'Espirit des Lois*, commented on the belief of the Greeks regarding the influence of music in the state, as did Voltaire and Rousseau. These philosophical ideas, particularly those of Rousseau emphasizing the senses, were all the more important because three-quarters of the French population (including many of the aristocrats!) were illiterate. Thus one can understand Mirabeau's comment,

> Man obeys his impressions rather than his reason. It is not enough to show him the truth; the important point is to rouse his passion for it.

Therefore after a provision for national festivals was actually written into the Constitution of 1791, by unanimous vote, in one form or another the government and various political parties would henceforth use the festivals as a means for mass communication.

The Ceremony for Voltaire

One of the most interesting of these early festivals, from the perspective of the band music, was one for the return of the remains of Voltaire to Paris in 1791 (because of his association with the Enlightenment he had been refused a Christian burial). Dating from this ceremony, the festivals often became richly theatrical in character, primarily because of the influence of Jacques-Louis David who had become involved as a planner of these events. The foremost French painter of his generation, David was attracted to the revolution as an opportunity to free art from the prejudices of the old regime and to return it to the idealized concepts of Greece and Rome. His involvement in this ceremony is clear, as its theme was 'to emulate the pomp and grandeur of the Greek apotheoses and the Roman consecrations.' Paraphernalia, costumes, and even new musical instruments, were all constructed after sketches which David, when studying in Rome, had carefully copied

Jacques-Louis David, self-portrait, 1794

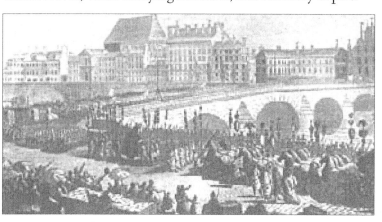

Funeral procession designed by Jacques-Louis David on the death of Voltaire

from figures on the famous Trajan column. In the autograph score of a work composed by Gossec for this festival, his *Patriotic Chorus*, these new instruments designed by David are called '*petites et grandes trompes antiques*,' but they soon became known as the '*buccin*' and '*tuba curva*.' A newspaper commented on their sound in this first appearance.

> We think we owe to those interested in the progress of the arts a note on the instruments antiques which were used under the direction of M. Sarrette, through who's zeal and intelligence the funeral of Voltaire was made so interesting. The largest are those which the ancients called cornua curva—they have the sound of six serpents. The smallest are called buccins—they have the sound of four demi-cors.

In view of the absence of sufficient surviving specimens, one can not know today what these new instruments were like. The larger of the two seems to have been a variant of the large French style hunting horn, but without the completed circle.

The Funeral of Le Peletier

An example of the political purpose behind most of these great civic festivals can be seen in one of several which were intended to help create 'Republican Saints.' The first of these honored a deputy who had voted for the death of the King and was then murdered by a former royal bodyguard. His colleagues in the Convention, believing themselves similarly threatened, decided to form their protection by arousing public opinion against any remaining royalists. To do this they made pronouncements to the public ('It is not against the life of a deputy that the blow has been dealt but against the life of the nation') and called for David to organize a great public funeral ceremony which would underline this point.

This ceremony began on 24 January 1793, at the home of Le Peletier's brother in the Place des Piques. A platform was erected upon which were placed a black foundation, studded with tears of silver, upon which was set the actual bed upon which the victim had died. Upon its bloodstained sheets was placed the body, stripped to the waist, displaying the gaping wound on the left side all clotted with blood and with the arm hanging out. By the side of the body lay the victim's clothes and the murderer's blade, besmeared with [fresh] blood. David had taken up a position nearby where the crowd could watch him paint this scene, on a canvas now lost. All this occurred to choral music and the muffled roll of drums.

At about noon the Convention and the National Guard marched to the site. The President mounted the platform and placed a crown of oak-leaves upon the dead man's brow and speeches followed. While the body was being prepared for the procession to follow, a composition by Gossec, *Hymn to the Divinity of Nations*, was sung by a thousand voices.

This was followed by a procession to the Pantheon where additional music for chorus and band was heard.

The Festival of Reunion

By the Summer of 1793 the young republic was at a low ebb. In addition to the civil problems in Paris, there were food shortages, civil revolts throughout the country, fears of a military invasion by Austria, and a general lack of confidence in the government. Thus it was that the Convention decided a demonstration of national solidarity was needed to restore unity and confidence.

David wanted the procession for this Festival of Reunion to begin at four o'clock in the morning in order that the sunrise itself would be part of the ceremony—representing The Illumination of Truth. The procession consisted of all the usual popular societies with their banners, etc., and the members of the Convention, who carried an official copy of the constitution in an ark. The one unusual aspect of the procession was a large group of people who, to emphasize the 'unity' theme, were to appear indiscriminately massed together. David's plan for this group read as follows:

> Thus shall one see the president of the provisional executive council abreast with the blacksmith; the mayor with his scarf side by side with the wood-chopper or mason; the judge, in his robes and his plumed hat, next to the dyer or shoemaker. The black African, differing only in color, shall walk beside the white European. The interesting scholars of the institution for the blind, drawn on a moving platform shall present the touching spectacle of misfortune honored. You, too, shall be there, tender nurslings of the foundling asylum, carried in white bassinettes: you shall begin to enjoy your civil rights which you have so justly recovered. And you, worthy labourers, you shall carry in triumph the useful and honorable tools of your calling. Finally, in the midst of this numerous and industrious family, one will especially notice a truly triumphal wagon formed by simple plough on which will be seated an old man and his aged wife, pulled by their own children—a touching example of filial devotion and the veneration of old age.

The procession made five official stops as it crossed the city. The first was at the site of the former Bastille, where a 'Fountain of Regeneration' had been constructed in the form of a colossal statue of 'Nature.' Around its base were the words, 'We are all Nature's Children,' and from two ample breasts spurted forth jets of water into a vast ornamental basin—an emblem of nature's fecundity. The President of the Convention took a superb agate goblet, filled it from a breast, and said,

> O Nature, Sovereign both of savage man and civilized nations! This immense people gathered together before your image at the first rays of the dawn is worthy of thee—it is free. O Nature! may the expression of the eternal attachment of Frenchmen to thy laws be acceptable to thee, and may this beneficent water which gushes from thy breasts, may this pure beverage with which our first parents quenched their thirst, consecrate in this cup of Fraternity and Equality the oaths which France will take on this, the fairest day that has ever dawned.

The first stop on the Festival of Reunion: a female statue of Nature in the form of the Egyptian goddess Isis

The second stop by the procession was at a great triumphal arch on the Boulevard Poissonniere, commemorating a march by the public on Versailles early during the revolution. Around its base were phrases such as, 'The People's justice is terrible!' and 'But its mercy is great!' On the sides were paintings of the heads of the massacred bodyguards at Versailles and under the arch, seated on guns, were heroines of the march carrying olive branches. Here the President exclaimed,

> What a glorious sight is this! Here we have the weakness of women allied to heroism! O Liberty! these are thy miracles! ... O Women!

Next the procession halted at the Place de la Revolution, where formerly a statue of Louis XV had stood. Now on the same pedestal stood a plaster figure of Liberty, surrounded by young oak trees decorated with tributes to the goddess. At the base a pile of wood was arranged upon which were ornaments of the monarchy: a model throne, crown, sceptre, escutcheons, arms, etc. The President announced,

> Here it was that the blade of law struck down the Tyrant. Let them be also destroyed, these shameful insignia of a slavery which despots have sought to perpetuate in every shape and form! Let the flames devour them!

Then taking a lighted torch he set fire to the wood pile, at which moment three thousand birds were released, each having tied around its neck a tricolor ribbon with the words, 'We are free—be like us!'

The fourth stop was at the Invalides, where there was a colossal statue representing the French people crushing Federalism. An inscription on the base read, 'Aristocracy has appeared under a hundred different forms, but the almighty people have everywhere crushed it.' Here the President heaped curses upon the 'monster of Federalism.'

Finally the procession reached the Champ de Mars, where two figures symbolic of Liberty and Equality stood, with a huge plane suspended between them (the national plane which was to bring all men to the same level). Here there were speeches, an extended ritual over the urn with the ashes of the dead heros, a fraternal banquet, singing, dancing, and a military pantomime of the siege of Lille which excited the emotions of the spectators.

Four new compositions for band by Gossec received their premieres as part of this major festival. Two of these deal with nature and were of course sung at the first stop by the procession, by the great statue of Nature: the *Hymn of Liberty* ('Touching, enchanting dawn, come relieve') and the *Hymn to Nature* ('Divinity, guardian of our lives and senses').

At the triumphal arch another new Hymn was sung, a rather short, untitled work, to the text:

> What an immense people around us hurries, do you hear the clairons? Let us go, let us go, let the festons of gladness adorn our foreheads.

Two earlier band works by Gossec were also performed, the *Hymn to the Statue of Liberty* and his setting of the 'Marseillais' tune.

Band Music during The Terror

On 30 August 1793, a deputy said, 'Let Terror be the order of the day,' and so it was. The Committee of Public Safety, now dominated by Robespierre, requested and received from the Convention the Law of Suspects. This allowed for the arrest of anyone who gave sign of opposition to the revolution and began the period with which we associate the use of the guillotine. Death sentences were handed out at the rate of about seven per day including many to recent leaders of the revolution—causing Vergniaud to say, 'The Revolution is devouring its own children.'

It was during The Terror that the anti-Church facet of the revolution came to a climax. In the provinces this concept caused a great division, for many peasants felt a stronger loyalty to the Church than to the revolutionary government in Paris. In Paris, long more indifferent to religion due to the influence of the *philosophes*, a determined effort was made in the Fall of 1793 to de-Christianize the country. This resulted in two extraordinary manifestations, the first being the declaration of a new calendar. Replacing the Christian calendar was the Revolutionary Calendar, in which the months were renamed for nature: vintage, mist, and frost for Autumn; snow, rain, and wind for Winter; budding, flowering and meadows for Spring; and harvest, warmth, and fruit for Summer!

Band Music for the Festival of the Worship of Reason

The second extraordinary manifestation of the all-out attack on the Church was the decision, in the Fall of 1793, to rename all churches 'Temples of Reason' and to hold services in honor of Reason. This actually happened for a while and is best characterized by the first of these celebrations, which was held on 10 November 1793, in Notre Dame. As part of the ceremony, the Declaration of the Rights of Man, the Constitutional Acts, and news from the armies was read and analyzed. The centerpiece, however, was the 'Goddess of Liberty,' who was,

> borne, at the sound of instruments, to the foot of the alter, and placed on the spot where the adoration of the faithful so lately sought the mystic bread transformed into a divinity. Behind her was a vast torch, emblematical of the light of philosophy, destined henceforth to be the sole flame of the interior of these temples. A mutilated statue of the Virgin was lying at his feet … Dances and hymns attracted the eyes and ears of the spectators. No profanation was wanting in the old temple.

Three band compositions all received their premiere performances at this ceremony, the *Overture in C* and *Ode Patriotique* by Catel and the *Overture* by Mèhul. Works by Gossec, but not specific titles, were also mentioned in the contemporary press.

Band Music for the Festival of the Supreme Being

The greatest of all of these French revolutionary festivals, and the highest triumph of the de-christianizing aspect of the Enlightenment, was the celebration of the Festival of the Supreme Being. The Committee of Public Instruction had begun to see that their ideal state of justice and virtue required a central moral force for the foundation of those ideas among the masses. Having discarded the Roman Catholic faith, and having mixed success with the substitution of the worship of Reason, a new alternative was clearly needed—a means of supplying both the people's longing for God and immortality and the state's desire to foster patriotism and civic order.

Robespierre announced the new philosophy in a major speech on 7 May 1793.

1. The French people recognized the existence of a Supreme Being and the immortality of the soul,
2. The kind of worship best suited to this Supreme Being consisted of doing one's duties,
3. These duties included hating bad faith, traitors, etc., doing good to one's neighbor, never being unjust, etc., and,
4. Festivals would be the vehicle to keep these ideas before the common man.

The official observance began at the National Gardens, the Tuileries. Here a kind of stadium had been built, with special seating for the Convention. The center-piece, in front of Robespierre's seat, was a colossal group of figures representing Atheism, Egotism, Nothingness, Crime, and Vice. The plan was for Robespierre, at the end of the Tuileries portion of the celebration, to light these figures made of combustible materials and as they were destroyed a statue of Wisdom would become visible.

Pierre-Antoine Demachy (1723-1807), 'Fête de l'Etre suprême au Champ de Mars (20 prairial an II – 8 juin 1794)', 1794

Robespierre arrived, carefully dressed to set himself apart from the rest of the Convention, carrying an enormous bouquet of flowers and wheatears, for his opening speech.

> Frenchmen, Republicans! at length has arrived the day forever fortunate, which the French people have consecrated to the Supreme Being! Never did the world which he has created offer to its Author a spectacle more worthy of his regard.
>
> …
>
> He did not create Kings to devour the human species; he did not create priests to harness us like vile animals to the chariot of kings, and give to the world the example of baseness, pride, perfidy, avarice, debauchery, and falsehood; but he created the universe to make known his power, he created men to aid and love each other, and to attain happiness by the path of virtue.

Robespierre, unknown painter, ca. 1790

After a lengthy speech in this style, there was a pause for music, the *Hymn to the Supreme Being* by Gossec, a work expressly written to be performed by the attending public. After the music was concluded, Robespierre descended from the stadium to set fire to the group representing Atheism. An ill-wind left the emerging statue of Wisdom blackened with smoke, to the delight of those gathered.

Band Music in Celebration of the End of the Monarchy

The overthrow of the monarchy had been scheduled to have been celebrated with a major national festival on 10 August 1794, but due to the political chaos surrounding the fall of Robespierre two weeks earlier only a hastily organized concert in the Tuileries occurred.

Two of the works performed by the band on this occasion are mentioned in a review by Duchosal, editor of the *Journal des théâtres et des fetes nationales*; first the Méhul *Chant du départ*:

> But the work which produced general enthusiasm was the Hymn of War by Chénier and Méhul. You undoubtedly recall the eulogy by Plato, in his *Livre des lois*, and Plutarch in his *Opuscules* produced at this Tyrtée verses which burned and the nervous animation of the music contributed to the success of the Spartans against the Messeniens. When one hears the Chant du départ, one thinks one hears the Athenian poet with these words: Tremble enemies of France … the rage was painted in all the faces, and the spectators all agitated.

Étienne Méhul by Antoine Gros, 1799

The same paper praised Catel for his *Battle of Fleurus*.

> This young composer who marches in the footsteps of his master [Gossec] has seized all the nuances of the poem by Lebrun. He has painted with striking truthfulness the combat, the *récit* of the combat and the song of victory, certainly he must have received from nature an uncommon and extraordinary amount of energy to render this couplet worthy of Pindare: Pareils aux flots.

Additional compositions for band which were performed during this concert were the Gossec *Hymn to the Supreme Being*, *Hymn to Equality* (formerly 'Hymn to Nature'), and *Symphony in C*; Catel's *Hymn to Victory*; and Méhul's *Overture*.

Band Music during the Final Years of the Revolution

On 7 May 1794, a decree set forth an extraordinary list of potential topics to which festivals might be dedicated:

> To the Supreme Being and to Nature; to the Human Race; to the French People, to the Benefactors of Humanity; to the Martyrs of Liberty; to Liberty and Equality; to the Republic; to the Liberty of the World; to Love of Country, to the Hatred of Tyrants and Traitors; to Truth; to Justice; to Modesty; to Glory and Immortality; to Friendship; to Frugality; to Courage, to Good Faith; to Heroism; to Disinterestedness; to Stoicism; to Love; to Conjugal Love; to Maternal Tenderness; to Filial Piety, to Infancy; to Youth; to Manhood; to Old Age; to Misfortune; to Agriculture, to Industry; to our Forefathers; to Posterity; to Happiness.

As it turned out, these festivals were held at only irregular intervals, if ever, for the day of the great festivals was over. Nevertheless, some of these festivals were responsible for a number of new and, in some cases interesting, original band compositions.

One of these was a state funeral for the twenty-nine year old General Hoche, whose death was widely considered a great loss to the nation. As head of the combined armies of the Meuse and the Rhine, General Hoche was head of the most extensive force under arms and was the only person who could have given the Directory the necessary support to oppose Napoleon.

Charles-Simon Catel by Louis-Léopold Boilly, 1817

Because of his youth, and the suddenness of his death, there was a rumor that Hoche was poisoned. This possibility was given further support by the post-mortem examination which found his stomach full of black spots. Some said the Directory itself was responsible, but others thought Napoleon was somehow responsible, for he had the most to gain. He answered,

> As there existed a party who seemed to think that all crimes belonged to me, endeavours were made to circulate a report that I had poisoned him. There was a time when no mischief could happen that was not imputed to me. Thus, when in Paris I caused Kleber to be assassinated in Egypt; I blew out Desaix's brains at Marengo; I strangled and cut the throats of persons who were confined in prisons; I seized the Pope by the hair of his head, and a hundred similar absurdities.

In any event, the Directory ordered a magnificent funeral in the Champ de Mars, which was attended by an immense crowd. This occasion produced one of the very best band compositions of this entire repertoire, the *Funeral Hymn on the Death of General Hoche* ('From the heights of the eternal vaults, the young heros receive our tears') by Cherubini.

Another interesting festival was in honor of art, but stolen art! For all the battles and wars Italy had suffered through for ages and for all the armies of many nations who had exacted their spoils of victory, never had she been conquered by so sophisticated an art lover as Napoleon Bonaparte.

Beginning in 1796, all of Italy suffered the theft of art masterpieces which were sent to Paris, not the least of which was the *Mona Lisa*! No longer would French art students need to go to Italy to study, Italy was being brought to Paris! Accordingly, on 27 July 1798, a festival was held by which the public could view the stolen art treasures.

Luigi Cherubini, unknown artist, ca. 1815–1824

> Float after float! Ten wagon-loads of manuscripts and books, thirty wagon-loads of paintings and statuary—the most civilizing possessions nations have—stolen by the armies that were to bring liberty and enlightenment, and paraded before the Paris populace ... accompanied by an honor guard of the professors of the College of France and the Polytechnic Institute, and the conservators of the Paris libraries and museums.

One new band composition was written for this extraordinary ceremony, the *Chant dithyrambique* ('Wake up lyre of Orpheus') by Lesueur.

As for the Italians, one must appreciate those people who, as they watched Bonaparte carry off their treasures, could utter that perfect pun on the name of this famous thief:

> Non tutti Francesi sono ladroni, ma buona parte!
> [Not all Frenchmen are robbers, but a good part are!]

PART V
The Nineteenth Century in Europe

17 Military Bands

NEVER DURING MODERN HISTORY has there been a century when the prestige of the military was so high as it was during the nineteenth century. Looking at nineteenth-century iconography, one would think the governments and the military were one, for even kings and emperors regularly wore military uniforms. It was the last century in which war could be a grand adventure.

This close connection between the military and society in general during the nineteenth century extends, of course, to military bands. Consequently, one can not speak of nineteenth-century court music without speaking of musicians in military uniforms, and the same can be said for church and civic affairs.

There are three rather natural periods for nineteenth-century military bands. First, there is the period from the beginning of the century through the Napoleonic Wars, when the military bands in most countries seem only to continue the fundamental *Harmoniemusik* approach of the eighteenth century. Second, beginning about 1820–1825, is a period of extraordinary developments in the construction of individual wind instruments, both old and new, and a corresponding growth in the size and instrumentation of military bands everywhere. Finally, this leads, by mid-century, to the 'Golden Age' of military bands.

Prussia

While no official policy for the instrumentation of Prussian infantry bands seems to have been made during the eighteenth century, one might suppose a typical infantry band at the end of the century consisted of pairs of oboes, clarinets, and bassoons with a trumpet. This instrumentation falls within the general categorization known as *Harmoniemusik* (usually six or eight players of pairs of oboes, clarinets, horns, and bassoons). Players being traditionally conservative, due to their many years devoted to learning one specific skill, one can understand that there was a certain sense of protection of this tradition on

Opposite page: An anonymous nineteenth-century engraving: A bassoonist holds off the enemy

the part of the established wind players. Thus the name 'Harmonie,' or 'Hoboisten,' remains associated with military bands long after there is any real resemblence to the old traditions themselves. One can see this in the titles of many nineteenth-century military band works which seem to point to a nucleus of 'Harmoniemusik' and in the Austrian custom of distinguishing (in uniform and sometimes in pay) between the 'Hoboisten' and 'Bandisten' within a single band.

Given this tradition, one can understand how the growth of military bands began first with the expansion of the *Harmoniemusik* idea. The first step, following the French taste, was the expansion in the number of clarinet players. The desire to expand the bands beyond the official limits set by the government led to private officers hiring civilian players to augment their own musicians. The earliest extant nineteenth-century Prussian government document which sets official policy for instrumentation mentions the possibility of a regiment having up to twelve of the extra hired musicians (*Hilfsmusiker*), while also setting the regular, maintained limit at twelve.

The music of the cavalry units, early in the nineteenth century, consisted of ensembles of natural trumpets, who played signals and perhaps simple repertoire works.

In 1820 Georg Abraham Schneider (1770–1839) was appointed to the supervisory position of Inspector of Army Bands (*Herresmusikinspizienten*) in Berlin. Schneider was not an innovator to the extent of his successor, Wieprecht, but he was a distinguished musician and great credit is due him for helping to establish an artistic climate in which contemporary and later men such as Weller, Neithardt, Piefke, Saro, Schick, and others, would produce Prussian military bands with artistic concert standards which were rarely surpassed by any symphony orchestra of the nineteenth century.

Based on the extant scores of Neithardt, Weller, and Schick, one might suggest a typical infantry band for the 1830s, that is just before the period of Wieprecht, including valved instruments for the first time:

Georg Abraham Schneider

    large and small flutes
    clarinets in F and Eb
    clarinets in C, Bb, and A
    Bassethorns
    oboes

bassoons
contrabassoon
English-basshorn
serpent
4 chromatic horns
4 chromatic trumpets
chromatic altohorn
tenor and bass trombones
Harmoniebass
large and small drum
triangle
cymbals

'Wieprecht is the *l'etat c'est moi* of Prussian military music,' said Hans von Bülow, one of the most important music critics of the nineteenth century. This association with Louis XIV is not altogether inappropriate, for it is difficult to think of any military musician who was more influential. Wilhelm Wieprecht came from a very musical family, his grandfather, father, and four uncles all being professional musicians. His father, it was said, could play in the third octave of the Eb clarinet so softly that one could not distinguish it from a flute. Wieprecht was born in 1802 and a rigorous musical education administered by his father soon began. He studied trombone and arrived at such a degree of proficiency that by age twenty he could rival the most famous trombonist in Leipzig.

After service as a civic musician in his hometown he held court positions as a trombonist in Dresden, Leipzig, and finally in Berlin. It was in Berlin when the turning point in Wieprecht's life occurred. This metamorphosis began with his chance hearing of a Prussian military band performing the Overture to *Figaro* by Mozart. Wieprecht remembered this moment:

Wilhelm Wieprecht

> When I heard in Berlin for the first time an infantry band in its full instrumentation, I was seized by an emotion I have never been able to explain to myself. Was it the rhythm, the melody, the harmony, or other elements which affected me so deeply? As I then followed this band on their march to the watch parade, and there heard them play the Overture to Mozart's *Figaro* in a closed circle, there came into my heart the firm decision that I would dedicate myself from now on to military music.

The reader may find confusing this confession that a professional orchestral musician, with experience in the royal operas of Dresden and Leipzig, could be so taken by the performance (outdoors) of a military band. But the reader must remember we speak of a time when most orchestras were opera orchestras; the great repertoire orchestras we know today had not yet emerged. The better military bands sometimes were more disciplined (due to the military) and performed at a higher technical level than these small opera orchestras.

As a person from outside the military establishment, Wieprecht seems to have understood that his most opportune entrée into military music was through the one kind of band most musicians at that time were less interested in—the trumpet corps of the cavalry. Perhaps he also intuitively understood that it was the brass instruments, not the old court oriented *Harmoniemusik* (which lay at the heart of the larger infantry bands), which were more perfectly suited, psychologically, to express the exuberance and pride felt everywhere by the citizens now in the process of rebuilding Prussia.

Through an acquaintance with a Major von Barner, of the Guard Dragoon Regiment, Wieprecht began his career by composing for this regiment six marches, which were very highly regarded. The great harmonic limitations imposed by the instrumentation (natural trumpets in G, F, and C, and trombones) led him to persuade the Major to buy instruments with valves, which at this time were not used in Berlin cavalry units. The band in question had thirteen regular members, for whom Wieprecht chose the following instruments:

1 high Bb valve trumpet
2 keyed trumpets
1 alto trumpet in Eb with valves
2 tenorhorns in Bb
1 tenor-bass horn in Bb
4 trumpets in Eb with valves
2 bass trombones

The band was allowed an additional seven 'hired' players. Wieprecht writes, 'for these I used four more trumpets, one high Bb trumpet, one alto trumpet, and another bass trombone. Now I had a full "Blech-instrumental-harmonie" with which I could modulate in all directions.'

The success of this new instrumentation gained immediate attention in military circles and before long (in 1838) he became the director of all the military music of the Berlin Guard. Soon after this appointment the king desired a great *Festmusik* for the occasion of the visit of Kaiser Nicholaus of Russia and asked Wieprecht how many bands he trusted to participate in this. 'Every band quartered in Berlin,' answered Wieprecht and thus occurred the first of the 'Monster Concerts' which would make Wieprecht one of Berlin's best known persons. The concert was held in an open square before the Berliner Schlosss by a combined band consisting of sixteen infantry bands and sixteen cavalry bands totaling more than a thousand musicians and two hundred percussionists. Wieprecht conducted the following program:

> Overture to *Rienzi* by Wagner, played by the full ensemble.
> 'Chorus' and 'March' from *Conradin* by Hiller, performed by the bands of the foot troops.
> 'Halleluja' from the *Messiah* by Handel, performed by the infantry bands.
> *March* by Möllendorf, performed by the cavalry bands.
> 'Coronation March' from *The Prophet* by Meyerbeer, performed by the full ensemble.
> *The Dessauer, Hohenfriedberger,* and *Coburger* marches, performed by the full ensemble.

In 1843 Wieprecht conducted another Monster Concert in Lüneburg, where he became acutely aware of the need for a standardized instrumentation, for in order to hold rehearsals he had to write out seventeen different versions of the infantry parts and nine different versions of the cavalry parts! For this performance he was awarded the Golden Service Medal by the King of Hannover, but as he was not an officer he had to receive the official permission of the Prussian aristocracy to wear it.

At home, Wieprecht was no doubt beginning to achieve at least some administrative control, if not yet a standardized instrumentation, as we can see in a report by Berlioz during this same year.

> As for the military bands, one would have designedly to avoid them not to hear at least some, since at all hours of the day, either on foot or on horseback, they are passing through the streets of Berlin. These little isolated bands do not, however, give any idea of the majesty of the

grand whole which the head bandmaster of the military bands at Berlin and Potsdam [Wieprecht] can collect whenever he chooses. Imagine, he has a body of upwards of six hundred musicians under his command, all good readers, all well up in the mechanism of their instruments, playing in tune, and favoured by nature with indefatigable lungs and lips of leather. Hence the extreme facility with which the trumpets, horns, and cornets give those high notes unattainable by our artists [in France]. They are regiments of musicians, rather than musicians of regiments. The Crown Prince of Prussia, anticipating my desire to hear his musical troops and study them at my leisure, kindly invited me to a matinee organised at his palace espressly for me, and gave Wieprecht orders accordingly … His Royal Highness had had the courtesy to order the concert to open with the *Franc-Juges* overture, which I had never heard arranged thus for wind instruments. There were 320 players, directed by Wieprecht, and difficult as the music was they performed it with marvellous exactness, and that furious fire with which you of the Conservatoire perform it on your great days of enthusiasm and ardour.

The solo for the brass in the introduction was especially startling, performed by fifteen bass trombones, eighteen or twenty tenor and alto trombones, twelve bass tubas, and a host of trumpets

… The middle and high tones of the tuba are very noble, not at all dull like those of the ophicleide, but vibrant, and very sympathetic to the tones of the trombones and trumpets, of which it forms the true double-bass, and with which it blends perfectly …

The clarinets seemed to me equal to the brass: they performed great feats in a grand battle symphony for two wind orchestras by the English ambassador, the Earl of Westmoreland. Afterwards came a brilliant and chivalric piece for brass only, written by Meyerbeer for the Court festivals under the title of *Torchlight Dance*, in which there is a long trill on the D, kept up through sixteen bars by eighteen cylinder trumpets, doing it as rapidly as the clarinets could have done. The concert ended with a very fine and wellwritten funeral march, composed by Wieprecht, and played with only one rehearsal!

In 1845, Wieprecht turned to the press in his attempt to generate support for the standardization of Prussian military bands. In one of these articles, published on 28 June, in a Berlin newspaper, Wieprecht proposed an extraordinary new concept for military band instrumentation. It called for a band of twenty-one different parts, with players doubling according to the dictates of his desired texture. The instruments were grouped into three registers, which were further balanced, resulting in what Wieprecht called an 'acoustic pyramid.' Given are the numbers of players for each part in both the Guard Infantry and regular Line Infantry bands.

	Guard Inf.	Line-Inf.
PIERCING REGISTER, TO BE PLAYED LIGHTLY		
flutes, large and small	2	1
clarinets in Ab or G	2	2
clarinets in Eb or D	2	2
clarinets in Bb or A	8	6
oboes in Eb or D	2	2
bassoons	2	2
baryphons	2	2
MIDDLE REGISTER, TO BE PLAYED STRONGER		
cornets in Bb or A	2	1
cornets in Eb or D	2	1
tenorhorns in Bb or A	2	1
bass horns (Baryton) in Bb or A	1	1
bass horns in F or Eb	2	1
LOW REGISTER, TO BE PLAYED VERY STRONG		
trumpets in Eb or D	4	4
trombones in Bb or A	2	2
bass trombones in F or Eb	2	2
bass tuba in F or Eb	2	2
triangle	1	1
cymbals	1	1
small drum	2	1
bass drum	1	1
Schellenbaum	1	1
Conductor	1	1

Thus, while a large concert band, such as the one given above, would have been unthinkable only twenty years before, large concert bands were no longer uncommon in Prussia by mid-century. Indeed, according to Georges Kastner, although a band of twenty-four men was in 1848 *de rigueur*, one in fact ordinarily found a band of fifty or sixty musicians. In addition each regiment now also had a soldier's chorus of sixty voices for performing national hymns with the band.

In 1860 the War Ministry created thirty-four new infantry and ten new cavalry regiments and gave to Wieprecht the responsibility for creating their bands. These he managed to recruit and supply with instruments in only three months.

This offered him the opportunity to publish yet another reorganization of Prussian bands. This was an ingenious system by which, through the addition of instruments, one could arrive at the instrumentation of the cavalry, Jager, artillery, or infantry bands. His idea was that if publishers would make compositions available which were scored in accordance with this plan (including the resultant unconventional score order), then the same piece of music could be purchased and used by any of the three basic types of bands.

Wieprecht's Unified Instrumentation System of 1860

	Cavalry	Artillery	Jager	Infantry
Cornettino	1	3	1	
Soprano cornet	4	6	4	2
Alto cornet	2	3	2	2
Tenorhorn	2	6	2	4
Baritone-tuba	1	3	2	1
Bass tuba	3	6	3	4
Trumpet	8	12	3	4
Horn			4	4
Flute				2
Oboe				2
Clarinet in Ab				1
Clarinet in Eb				2
Clarinet in Bb				8
Bassoon				2
Contrabassoon				2
Trombone				4
Cymbals				1
Small drum				2
Large drum				1
Halbmondtrager				1
Total	21	39	21	47

Aside from his contributions to the reorganization of Prussian military music, we must not forget his tremendous contribution as a composer and arranger of enormous numbers of complete symphonies and overtures for large infantry band. Among his original compositions is his extraordinary *Tone Poem* for three separate bands composed for a celebration of the 50th anniversary of the Battle of Leipzig.

The various contributions of Wieprecht were in large part responsible for the great popularity of Prussian bands through the end of the century. By World War I, no fewer than 541 separate bands were authorized for the various branches of the Prussian military (including naval bands) and on a summer evening in Berlin one could hear any of twenty to thirty different military band concerts!

The remaining principal states of what is today the modern Germany varied both in quality and in the degree to which they followed the lead of the Prussians. Berlioz, during his tour of Germany in 1842–1843, commented on some military bands which were lacking, such as in Dresden.

> The military band is very good—even the drummers are musicians; but the reeds did not strike me as irreproachable. Their intonation left much to be desired, and the bandmasters of these regiments would do well to order their clarinets from our incomparable Sax. Ophicleides there are none; the deep parts are sustained by Russian bassoons [the 'bass horn'], serpents, and tubas.

Some he admired, such as in Darmstadt.

> At Darmstadt there is a military band of about thirty musicians, for which I envied the Grand Duke. They play in good tune, with style, and with such a feeling for rhythm that even the drum parts are interesting.

Wieprecht found nothing to admire among Bavarian military bands during his travels there in 1845. He especially pointed out the lack of suitable instruments in the lower range, the tuba, in particular, being completely unknown there. 'This demonstrates,' says Wieprecht, 'how little care is given to military music in Bavaria.'

Austria

During the first half of the nineteenth century one finds in Austria a typical infantry band composed of a small nucleus of professional musicians, called the '*Hautboisten*,' after the baroque tradition; then perhaps thirty-five musicians called '*Bandisten*,' who were regular soldiers, and trained as musicians within the regiment; and finally civilians, hired as needed or as they could be afforded. An order of 1835 seems to worry that a band might develop beyond military function and become musical.

> The choice of instrumentation is left to the regiment, but the commander should observe that there is no unnecessary luxury or constant changes, so that the military music is sonorous but not require any musical virtuosity that goes beyond this purpose.

The outstanding musicality of the Austrian bands, to which many contemporaries testify, begins to appear as a characteristic after 1840 and may have been due in part to the fact that Austria turned to established civilian musicians for its military band leaders. By drawing on band leaders who were trained in the conservatories, rather than 'in the field,' Austria was able to profit from a particularly distinguished group of conductors, including Joseph Fahrbach, Philipp Fahrbach Snr, Philipp Fahrbach Jnr, Josef Gungl, Michael Zimmerman, Karl Komzák, Julius Fučik, Alphons Czibulka, and Joseph Franz Wagner.

By the 1840s one also begins to find the instrumental characteristics which one associates with nineteenth-century Austrian music, in particular the prominence of the brass instruments, the Eb trumpets, and the appearance of the Flügelhorns and euphoniums. Eugen Brixel gives a typical infantry band for 1845 as,

Josef Gungl, 1874

1 small flute
1 large flute
2 oboes
1 clarinet in Ab
2 clarinets in Eb
3 clarinets in Bb
2 bassoons
1 contrabassoon
1 trumpet in high Bb
8 trumpets in Eb
2 natural trumpets
2 bass trumpets in Bb
2 Flügelhorns in Bb
1 bassflügelhorn
1 'Obligatflügelhorn'
1 euphonium
3 trombones
4 horns (Eb, Ab)
3 bombardons
1 or 2 small drums
2 pair of cymbals

Philipp Fahrbach Jr

A large Austrian military band still included a sizable number of extra players, hired by the officers of the regiment. Kastner wrote of this period that, although they were only authorized thirty-five or forty musicians, Austrian infantry bands sometimes had as many as seventy or eighty players! Of

Julius Fucik

the musical characteristics of these Austrian military musicians during the 1840s, Kastner provides some very interesting contemporary observations.

> The musicians of Austria are very capable, and especially it is in the execution of marches where they have proved a rare energy and great precision which electrifies the troops. One should not fail to point out the admirable dexterity of the tambours. They play with taste and intelligence; that is to say they have style. The tambour part is written only as a general guide and the players improvise, pointing up the accents of the melody, etc. The snares of the Austrians are very small and have a very determined sound.
>
> …
>
> The Austrian musicians are blessed with a very good memory; they play by heart their marches and pas redoubles, and one is assured that there are regiments where the musicians have memorized nearly their entire repertoire, that is to say something like 50 or 60 works.

The great administrative figure in nineteenth-century Austrian military music was Andreas Leonhardt, who was appointed to a newly created post of '*Armeekapellmeister*,' thus giving Austria for the first time the centralized direction comparable to that found in Prussia and France. Leonhardt was a man of vision who immediately fought for larger bands and for the increased social status of the conductor, by giving him regular army rank and pay (in this he was not successful, however). His official duties included the supervision of instrument purchase ('the best and cheapest'), music, and he was supposed to have been consulted by regiments who hired civilian conductors. A typical advertisement of 1854 for such a civilian conductor reads,

> Conductor's Position to be had
>
> The Tuscany 8th Dragoon Regiment, stationed at Oedenburg, seeks someone qualified in every respect. The pay is 60 fl. per month, plus quarters and uniform. For the acquisition of instruments and other musical necessities, and for the recruitment of individual, knowledgable musicians, money will be put at his disposal in sufficient amounts.
> At first he will be hired on a provisional basis, but if in a reasonable period of time he proves himself capable he will be hired permanently and be given a bonus of 100 Gulden.

In a reorganization and standardization of all the army music in 1851, Leonhardt was able to achieve a basic infantry band personnel of forty-eight men, with another twelve who could serve as apprentices during peace time. In practice, individual regiments could still add 'extra' players at the officers' expense. Brixel gives the following instrumentation (expressed in numbers of parts, not numbers of players) as typical for this period.

1 piccolo in Db
1 flute in Db
1 clarinet in Ab
1 clarinet in Eb
3 clarinets in Bb
2 bassoons
4 horns
1 cornet in Eb
2 soprano Flügelhorns in Bb
1 alto Flügelhorn in Eb
1 bass Flügelhorn in Bb
1 euphonium
1 'Obligattrompete' in Eb
4 trumpets in Eb
1 bass trumpet in Bb
3 trombones
2 "Basse"
small and large drum
cymbals

Shortly after the 1848 civil disorders, the modern march appears in the heart of the Austrian–Hungarian Empire. By the end of the century this new march had become so popular that one finds its essential characteristics in not only marches composed in the Empire, but in Germany, America, and even Russia and China.

The *style* of this new march had its most immediate roots in the '*verbunkos*' (from the German root *Werbung*, 'to recruit'), a form of dance used to recruit troops in the Hungarian part of the Empire until the Austrian administration imposed conscription after 1849. The music of this dance had, of course, much older roots in Hungarian, Slav, and Balkan popular music. By the beginning of the nineteenth century, the *verbunkos* was a dance with varying tempi requiring good coordination. The recruiters would arrive in a village, assemble the young men of military age, and begin the music of the *verbunkos*. The young man who danced best was designated the leader of the young men recruited from that village, under the assumption that the demonstrated co-ordination represented more general potential. Had not Socrates said, 'The best dancer is the best warrior'?

The musical characteristics which carried over from the *verbunkos* to the modern march style are the very distinguishing characteristics of the march as we know it. The melodies were cast in widely arched, binary, nearly symetrical phrases, with complementary cadences. More important, I think, was the *character* of the melodies: a character more vocal than instrumental and, in fact, referred to at the time as 'song without words' (*hallgató-nóta*). There was an introduction and, at the end, a traditional cadence which represented the 'clicking of heels' (*bokázó*, or as we say today, 'stinger' or 'bump-note'). None of these musical characteristics are found in wind band marches of the eighteenth century. The adoption of these musical characteristics into the musical language of nineteenth-century Austria is a direct expression of that people's dawning interest in the Hungarian culture, something which had been subservient and repressed for years.

The actual *form* of the new march was not so different from the eighteenth-century march. Both consisted of a March in two sections, each repeated, and a Trio in two sections, each again repreated. The eighteenth-century march, however, always included a da capo. It is the absence of this da capo which makes the late nineteenth- and early twentieth-century march so peculiar at first glance—a form which ends in a different key than that in which it began!

It is in a deeper, psychological sense that one has to look for meaning in this unprecedented formal design. The *verbunkos* found a source of variety in contrasting tempi, something impossible in a functional march. Instead, the new march sought variety in the contrast of melodic styles between the more militant and exciting March and the more lyric and contemplative Trio. While there would be the traditional sense of satisfaction felt in the return to previous material through the da capo, this sense of satisfaction would be far out-weighed by the psychological jolt of the abrupt return to the strong militant style after one had reposed in the peace of the Trio.

Sousa once expressed his rationale for this form very nicely in an analogy with dining. When asked why he wrote marches which lacked a da capo, he answered, or so the anecdote goes, 'When you have finished the ice cream, who wants to go back for roast beef?'

France

There was little development of military bands in France during the period of Napoleon, for he permitted larger military bands only in those cases where it cost his government nothing, that is, where the bands were supported privately by the officers. In fact he eliminated cavalry music entirely for a time when he discovered the cavalry music required enough horses and supplies for four regiments of soldiers!

His own taste for military music was much more basic; for him the essential military music was only the trumpet signals necessary for troop movement. Therefore the *one* musical institution which Napoleon enthusiastically supported was the Trumpet School at Versailles. Here as many as six hundred trumpeters were schooled between 1805–1811, under the leadership of the German composer, David Buhl.

Among the more interesting innovations of Buhl were the first signals in more than two-parts, in this case four to six parts. Several specimens of these are still extant in the Bibliothèque nationale de France in Paris, scored for four trumpets, two horns, and trombone. The inspiration for these more musically complicated signals was not art, but rather a military necessity: the need for a means of transmitting more sophisticated instructions for troop movement. Another Frenchman working on this problem was a man named Sudre, who published a paper in which he claimed the potential for holding real conversations in the field through what he described as 'musical symbols.' He demonstrated his new system before enthusiastic generals on the Champ de Mars. Telegraph, which had appeared at the end of the eighteenth century, soon eliminated all need for music as a means of field communication and Sudre and his system were forgotten. The name he coined for his system of musical communication, however, remains in the language of all peoples to this day—*la téléphonie*!

It was during this period of small bands that Anton Reicha composed his 'Commemoration Symphony' for *three* military bands, each band consisting of piccolo, pairs of oboes, clarinets in C, horns, trumpets, bassoons, string bass or contrabassoon, with percussion and cannons.

Further growth during the Napoleonic period was impossible due to the losses which occurred during his campaigns. It seems almost impossible to imagine, but it is said that more than two thousand French military musicians perished during the murderous offensive in Russia alone!

One institution which tended to preserve the old traditions, no matter how inferior they might have been, was the *Gymnase de Musique Militaire*.

Founded in 1836, under the leadership of musicians such Berr, Klosé, and Carafa, the school was open to talented members of all French regiments for the training of both players and conductors until it was closed in 1870.

This institution was devoted to preserving the old military instrumentation, based on the traditional *Harmoniemusik* instruments. In this regard it was closely allied with the Parisian instrument makers, who were geared up to produce only these traditional instruments.

Thus the *Gymnase de Musique Militaire* and its Director, Michele Carafa, represented all that was comfortable and traditional about French military music and was a formidable establishment against whom a young foreigner named Adolphe Sax had to battle to win his revolution in French military music.

Sax was a talented young instrument maker in Brussels when he came to the attention of the French Général de Rumigny, an aide-de-camp to Louis Philippe. It was probably Général de Rumigny who was largely responsible for sponsoring Sax's move to Paris in 1842, for almost immediately Sax began a correspondence with the Minister of War relative to the poor condition of the instruments of French military music, the social status of the players, etc. Sax, however, was in immediate conflict with the traditional school, led by Carafa, who at once attempted to undermine his ideas and his new business in Paris. Sax was subjected to vicious press campaigns, his best workers were tempted away by higher salaries, a mysterious fire destroyed part of his factory, and he was even attacked physically. Berlioz described all this in his *Memoirs*.

Michele Carafa by Antoine Maurin

And yet, will it be believed that this ingenious young artist has all the trouble in the world in making his way and maintaining himself in Paris? Persecutions worthy of the Middle Ages are inflicted on him, corresponding perfectly to those Benvenuto Cellini had to endure from his enemies. His workmen are enticed away, his designs are stolen, he is accused of madness, and driven to litigation. A trifle more, and they would assassinate him.

It was in this rather inflamed atmosphere that the Minister of War appointed a commission in 1845 to study the conditions of French military music. Their discussions led to a concentration on the question of size and instrumentation and the isolation of three fundamental questions:

1. How many players are strictly necessary for infantry and cavalry bands?
2. Which instruments, either old or new, should be adopted for these bands?
3. How many of each instruments (doubling) are necessary for a desirable sound?

The commission also invited makers to demonstrate new instruments and for interested persons to submit suggested instrumentation ideas. Rather than attempt to resolve the question on an abstract basis, they decided to conduct a live field test. This offered not only the opportunity to test the instrumentation plans in an outdoor environment, as would be typical for a military band, but would offer a wide segment of the interested public the opportunity to make first-hand judgments. The date for this event was set for 22 April 1845, and the place selected was the spacious military parade ground known as the Champ de Mars (where today the famous Eiffel Tower stands).

The commission decided to test primarily the instrumentation plans submitted by Carafa and Sax, as best representing both the older traditional ideas and the entirely new. To this end, both Sax and Carafa were asked to recruit a band and both bands would perform music prepared for the occassion by commission member Adam, in addition to music of their choice.

It had been agreed beforehand that each of these bands was to be limited to forty-five players, in order to fairly compare the difference in the instrumentation. Carafa had one important advantage for his players (the professors and best students from the *Gymnase de Musique Militaire*) were playing on traditional instruments, whereas the players of Sax were playing, in some cases, entirely new instruments they had only seen for the first time the day before!

Carafa, who believed his entire reputation to be at stake, was determined to stop at nothing to win. Accordingly, he not only arrived with four additional players beyond the agreed limit, but had his agents kidnap seven key members of Sax's band. The commission refused to allow Carafa his extra players, so he gave up two bugles and two flutes, performing with the following instrumentation:

1 piccolo
1 small clarinet
16 clarinets (divided 2, 7, 7)
4 oboes
4 bassoons
2 natural horns
2 valve horns
2 valved trombones
2 cornets
3 trumpets
4 ophicleides
4 percussion

Sax, trying without success to locate his missing players, arrived late for the contest, carrying two instruments which he himself alternately played in an attempt to cover the missing parts. The thirty-eight players which he had at his disposal for the contest included,

1 piccolo
1 Eb clarinet
6 Bb clarinets
1 bass clarinet
2 cornets
2 Eb soprano saxhorns
4 Bb soprano saxhorns
4 Eb alto saxhorns
4 Bb bass saxhorns
2 Eb contrabass saxhorns
2 trombones
2 ophicleides
4 percussion

Adolphe Sax

Anyone with experience in the performance of bands outdoors will not need to be told who 'won' the contest. Carafa, even with his greater number of players, had a band which was 60% woodwinds, some of which (oboes and bassoons) were of virtually no use in the open air. Sax's band, on the other hand, was only 24% woodwinds and furthermore was much stronger in the lower register. As a result we may be sure that Sax's band sounded darker, more homogeneous, and with a bigger sound. It was no contest.

Carafa began, performing an 'Antante' composed for the occasion by Adolphe Adam.

> This piece, perfectly played by the principal students of our ancient school of military music and by several professors of the same establishment, was heard with lively attention. The audience applauded, but without enthusiasm.

Then Sax's band, conducted by A. Fessy, music director of the 5th Regiment of the Parisian National Guard, performed the same composition.

> Almost immediately followed the music of Sax, playing the same Andante. This good military music was bold, open, sonorous, noble, sustained, less varied in timbre, without a doubt, but more homogeneous, equal throughout, and infinitely more adaptable to soldiers on the march or on the field of battle ... The piece played by Sax was followed with cries of enthusiasm and applause.

The commission decided in favor of Sax, but political factors prevented any practical application of his ideas until 1854 when a government ordinance set the official instrumentation for the infantry and cavalry (brass) bands. Here we see the first official appearance of the new saxophones.

Infantry
2 flutes or piccolos
4 Eb clarinets
8 clarinets in Bb
2 soprano saxophones
2 alto saxophones
2 tenor saxophones
2 baritone saxophones
2 cornets
4 trumpets
4 trombones

2 soprano saxhorns in Eb
2 soprano saxhorns in Bb
2 alto saxotrombas
2 baritone saxhorns in Bb
4 bass saxhorns in Bb
2 contrabass saxhorns in Eb
2 contrabass saxhorns in Bb
5 percussion

Cavalry
1 sopranino saxhorn in Bb
2 soprano saxhorns in Eb
4 soprano saxhorns in Bb
2 alto saxhorns in Ab
2 alto saxotrombas in Eb
2 baritone saxotrombas in Bb
4 bass saxhorns in Bb
2 contrabass saxhorns in Eb
2 contrabass saxhorns in Bb
2 cornets
6 trumpets
6 trombones (AATTBB)

This essentially was the instrumentation which had so wide an influence on all continental military bands during the second half of the nineteenth century. The saxhorn family contributed one permanent member of today's bands, the baritone or euphonium. The use of the new saxophone family was not immediately adopted in every French regiment, but they too are part of today's band.

England

During the earliest years of the nineteenth century, military music in England seems to have been completely supported by the private officers and not from the government.

During the period of 1820–1845, Prussia, Austria, and France experienced a vigorous period of experimentation with new instruments, resulting in a series of official orders dealing with military band instrumentation. England's story is somewhat different, primarily because she lacked during this period a strong personality, like Wieprecht in Prussia, Leonhardt in Austria, or Sax in France, to influence the thinking of the military as a whole. Lacking a centralized policy, the instrumentation of the regimental bands was left to the individual bandmasters during this period. Moreover, the bandmasters were frequently civilians who owed their appointments to well-placed influence by one or other of the various instrument makers. The newly appointed bandmaster would immediately replace all the instruments with those made by his industrial partner. Thus the guiding force was commercial and not an aesthetic one as in Prussia.

Another commercial influence on the developing English military band instrumentation was the proliferation of band 'journals', beginning just before 1850. Here the influence was indirect, in so far as this was not the immediate purpose of the publisher. However, bands quickly adjusted their instrumentation as necessary to perform the works of the journal to which they subscribed. Therefore, the more popular journals tended to indirectly contribute to the standardization of band instrumentation.

The first of these journals was printed at his own expense by Carl Boosé, bandmaster of the Scots Guards, in 1845. Boosé was another 'imported' German bandmaster, who was born, studied, and served as a professional and military musician in the Darmstadt area before coming to England. The instrumentation he set forth in his journal was, of course, based on the Prussian–German model and was largely influential in pointing England in that direction, rather than after Austrian or French models. In his journal for 1856 one finds an interesting note that he also offers a group of works available in manuscript, including the complete Mendelssohn *Third Symphony*, the *Fifth* and *Sixth* of Beethoven, the *G minor* Mozart and overtures of Wagner and Mendelssohn.

After mid-century there was a growing concern over the quality and organization of English military bands, and especially the tradition of civilian bandmasters. Farmer summarizes this critical period:

> The Crimean War opened the eyes of the authorities to the evils of the civilian bandmaster system. When the war broke out, our bands, deserted by their bandmasters [civilians who wanted nothing to do with battle], were soon disorganized. The French, on the other hand, maintained their bands at a high state of efficiency throughout the campaign. The final humiliation came at Scutari in 1854 when, at the grand review of honour of the birthday of Queen Victoria, with some 16,000

men marching past in perfect order, our bands later struck up 'God Save the Queen,' not only from different arrangements, but in *different keys*, and this before the general staff of the allied army.

It was such concerns which led to the founding of the famous Kneller Hall military school in 1857. In terms of instrumentation, however, the English military bands continued to resist the brass orientation of the Austrian bands. The Royal Artillery Band in 1857 consisted of:

2 flutes and piccolo
4 oboes
4 Eb clarinets
22 Bb clarinets
2 Eb saxophones
2 Bb saxophones
4 bassoons
4 cornets
2 trumpets
2 soprano Eb cornets
2 Flügelhorns in Eb, 2 in Bb
4 horns
2 baritones
2 euphoniums
4 trombones
4 bombardons
percussion

Kneller Hall

Russia

It was the employment of foreign, especially Prussian, bandmasters which brought rapid modernization to Russian military music. The most famous of these persons was Anton Dorffeld, who became Director of the entire Kaiser's Guard Corps.

One of the great figures of the nineteenth century, Rimsky-Korsakov, was associated with the music of the Russian military. He was appointed Inspector of Navy Bands in 1873, a post he was to hold for more than ten years. In this position he suddenly acquired rather absolute authority over the instruments, music, and the education of the players and conductors under his supervision.

Nikolai Rimsky-Korsakov by Valentin Serov, 1898

> In the bands of musicians I was met as superiors are met: stand up front! I made them play their repertory in my presence; caught the wrong notes; detected the slips (and there were very many of them) in the instrumental parts; examined the instruments and made requisitions for new or additional ones … occasionally I grew rather peppery and humiliated some bandmasters undeservedly or ridiculed pieces which I did not like, though the performance of these was necessary and unavoidable in military bands.

The transcriptions which Rimsky-Korsakov himself made for these bands are one portion, perhaps only a very small portion, of what may be a vast repertoire of interesting music unknown in the West today.

Italy

In Italy, political strife retarded the opportunities for the military bands to follow the exciting developments in new instruments which had taken place in Prussia, France, and Austria. The degree to which some of these states were still behind continental developments can be seen in Florence, where a commission on military music was formed in 1848. Presided over by Teodulo Mabellini, the commission set the instrumentation for a regimental band at only eight regular players (piccolo, clarino, two trumpets, ophicleide, trombone, horn, and bass drum), with the possibility of additional 'extra' hired players.

In 1865 another commission on military band instrumentation was appointed, this time chaired by Mercadantes. This commission recommended a standard infantry band instrumentation of,

small and large flutes
oboe
clarinet in Ab
2 clarinets in Eb
solo clarinet in Bb
6 clarinets in Bb
2 bass clarinets in Bb
2 cornets
2 Flügelhorns
5 trumpets
3 horns
3 tenorhorns
3 trombones
3 bombardons
contrabassoon
4 'Basses'
percussion

For the cavalry band, the commission recommended thirty players:

2 trumpets
3 cornets
3 Flügelhorns
5 trumpets in Eb
4 horns
3 tenorhorns
3 trombones
3 bombardons
4 'Basses'

Missing in this instrumentation (which had a distinctly Austrian flavor) were the new instruments of Sax. One who campaigned for the adoption of these instruments was the famous Rossini. When he was made a member of the 'Grand Knight of the Order of the Crown of Italy,' by Victor Emanuel II, Rossini composed, in return, his *La Corona d'Italia* for military band. When the score was sent from Paris, Rossini included the following note:

> Instrumenting this little piece of music, to be performed, be it well understood, on foot, I took advantage not only of the old instruments of Italian bands, but also of the excellent new ones we owe to Sax, their celebrated inventor and maker. I cannot imagine that the leaders of Italian bands have not adopted these instruments (as was done everywhere). If by any chance this *only advance of our days* was not embraced by them (a thing that would pain me), I beg Your Excellency to be willing to entrust my score to a good composer of military music so that he may adapt it to the standard instruments.

Another attempt at reforming the instrumentation of Italian military bands occurred in 1884 when a commission was appointed to meet in the Palazzo del Comando, of the Second Army Corps, in Milan. This commission met from February through August, 1884, and published comments on repertoire and instrument design, as well as their recommendations on instrumentation.

Their instrumentation plan was based on a concept by which all instruments would serve primarily one of three basic functions: melody, accompaniment, or bass (*Cantabili, accompagnameti e bassi*). To cite some examples, within the 'melody' category the cornet was assigned the soprano and mezzo-soprano roles, with the first Eb trumpet serving as the contralto (the remaining three Eb trumpets were 'accompaniment' instruments for the middle range.) Similarly, the first trombone was the 'melody' instrument of the tenor range, with the three remaining trombones filling 'accompaniment' roles. Two flicorni and two bombardini, representing SATB, were also considered as 'melody' instruments.

Military Bands in Public Concerts

I believe general studies of nineteenth-century European music have failed to give credit to military bands for their contribution to aesthetic music. One can understand why the late nineteenth- and twentieth-century authors closed their ears to the medium, for by the end of the nineteenth century military bands had often elected to perform only an entertainment function for society and in that role performed literature of so little aesthetic value that the wind band is to this very day struggling to free itself of the stigma. But to be perfectly fair and honest about nineteenth-century music, one would have to admit that there was an 'entertainment' facet in even the most highly regarded of society's aesthetic jewels. Let us not forget that the Vienna premiere of Beethoven's *Seventh Symphony* shared a program with a mechanical trumpeter! Neither was the keyboard exempt, as one can see in an organ recital given in September 1807, in Frankfurt, by the highly esteemed teacher of Carl Maria von Weber and Meyerbeer, Abt Vogler.

Part I
1. Chorale: How Brightly Shines the Morning Star
2. Song of the Hottentots, which consists of three measures and two words: Magema, Magema, Huh, Huh, Huh!
3. Flute Concerto: Allegro, Polonaise, Gigue

Part II
1. The Siege of Jericho
   a) Israel's Prayer to Jehovah
   b) Sound of Trumpets
   c) Crash of the Walls
   d) Entrance of the Victors
2. Terrace Chant of the Africans, when they seal their flat roofs with lime, during which one chorus alternately sings and the other one stamps
3. The Pleasure Ride on the Rhine, Interrupted by a Thunder-storm
4. Handel's Hallelujah, treated as a fugue with two subjects and counterpointed with a third subject

I only wish to make the point that with wind bands, even as it was so with symphony orchestras and keyboard artists, such concerts were not the *whole* story during the nineteenth century. There *were* bands and band conductors who had aesthetic goals which were quite as serious as those of any other artist.

One factor which helped create the success military bands had with the public was their technical excellence. In the years before the impact of the conservatories was widely felt, and before the modern, well-disciplined symphony orchestras appeared, the military band may often have exceeded the local orchestra in many technical performance qualities. The reason for this, of course, was because the military bands enjoyed a residual military discipline as the foundation for their music making. The aesthetic significance of this was recognized by the famous nineteenth-century critic, Eduard Hanslick.

> In this form, the regimental band emerges out of its purely military role and reaches higher artistic purposes. These are the so-called 'Garden concerts' by which the military bands offer the court a favorite

recreation and often give small cities a full artistic musical experience. The many and strenuous rehearsals for this concert [a concert of the music of Berlioz, given in Prague] allow us to see the value of military subordination for artistic reasons; no conductor of any civic orchestra would have been able to manage this performance at that time. It may go against some idealistic theories that art could be encouraged through something so very different from personal freedom as subordination, however it is so. Every art has in its technique one facet which can only be developed through constant work, and this technical side is even more important in the work of many together than by the individual virtuoso. The conductor's baton and the corporal's stick both have the purpose of bringing many heads together under one hat ... where the artistic subordination joins with the military subordination, 'a good sound results.' In the Garden concerts or other non-military performances the military bands are in a better position than other mediums to pursue purely artistic goals. The position of the conductor appears here more independent, the selection of the repertoire more free, and the means more complete. In any case, from these favorable conditions springs a stronger obligation to art.

Eduard Hanslick, 1894

From the 1830s until the end of the century, one finds an increasing number of references to public concerts and an ever larger number of extant serious, original works for military band. These military bands, as bands still do, continued throughout the century to perform transcriptions of major orchestral works. These performances seem rarely to have been debated with regard to the principle of transcriptions, but rather seem to have been accepted on the same level as orchestral performances. The key to the latter was found in the high quality of performance, especially by the Prussian bands, as one can see in an 1858 review of a concert conducted by Piefke, by the very distinguished musician and critic, Hans von Bülow.

> We had the satisfaction on numerous occasions to attend the accomplished performance of his band and we were always surprised by the technical perfection, the painstaking nuance of every detail, the majestic power of the mass impression and finally the fresh full vibrating spirit of the noble performances.
>
> The A Major Symphony by Beethoven, Wagner's Overture to Tannhauser, the transcription of the first Finale, Pilgrim's Chorus, Prayer, and Romance from Act III of Lohengrin which we heard were satisfying, as one would not have thought in this sphere and brought to the conducting and the entire band the highest honor. The choice of the Seventh Symphony of Beethoven appeared to us genuinely successful; this apotheose permitted a unity of character with that which had been

played earlier, for example the transcription of Beethoven's C Minor Symphony by Wieprecht—a work by which he had obtained his great reputation. The Scherzo and Trio, as well as the last movement, were in this transcription of such an overpowering and compelling effect that it was possible for one at the moment to completely forget the original instrumentation.

The opportunity to have their works given such fine performances before vast audiences attracted the attention of many major composers. Berlioz, for example, speaks of his arrival in Mainz.

On my arrival in Mainz, I hastened to make inquiries as to the Austrian military band which had been there the year before, and ... had performed several of my overtures with great verve and power, and immense effect.

Wagner, too, enjoyed hearing fine bands perform his music, as we can see in a letter of appreciation he wrote to the conductor of an Austrian band he heard in Venice in 1858.

Honorable Conductor,
    I could not find you in the Piazza yesterday to thank you for the wonderful performance of the *Rienzi Overture*, so today I do this in this written form. I appreciated it very much that your musicians had noticed everything, had marked everything so well and brought everything out correctly.

Many extraordinary reviews are extant which document both the quality of the Austrian bands and their impact on the public, even in foreign countries. For example, an account in the Austrian army newspaper, *Der Soldatenfreund*, quotes contemporary reviews from Germany in 1864.

[*Hamburger Nachrichten*]
The Austrian military band opened the planned cycle of six concerts in the Great Hall of the Sagebiel'schen Kolosseum the evening before last. The rush of the public was so stormy that already during the first piece the places were full and those arriving late had to turn and leave the filled hall ... Fifty well-rehearsed members were received very thankfully. The public especially recognized with applause the piece by the conductor, Herr C. Siede, *Konigsberg-Siegesmarsch*, which opened the concert. In the following opera pieces there was great precision and ensemble and in the solo pieces one recognized the masterful handling of the brass instruments, so characteristic of the Austrians.

[*Bremer Zeitung*]
The Austrian military band of IR [Imperial Regiment] 72 in their two concerts in the Schützenhof and in the Union went beyond the greatest expectations. The perfection of the instruments and the precision with which the presentation took place allows us to praise the musicians as well as their hard-working and intelligent bandmaster, Scharoch, without reservation. Like a cloud-burst everything comes out, even the most difficult passages, and the repertoire is to be remembered by its variety and richness.

An audience which was as select as it was receptive gave stormy applause and desired numerous repetitions.

If one can judge by the extant repertoire of the French military bands during the second half of the nineteenth century, they too must have had very active concert schedules. The extant *published* repertoire alone includes many hundreds of *original* symphonies, overtures, fantaisies, solo and ensemble works with band accompaniment, not to mention thousands of orchestral transcriptions. One of the most interesting forms in France was the *Air varié*. This is typically a set of variations with each section of the band having its own variation to 'show off.' Many of these are of extraordinary difficulty, indeed one can not examine these without coming away astounded at the technical level of these nineteenth-century French bands.

In England something seems to have gone wrong, aesthetically. There were serious compositions and performances by wind bands in England through the Baroque, but during the Classic period one finds a strange absence of the original *Harmoniemusik* which was so prominent on the continent. What went wrong in England? Certainly there can be no doubt with regard to the band's popularity with the public. Military bands were as popular in England as elsewhere during the nineteenth century and important for this reason, for they reached a broad public, an entire working-class of people, who did not feel welcome in the fashionable concert halls. But, the appearance of some fine orchestral transcriptions in the band 'journals' notwithstanding, the broader evidence seems to suggest that in England the bandmasters did not take advantage of the great popularity of their medium to seek to raise the musical understanding of the public, but rather sought to expand the band's popularity by reaching down to select their repertoire at the level of popular taste. The aesthetic aim of most military bands during the second half of the nineteenth century in England is perhaps best defined by an expression one used to hear regarding 'concerts' given in Crystal Palace by the best of the London military bands. According to Farmer, one would commonly hear,

> There is no concert to-day, but the band is going to play!

At no time during the nineteenth century did military bands so capture the attention of the general public as they did on 21 July 1867 when ten bands, representing nine countries, met in Paris for the purpose of artistic competition. This event, organized by Georges Kastner, was held during a great international exhibition and offered a first prize of a gold medal and 5,000 Fr. The jury consisted of twenty men recommended by the participating countries and one of them, the distinguished critic Hanslick, left his impressions of this afternoon. In particular, he captures for us the enthusiasm of the public, an enthusiasm that almost reads as the description of a great 'popular' concert today!

> It was a tiring piece of work to listen attentively to twenty military band performances in a hall filled with at least 23,000 people, from 1:00 P.M. until 7:00 P.M. My favorite overture, *Oberon*, was made so repelling [through so many performances] at this event that I had to avoid it for several years. But the hard work [of listening] was [repaid] by the shining success of our Austrians. I have never experienced so strongly in myself the feelings of patriotism, which at home so often are asleep or turn critically to the opposite, as at that instant immediately after the astounding performance by the Prussians when our white coats [the traditional dress of the Austrian military] stood themselves in a half-circle. The Prussians had a harvest of applause which could not be exceeded, but after the Austrians played, the hall howled as if in a hurricane; everyone screamed and waved hats and scarves. There was still one serious virtuoso rival, that of the Paris Band, which possessed very good virtuosos and the new Sax instruments; they played with the precision of a clock. It was not easy to decide among these three, so we decided to give three first prizes in equal value to the Austrians, the Prussians, and the French.

As Hanslick indicated, the jury elected to award three first prizes, but it should be noted that the Prussians clearly were the real winners, having received twenty votes in the original balloting, to eighteen for the French and seventeen for the Austrians. The second prize was shared by Bavaria, Russia, and the French Imperial Guards. The third prize was shared by the Dutch, Baden, and Russia and the fourth prize went to Belgium and Spain. Wieprecht, conductor of the Prussian band, heard in the Austrians a great musicianship; in the French, virtuosity; and attributed his own victory to the Prussian's 'superior musical education, understanding, and technique.'

A final measure of the enthusiasm of the public can be seen in a 'farewell' concert given by the visiting Austrian band in the famous Tuileries Gardens. It was estimated that 200,000 Parisians (one in five of the inhabitants at this time!) tried to attend this concert.

Military Bands and Opera

The numerous and successful military band concerts created a wide interest on the part of the public. This was a fact not lost on the the super-showman, Rossini, who introduced a military band on stage during a performance of *Ricciardo e Zoraide* in 1818. This, in the view of one present day opera scholar was 'clearly a dark day ... for Italian opera,' because the appearance of military bands on stage rapidly became a popular demand.

Gradually the use of the military band in opera began to evolve from mere stage business to a more involved musical role, as one finds in Meyerbeer's *Il Crociato in Eqitto* where a band on the stage alternates with the theater orchestra and in one case two bands on stage play antiphonally. Later, in *Le Prophete* (1849), Meyerbeer scored for a full cavalry band in alternation with the pit orchestra. In this case one sees all of the new Sax instruments which had only recently been adopted by the military.

> 2 petite saxhorns in Eb
> 2 first contra-alto saxhorns in Bb
> 2 second contra-alto saxhorns in Bb
> First and second cornets with cylinders in Bb
> First and second trumpets with cylinders in Bb
> 2 first alto saxhorns in Eb
> 2 second alto saxhorns in Eb
> First and second baritone saxhorns in Bb
> 4 bass saxhorns with cylinders in Bb
> 2 contrabass saxhorns in Eb
> 2 'Tambours militaires'

A similar, musically independent, cavalry band is found in the pages of *Rienzi* by Wagner, here scored for six valve and six natural trumpets, six trombones, four ophicleides, and eight drums. How important was this kind of stage business to Wagner? In a letter of 1842 to a court official, Wagner writes,

> I am not ready to forfeit a single detail of the musical pomp on the stage; it is absolutely necessary and can easily be managed with the help of the military and other musical bands—certainly my requirements are not the usual ones—I demand an extraordinary band, not put together like the ordinary band ... See to it that the trumpeters and trombonists accompanying the warlike cortege of Colonna and Orsini in the first act are chosen from the cavalry and appear on horses ... in operas like mine, it must be all or nothing.

In Paris and elsewhere the popularity of the increasingly larger and larger wind bands on stage by mid-century threatened to drown out the music of the opera itself. By 1863 one finds in Berlioz's *Les Troyens* no less than two bands and a wind ensemble, although all were behind the scenes. Verdi, faced with this kind of esculation of instrumental forces in Parisian productions, suggested that the rather innocent off-stage *Harmoniemusik* of the original might be doubled, tripled, or quadrupled as needed, rather than 'modernizing' the band.

> You must adhere strictly to the instruments composing the small orchestra beneath the stage. This little orchestra of two oboes, six clarinets, two bassoons and a contrabassoon produces a sonority that is strange and mysterious, and at the same time calm and quiet, such as other instruments cannot do.

One can see how out of control this all became in a remarkable passage written by Rimsky-Korsakov. He had been asked by the sister to Glinka to reorchestrate that composer's opera, *Russlan and Ludmila*, as the original score had been lost in a theater fire.

> For my part, I was carried away by enthusiasm and did many impractical things, in orchestrating for a military band the respective parts of *Russlan*. Thus in the Introduction to Act I, the band on stage was to be brass, in Glinka's scheme; I followed his idea accordingly, but took a brass band with the full complement current in our Guards regiments. For Act IV, again in accordance with the composer's intentions, I wrote the orchestration for a mixed band of brass and woodwind, both again with the full complement current in the Guards. Thus a performance

of *Russlan* called for two complete hetergeneous regimental bands. Glinka himself hardly wanted this! But that is not all. In Act V, I had the imprudence to unite the two bands in full complement—the brass band and the mixed band. The result of this was sonority so deafening that no theatre orchestra could hold its own against it; and this was manifested once, when Balakireff gave the whole *Russlan* finale at a concert. The theme and all the figures for the strings were completely drowned out by the military bands which performed their parts in my orchestration.

'Popularizing' Orchestral Music

The great bond between military bands and the public, which the above material typifies, did not go unnoticed by composers and publishers, especially in Germany. Several important composers sought out opportunities to have their works arranged for military bands in the hope that the subsequent performances would help to build an audience for the original versions of their music! Thus Liszt, Meyerbeer, and Spontini all asked Wieprecht to transcribe their music for this purpose. Wagner's music was, of course, popular with military bands and, remarkable as it may seem, part of *Lohengrin* was performed by a military band in Berlin before the premiere of the opera itself by Liszt and the Weimar Court Opera in 1850! Wagner, himself, makes it quite clear in a letter to Count Redern in Berlin, that he supported such transcriptions.

One nineteenth-century transcription of 'Brunnhilde's Awakening,' from *Siegfried* is of particular interest. It was done by Anton Seidl, one of Wagner's closest protégées and later a famous conductor, together with Gottfried Sonntag, a senior government auditor in Bayreuth. The extant published score (Hannover, Oertel) is a newly orchestrated one by Oskar Junger, but carries a very interesting note relative to the original arrangement.

> This work was arranged for military band during the 1770's by Anton Seidl and Gottfried Sonntag for the band of the 7. Bavaria Infantry Regiment in Bayreuth with the *approval* and *under Richard Wagner's Supervision*.

The civic band of Cioia, Italy

18 Civic Wind Bands

Germany

These pages have traced in some detail the tradition of European civic wind bands during the Middle Ages, Renaissance, Baroque, and Classic Periods. Toward the end of the eighteenth century these institutions, and the ancient guilds which supported them, fade from notice somewhat. This was due primarily for economic reasons, but the rising popularity of civic orchestras played a role as did the presence of military bands quartered in or near many towns, who offered an alternate, less expensive, source of wind music for many of the functions formerly filled by the city musicians.

The period of 1785–1815 saw the development of a new civic institution, the civic milita, sometimes called 'Schützenkompagnien' in Germany and 'Volunteers' in England. These units of civilian-soldiers reflected a political and social scene which was very much dominated by the military and the natural desire of the public to be involved. These militia bands should be thought of as civic bands, and not as authentic military bands, although some of the characteristics of the military they imitated would remain characteristics of German civic bands to the present day (such as the style of the uniforms). The instrumentation of these new civic militia bands was based on the French version of *Harmoniemusik*, an ensemble in which the clarinet was the principal melodic instrument.

The by-laws of some of these early German militia bands contain principles which seem very familiar to the organization of large ensembles today. Consider, for example, the statutes of the band in the German village of Oppenauer in 1824.

[1] Each member is required to give the bandmaster his most respectful attention.
[2] Everyone must take care of his own instrument. If a [city] instrument is damaged during official service, it will be repaired and paid for from the military or church funds. If it is damaged when not in official use, the player must pay for the repairs.
[3] Everyone is responsible for his music; if the music is lost, the player must pay 2 kr per page for copying.
[4] Everyone must attend rehearsals as required.

[5] All conversation is forbidden during the time music is being played.
[6] The bandmaster will determine the repertoire.
[7] Playing without direction ("Nebenblasen") is forbidden unless permission is given.
[8] If one appears and his keys are not working, and this also applies to horn and other [brass] players, he will be fined 12 kr.
[9] Talking about the society is forbidden.
[10] No one is allowed to take offense at the directions of the director.

It was these bands which began the great tradition of civic bands which still exists throughout the German-speaking countries today and they were valued by the town not only for their concerts, but also for their services in civic celebrations, in the church, and as a means of offering music education to the young people. A civic document from Zell am Harmersbach saw in addition an economic value for the town.

> [This band], when it is in a state of perfection—which is possible only through frequent rehearsals, very often draws, on the high festival days, many visitors to the community, which has economic importance for every citizen.

One of the largest portions of the extant repertoire of the civic bands in the German-speaking countries from the first half of the nineteenth century, and certainly the most musically valuable portion of that literature, is the music composed for performance together with civic, amateur choral societies. These singing societies had their origin in small societies called *Liedertafeln* which, toward the end of the eighteenth century, met once a week in a local *Gasthaus* for beer and singing. In the years following the Napoleonic Wars, these societies spread rapidly and often became very nationalistic. These compositions were written for normal concert appearances as well as for celebrations of a nationalistic, artistic, or civic nature, together with more specialized events revolving around Freemasonry, hunting, student life, and gymnastics. This great body of choral repertoire includes numerous works with band accompaniment, a repertoire all the more valuable as it includes contributions by some of the greatest nineteenth-century masters, including Brahms, Schumann, and Mendelssohn.

The civic militia bands could not avoid becoming involved in the civil strife of 1848 and this resulted in their being banned, together with the civil militia itself, after that date.

However, a new law of 1851, the Land Club and Assembly Law, allowed the establishment of civic bands, provided they were organized only as civic clubs. Now the by-laws seem more democratic in nature. The 1878 statutes of the civic band in Neuenburg, for example, allowed the members themselves to decide, by ballot, on the acceptance of performances. They limited membership to persons of irreproachable character over the age of fourteen. The prospective member submitted an application which the members accepted or rejected by secret ballot. Members were fined 10 pfenning for missing rehearsals without an excuse. A heavier fine of 3 Marks was assessed to those who failed to live up to the standards of deportment, which called for behaving tactfully and the avoidance of drinking, dissension, and fist-fighting!

Another paragraph is very interesting. Since the new civic bands were now more democratic and were free of the functional obligations which were the foundation of the ancient civic bands, it was now possible for a band to consider its primary purpose as being performance as an art. This was clearly an important objective for this band in Neuenburg, as one can read in the definition of their purpose.

> The purpose of this club is to awaken the sense of that which is lovely and noble in the people through the performance of selected musical compositions and to entertain and bring pleasure to said people.

The use of the word 'entertain' (*unterhalten*) here was in the sense of 'delight.' The civic militia bands in Vienna, however, not only continued into the second half of the nineteenth century, but were truly entertainment bands in the modern sense, participating in the famous waltzes and marches which one still identifies with that city.

The most valuable information on the spread of the popularity of civic wind bands during the second half of the nineteenth century is found in a world survey of civic band organizations, conducted just after the beginning of the twentieth century by the Orphéon Society in Paris. Unfortunately, this survey only reflects the reports which were returned from correspondents and is quite incomplete for Germany as a whole. The correspondent from the area of Alsace-Lorraine (then part of the German-speaking region), for example, gave the names of nearly forty wind band societies. Most were thirty members or so in size, but several were larger than fifty and one, the *Harmonie de Schiltigheim*, was a band of seventy. The participation in music in general can be seen in a reference to Mannheim, which with a population of only 160,000 had fifty-three adult musical societies (choral, orchestral, and band).

The correspondent from Switzerland cited an astounding total of eight hundred civic wind band (*Harmonie*) and civic brass band (*Fanfare*) societies! The same correspondent also gave very interesting details regarding the national civic band contests sponsored by the *Société fédérale*. The regulations for this contest included the following:

[1] Each band was to tune to A=435
[2] Each band performed a work of their choice, another selected by the National Federation, and had to sight-read a third.
[3] Bands were entered in categories according to the numbers of band members who were professional musicians.
[4] The adjudicators were three bandmasters, either foreign or Swiss, who were not participating in the competition.
[5] The performances were judged on the basis of "harmony, rhythm, dynamics, artistic conception, and total effect."

This same survey gives an insight into the extraordinary brass band popularity during the second half of the nineteenth century. For Germany, a correspondent from Württemberg counted no fewer than one thousand five hundred and sixty civic brass bands! No less surprising is the size of some of these bands, the one in Strasbourg given as ninety players!

France

The great impetus of civic band music begun in Paris in 1790, which resulted in great civic festival compositions for band and chorus, as well as serious and important overtures and symphonies for concert use, unfortunately came to an abrupt end with the arrival of Napoleon just before the nineteenth century. There continued, however, occasional civic fetes in the spirit of those of the revolutionary days and two of those resulted in band compositions which are quite extraordinary.

The first of these was a ceremony to accompany the removal of the remains of Louis XVI and Marie Antoinette to a more appropriate location. It is one of the interesting ironies of history that the French would celebrate this king, whose head they had so recently removed. Nevertheless, the ceremony occurred on 21 January 1815, and the central musical work was a great *Requiem*, in fifteen movements, for chorus and band by Charles Nicholas Bochsa.

The second of these extraordinary band works was commissioned for a similar fete, this one involving the removal of the remains of the heroes of the Revolution of 1830 to a newly constructed monument in the Place de la Bastille. The government minister in charge, M. de Rémusat, commissioned a Symphony for band by Berlioz as the centerpiece of this celebration.

The only insights Berlioz left us regarding the actual composition of this Symphony are his rather patriotic sounding ideas on the relationship of his music with the ceremony itself and a very interesting discussion of his struggle to compose the beginning of the third movement.

Charles Nicolas Bochsa

> When I had finished the march and the funeral oration, and found a theme for the apotheosis, I was delayed for some time by the fanfare, which I wished to bring up by degrees from the very depths of the [wind] orchestra to the high note where the apotheosis breaks in. I don't know how many I wrote but I liked none of them. Either they were too common, or too narrow in form, or not sufficiently solemn, or wanting in sonority, or badly graded. What I imagined was a sound like the trumpets of archangels, simple and noble, ascending radiant and triumphant and grandly resonant, as it announced to earth and heaven the opening of the Empyrean gates. Finally I decided, not without some trepidation, on the one now in the score; and the rest was soon written.

For the day of the ceremony (28 July 1840), Berlioz was able to secure the services of several military bands, numbering, he says, two hundred players. Apparently the first movement, or perhaps some form of it, was played as a procession moved through the streets of Paris. The entire Symphony was undoubtedly performed before the public at the monument, although Berlioz assures us that due to the general noise and confusion, 'not a note of it could be heard.'

One person who did hear it, however, was Richard Wagner. He confirms that the performance occurred at the monument, that it was by combined military bands, and reveals that Berlioz himself conducted.

Hector Berlioz by André Gill, nineteenth century

> It was, however, the latest work of this wonderful master [Wagner had been speaking of the *Symphonie fantastique* and the *Harold in Italy*], his 'Trauersymphonie fur die Opfer der Julirevolution,' most skillfully composed for massed military bands [kombinierte Militärmusik] during the summer of 1840 for the anniversary of the obsequies of the July heros, and conducted by him under the column of the Place de la Bastille, which had at last thoroughly convinced me of the greatness and enterprise of this incomparable artist.

Berlioz, of course, was too experienced a musician to leave this extraordinary Symphony to the fate of being judged by the musicians and critics of Paris in an outdoor premiere. Accordingly, he planned long before to have an indoor first hearing. At least two such concerts did, in fact, occur in August 1840, as we know from a letter Berlioz wrote to Queen Maria-Amelia. According to Berlioz, the public reception of the Symphony at these concerts was quite enthusiastic.

> At each performance of my new work the public seemed to appreciate it beyond any of its predecessors, and indeed praised it extravagantly. One evening, at the Salle Vivienne, after the final movement some young fellows [were so excited that they] took it in their head to smash the chairs against the floor, with shouts of applause.

During the years before mid-century the reorganization of civic bands begins. The Armentières civic band, for example, had thirty-five members in 1806 and was already participating in band contests by 1807. Some civic bands, such as those in Douai and Maubeuge also began their own music schools to prepare young people for future membership.

After the political turmoil of 1848 there was a tremendous growth in the development of civic bands in France. This development was helped by the creation of band societies in imitation of the successful civic choral organizations, called *Orphéon*, who had become nationally organized in 1833. In the following decade a division of *Orphéon* for bands was formed. In addition to providing a model for the organization of a band society, the national *Orphéon* society evidently sponsored composition contests for original band literature and published many band compositions. A contemporary description of the social status of these *Orphéon* band societies was given by the famous critic, Eduard Hanslick.

> Every city and village in France has their 'Musique d'harmonie,' or at least a 'Fanfare' [brass band]. In general, they recruit from the same social levels as the Orphéons [the choral societies], from craftsmen, businessmen, lower government officials, etc ... The government sponsors competitions, organized in higher and lower levels of ability.
>
> As to the artistic meaning of these groups, like the Orphéons, they stand in the second rank with the social clubs. Only the best of the French Harmonie Societies [bands of woodwinds and brass] achieve that which is musically perfect or even special, but even the least of them can take pride in drawing some souls away from drink and card playing. For the working man, even a crude encounter with art has something which frees and ennobles.

At the time of his writing, Hanslick indicates there were two thousand such civic band societies in France. The *Orphéon* survey at the end of the century lists a staggering total of seventeen hundred and eleven '*Harmonie*' societies (Paris alone having sixty-eight!), of which sixty-two are classed '*Division d'Excellence*' (one of five categories). A number of the individual bands had more than one hundred members. The *Musique municipale de Reims*, for example, by the end of the century used 5 flutes, 3 oboes, 47 clarinets of various sizes, 10 saxophones, 2 bassoons, and 61 brass. Some of these bands rehearsed several times per week and some gave as many as four concerts per week during the entire year.

The availability of chromatic brass instruments, especially those of the saxhorn family, made possible a tremendous development of brass bands in France after mid-century. The *Orphéon* survey lists more than four thousand brass band societies and noted that no community in France was so small as not to have at least a fanfare ensemble. Again, some of the brass bands are of extraordinary size, with more than one hundred players.

In addition to the development of these large bands, one must not fail to acknowledge France's contributions to smaller wind ensembles during the nineteenth century. In this regard it is, of course, the *Quintets*, op. 88, 91, 99, and 100 of Anton Reicha which first come to mind. Later during the century another extraordinary chapter in French chamber wind music begins with the creation of the *Société de Musique de Chambre pour Instruments à Vent*, founded by Paul Taffanel (1844–1908). This series of concerts, begun in 1879, had for fourteen years a tremendous influence throughout Europe. This Society was responsible for commissioning a number of substantial new works for wind ensemble, among them, the Gounod *Petite Symphonie* (1885), the Lazzari *Octuor* (1889), the *Octuor* and *Suite Gauloise* by Gouvy, the two *Suites* by Dubois, and the *Sextuor* by Boisdeffre. The great value of this activity was to keep alive the potential of the wind ensemble as absolute music, during a time when the military bands had elected to serve primarily as an entertainment medium.

Italy

James Herbert, one of the few scholars who has done research in Italian civic archives with respect to the development of civic bands before mid-century, summarizes this period as follows:

Conductor and composer Paul Taffanel

> During the first half of the nineteenth century, the town bands of Italy, similar to the one conducted by Giuseppe Verdi in Bussetto, consisted of whatever instruments and players that were available at a given time. Ranging in size from just a few players to a larger band of fifty or more, the instrumentation not only varied greatly from town to town, but from year to year, as players joined.

The period of real growth and expansion in Italian civic bands occurred after the period of the unification of Italy, known as the '*risorgimento*' (1860–1870). This period also saw an increase in the composition of original works for band, particularly those of a patriotic nature.

During the second half of the nineteenth century many civic bands had come into existence. According to one contemporary, by 1888 there were some six thousand civic bands in Italy! Some of the larger of these are cited in the *Orphéon* survey, including the *Musique municipale de Milan*, which, according to a correspondent, had a repertoire of some two thousand works; the *Musica civia de Novare*; and the *Musique municipale de Turin*, the repertoire of whom also included contemporary works.

The *Banda Municipale di Roma* had been formed as the *La Banda di Roma* after the *Banda della Guardia Nazionale* was disbanded. Under the conductor, Giuseppe Mililotti, the band was then divided into two sections, each with fewer than forty players, who performed separate services and together for important occasions.

The *Banda musicale di Bologna* performed 'various symphonies' for Pope Pius IX; in Naples there were three separate bands organized under the '*Banda Comunale,*' and similarly two bands in Rome.

Alessandro Vessella (1860–1929), together with Raffaele Caravaglios (1860-1941), conductor of the *Concerto Civico di Napoli*, was one of two important Italian band conductors who were conservatory trained musicians and who were active in teaching (Vessella in the *Santa Cecilia* in Rome and Caravaglios in the *Conservatorio San Pietro Maiella* in Naples) future band directors.

In 1894, Vessella published a proposal for a standardization of instrumentation, based on the concept of 'families' of instruments, which had an influence on Italian bands lasting well into the twentieth century.

England

After the Napoleonic Wars, the strong tradition of local civic militia bands in England gave way to more regular civic bands, called 'reed bands' by present day English writers to distinguish them from the strong tradition of the brass bands which replaced them. Some of the most famous brass bands of the century also began as regular civic bands with woodwinds, for example the Black Dyke Mills Band only became a brass band in 1855.

The normal civic bands were swept aside in an extraordinary wave of enthusiasm in England for the brass band. For the moment, consider, as an indication of this early enthusiasm, the reaction of one who heard the the Besses o' th' Barn.

> The effect was marvellous; my hair stood on end; I was in ecstasies; my soul was raptured; all around me seemed a vision of Heaven. Oh, what joy!! What bliss!!

The origins for a band which could have had such an impact is found in the densely peopled manufacturing districts of Yorkshire, Lancashire, and Derbyshire. There the cottage industries were giving way to new industrial centers with mills, workshops, miles of slums, smoke, and noise. There the poorly paid worker, often displaced and homesick for the fields of his village, toiled for twelve to fourteen hours a day.

The first of several factors which made possible the civic brass band development was the arrival of the new instruments fundamental to it, beginning in the 1830s with the cornet, first called the 'cornopean' in England. Here was a melodic instrument capable of considerable musical effect and tonal accuracy which was not too difficult for a working man to learn in his little spare time.

Shortly thereafter came the new family of saxhorns, which gained almost immediate popularity due to the extraordinary success of the tours of the Distin family quintet. This ensemble was founded by John Distin (b. 1798), who was a member of the South Devon Militia Band, and later the court band of the Prince Regent in London. The significant turning point, both in terms of the fortune of the family quintet and the British brass band movement, came when the quintet discovered the saxhorn while on tour to Paris in 1844. Their return with these instruments had a profound influence on the spread of these instruments in England and, in turn, helped make possible the growth of brass bands there.

Another source of encouragement for the development of brass bands came from religious institutions, who were interested in improving the leisure activities of the workers, who otherwise were tempted by drink and gambling. Thus a number of bands were founded by the temperance movement, beginning with the Bramley Band of 1836. Related to this was the rise of Salvation Army bands which also played a great role in the development of the brass band movement. The first of these was formed in 1878 by the Fry family, a father and three sons, who played cornets, trombone, and euphonium. Soon General Booth encouraged his Army to take up bands (including women) and within six years there were four hundred Salvation Army bands (today there are more than thirty thousand participants).

Band contests in England date from at least 1818, well before the arrival of the brass band movement with which they are so much associated today. The early contests were local and small, often organized spontaneously on occasions where several bands gathered together in various civic celebrations. With the brass bands of the workers the idea spread quickly, for it made the band the subject of wider civic interest and stimulated civic ambition.

Interest in brass bands was beginning to spread during the 1840s and led to the first brass band contest on a larger scale, the Belle Vue Brass Band Contest of 1853 in Manchester. This contest had three judges, who were screened from the view of the players—a basic element of these contests ever since. Although there had been considerable fear that the public would not support such a contest by amateur musicians (because the Manchester orchestra under the famous Charles Halle had only slowly been able to build an audience); in fact some sixteen thousand people formed the audience.

The front entrance of the Crystal Palace, Hyde Park, London, that housed the Great Exhibition of 1851

Truly national contests began with the Crystal Palace Contest of 1860, the first great contest to be held in the South of England. As a measure of the growing interest in brass band contests, one might note that seventy-two bands made application for participation in the first of the two-day contest. The audience, too, was growing, for twenty thousand persons heard the bands on the second day! The size of the Crystal Palace made possible a contest with so many bands, for it was possible to have six stages, each with three judges, operating simultaneously.

During the final twenty years of the nineteenth century the contest tradition grew to extensive proportions. By 1889 the *Daily News* observed that between Easter and August 'some hundreds of brass band contests take place.' By 1895 there were two hundred and twenty-two contests in Great Britain and by 1896 two hundred and forty!

One of several journals devoted to brass bands which came into existence during the final twenty years of the nineteenth century, the *Cornet*, remarked on the positive influence of the contest system.

> Without a doubt the main factor in this all-round advancement is the contesting movement. Contesting has literally revolutionized the whole world of brass music, and its beneficial influence has more or less affected every brass band in the country. Bands everywhere are awaking and striving to improve their position; the introduction of contests has imbued them with a commendable desire to press to the front; and as a result we have better instruments, better music, better teachers, better officials, and better bandsmen.

The repertoire of these bands consisted of a great deal of trivial music, but also major transcriptions of important orchestral music. Although all this activity did not attract original composition by major composers during the nineteenth century, there is nevertheless something impressive in the fact that the brass band movement introduced thousands of working men (by the end of the century there were an estimated twenty thousand of these bands) to the music of Mozart, Mendelssohn, Verdi, and Wagner.

František Krommer, český skladatel. Kreslil K. Maixner.

19 Court Wind Bands

Austria

The financial costs of the Austrian–Bohemian participation in the Napoleonic Wars brought an end to many luxuries in the smaller courts, among them the aristocratic *Harmoniemusik* wind bands which had so flourished during the Classic Period. If this activity was no longer so wide-spread, nevertheless the two most famous of the Viennese *Harmoniemusik* ensembles remained active during during the first third of the nineteenth century.

The Liechtenstein *Harmoniemusik* continued under the leadership of Joseph Triebensee until shortly before 1812. Triebensee was highly regarded for his skill in transcribing major orchestral works and operas for *Harmoniemusik* and he attempted to sell such works, in manuscript form, to other aristocrats. He apparently had at least limited success for his transcriptions can be found in a number of European libraries today. In doing all this work Triebensee absorbed a considerable opera repertoire and at the end of his career he was the successor to von Weber as head of the Opera in Prague.

In 1812 Prince Liechtenstein reorganized his *Harmoniemusik* and from this date nearly all its transcribed repertoire is by Wenzel Sedlak. Sedlak produced at least fifty major (many are twenty movements or more) opera transcriptions, including the major operas of Rossini, Bellini, and Donizetti. Among these is his *Fidelio*, which was published in 1814 by Artaria in Vienna under the supervision of Beethoven (according to the composer).

After the retirement of Johann Wendt, the kaiser's *Harmoniemusik* continued and included among its membership many of the leading wind players of this time in Vienna. One insight into the repertoire of this *Harmoniemusik* is found in the publications of the imperial printing bureau (k.k. priv. Chemischen Druckerey). A preface to one of these carries an interesting note reflecting on the importance of this repertoire.

Opposite page: Portrait of Franz Krommer (1759–1831) by Karel Maixner, 1871

'Fidelio' arranged for winds by Wenzel Sedlak, under Beethoven's supervision

> Our custom, as always with acknowledged and famous masters, is to work from autograph scores and with special diligence and exact knowledge of the characteristics of wind instruments ... We will stand by this Harmonie publication before any other publication as the proof sheets have had special priority. No master of art has been so often consulted with each exact and painstaking correction. Only once have we permitted an embellishment to be undertaken, and that was determined by the master himself in his own authentic version.

The most valuable portion of the repertoire of this *Harmoniemusik* is the group of partitas by Franz Krommer, the Viennese court chamber composer. These works are quite above average in quality, some ranking with the very best of this genre. They are more advanced harmonically than the works of the late eighteenth century and can be said to be a genuine harbinger of Romanticism. In addition, the Partitas of Krommer have much more advanced technical demands for each instrument, documenting a technical level of performer equal to the very best today.

Germany

As in Austria, the aristocratic *Harmoniemusik* tradition continued in Germany for about the first third of the nineteenth century. One of the best-known of these served the Duke of Sondershausen from 1802 until 1835. In this court the twelve-member wind band was the only court ensemble, with the famous clarinetist, Simon Hermstedt, serving as *Kapellmeister*. An article by Gerber in the *Allgemeinen Musikalischen Zeitung* for 1809 states that the typical repertoire consisted of a 'grand partita in the manner and form of a Haydn Symphony,' followed by operas transcribed for *Harmoniemusik*. The concert Gerber heard included, 'some of the bigger twelve-part [!] partitas by Krommer, the Dresden Schubart, and Schneider, together with several movements from the works of Haydn and Mozart arranged by Hermstedt.'

Another important *Harmoniemusik* was founded in 1801 by Duke Friedrich of Mechlenburg-Schwerin. The ensemble wore green uniforms and for a time carried swords, however, the duke ended this practice after one of the hornists, Bode, in a drunken condition, struck his wife with his sword! According to Clemens Meyer, this ensemble was formed for the purpose of art music and performed with distinction, especially in the

Johann Simon Hermstedt

Friedrich Franz I, Duke of Mechlenburg-Schwerin by Matthieu, 1776

Summer to the delight of the guests at the baths at Doberan. The reader may perhaps recall that Mendelssohn was inspired to compose his *Notturno* for eleven winds (known today as the *Overture*, op. 24) for this band after hearing them perform in Doberan. Wilhelm Wieprecht also reported being impressed with hearing this 'so-called Harmoniemusik' perform there.

Prince Ludwig Friedrich of Rudolstadt also had an important *Harmoniemusik* which gave two-hour concerts every Sunday, with the repertoire again partitas and opera transcriptions.

The traveling Englishman, Edward Holmes, heard in Munich what must have been an aristocratic *Harmoniemusik* in 1827. His touching account describes a concert in which it is evident the players were both excellent technically and sensitive.

> A friend invited me to an evening concert, in which were performed the overtures and various pieces from the Don Juan and Clemenza di Tito of Mozart, excellently arranged as sestetts for two clarionets, two bassoons, and two horns; there was not power enough for the full pieces, but the airs pleased me extremely, being blown with so subdued and mellow a tone as might have been borne in a small room. This *harmonie musik*, as it is termed, is a species entirely of German cultivation, and I suspect that the wrath of old Dominico Scarlatti against wind instruments might be appeased, were he to hear how skilfully they are tempered. One of the performers gratified me with a piece of sentiment which I did not expect from a person of his appearance; after playing a tender air from an opera of Mozart, he said, 'I think the composer means that the lady feels pain here,' placing his hand on his heart.

At least one *Harmoniemusik* in Munich seems to have performed a great deal of functional music, judging by an enormous bound collection of more than five hundred numbered transcriptions and compositions by William LeGrand. There is also an extant review of a *Harmoniemusik* concert in Dresden.

> The most noticeable music here given was some of the sinfonias of Beethoven and Haydn—the overtures to Fidelio and Anacreon, Mozart's finales to Don Juan and Figaro, ably adapted, and the voice parts taken in for a band by Meyer, brother of the celebrated composer of that name. I will not say that this music was so dashingly played as it might have been by our Philharmonic orchestra, but it was complete enough for those who enjoy the display of an author's mind more than the pride of perfect *fiddling*.

After mid-century in Germany the full military band provided many of the functional needs of the aristocrats. It is in this light that one can understand the existance of the functional works composed for the Berlin Court by Spontini and Meyerbeer for large bands. This predilection in Berlin for large military bands playing indoors for the aristocracy seems astonishing when one thinks of those palace banquets which had formerly been accompanied by only eight wind players. An eyewitness describes the resultant sound during a dinner for Bismarck in 1890.

> I sat opposite the Empress, and between Molke and Kameke. The former would have been very talkative, but was disturbed by the continual music, and was much annoyed therat. Two military bands were placed opposite one another, and when one stopped the other began to blare. It was scarcely bearable.

In Prussia one still heard the ancient aristocratic trumpet choir during the nineteenth century and works were composed for massed trumpets by Weber and Spohr, the latter for fifty-three trumpets! Spohr describes this work in his autobiography as follows:

> [For the celebration of the marriage of the Duke of Saxe-Meiningen] I had besides to compose a grand march with introduction of the melody of the old German ballad: 'Ond als der Grossvater die Grossmutter nab,' together with a torch-light-dance for fifty-three trumpeters, and two pair of kettle-drummers (for these were the numbers to be found in the music bands of the army of the Elector of Hesse); and as for the sake of the modulations I was obliged to take various tones of the trumpets, and the trumpeters of the bands not being very musical, I was obliged to practise them also beforehand in this torch-light-dance.

Before leaving this discussion of military bands in the Prussian Court, mention must be made of a newspaper item from 1881, relative to the court in Russia—which had, of course, been greatly influenced by Prussia since the time of Peter the Great. The implication of this extraordinary information, which some scholar *must* pursue, is that the aristocrats themselves performed in their own band!

> From St. Petersburg: The musical soirees for brass instruments, established by the Emperor Alexander III, when hereditary grand duke, are to take place again regularly every three weeks during the winter. The participants are the amateur grand dukes, the bandmasters of the regiments of the guard, and *dilettants* of the first families of the nobility, altogether about fifty persons.

Although court composers in the eighteenth-century tradition no longer receive much space in music history texts in their discussions of nineteenth-century music, the libraries of Germany are filled with occasional works for aristocratic welcomes, birthdays, and marriages, etc., which remind us that there *were* still court composers. Wagner was such a court composer and he has left several works for large band or brass ensemble composed for such functional purposes. One of these was his *Weihegruss* (1843) for the unveiling of a statue of King Friedrich August I in Dresden. Wagner also mentions, in his autobiography, a lost work by Mendelssohn which had been composed for the same ceremony.

> I had written a simple song for male voices [and brass] of modest design, whereas to Mendelssohn had been assigned the more complicated task of interweaving the National Anthem, 'Heil Dir im Rautenkrantz' ('God Save the King,' in English) into the male chorus he had to compose. This he had effected by an artistic work in counterpoint, so arranged that from the first eight beats of his original melody the brass instruments simultaneously played the Anglo-Saxon popular air … Mendelssohn's daring combination quite missed its effect, because no one could understand why the vocalists did not sing the same tune the wind instruments were playing.

Similar works for full band include his *Greeting of Friedrich August the Beloved by his Faithful Subjects* (1844) and the *Huldigungsmarsch* (1864).

Italy

Court *Harmoniemusik* in Italy seems to have vanished as the influence of Napoleon replaced that of Austria. A rare reference is of a concert by an Italian *Harmoniemusik* heard by Spohr when he visited Naples in 1817.

There was a famous band in Naples early during the nineteenth century, the band of the *Veliti del Regno di Napoli*, belonging to the Grand Duke Leopoldo II, which often played for the public in the gardens of the Boboli and for the duke and his family before his window in the Palazzo Pitti.

The long and extraordinary history of papal wind bands in Rome reaches its final chapter with the ensembles under Pope Pius VII. As the century progressed, apparently the Church also employed military bands for entertaimnent purposes, for one account mentions hearing two bands playing waltzes in the Palazzo di Venezia in Rome during a reception for a new German cardinal (Cardinal Haulik of Agram) in 1851.

Leopoldo II by Pietro Benvenuti, 1828

France

Court wind bands in the traditional sense died in France with the Revolution of 1789. During the nineteenth century their functions, when required, were filled by military bands as in Germany. These pages, therefore, would be unnecessary but for the impossibility of passing by Napoleon without some comment on his relationship to wind band music.

To one interested in the history of wind band music, Napoleon represents the greatest of disappointments. He came into power following one of the finest moments in the history of the wind band, the period of aesthetic music for large bands during the revolutionary years. He employed as his official court composers two men who had been successful composers of band music, François Lesueur and Giovanni Paisiello. The other composers he was interested in had also been previously successful as band composers, among them Cherubini, Catel, and Méhul. And yet, the fact that none of these composers produced a single important work for band, or any other significant court music, is an unfortunate reflection of the fact that Napoleon, although so unusually interested in literature and painting, had no strong interest in aesthetic music.

He did surround himself with appropriate ceremonial music, but the music was never more than functional in nature. Of his coronation, an eyewitness reported,

> The military bands were innumerable, and under the orders of M. Lesueur; these executed heroic marches, of which one, commanded by the Emperor from M. Lesueur for the army of the Boulogne, still ranks, in the judgement of connoisseurs, among the finest and most imposing of musical compositions. For my part, this music made me turn pale and tremble; I shuddered from head to foot in listening to it.

Jean-François Lesueur (1760–1837)

England

The last important private aristocratic wind band in the tradition which began during the Middle Ages belonged to George IV of England (1762–1830). Here was a noble with a strong natural talent for music and who was an active performer on the cello. One who knew him said, 'he was not only a musician among princes, but a prince among musicians.' He began his band when he was still Prince of Wales, sometime before 1811, and there is extant repertoire from this period by C. F. Eley and Henry Pick.

The name of the band changed to the Prince Regent's Band between 1811–1820, to conform to the change in the title of the sponsor. The band is described during this period as being 'esteemed the finest in Europe' and one source gives the instrumentation as,

King George IV when Prince Regent (1762–1830), facing left in the red uniform of a Field-Marshal, by Henry Bone, 1816

3 flutes
3 oboes
12 clarinets
4 bassoons
2 corni di bassetti
4 horns
4 trumpets
2 serpents
4 trombones (ATTB)
2 percussion

Musically, the turning point for this band came with the employment as conductor and arranger of Christian Krammer, from Hanover, Germany, and a pupil of Winter. He was a prodigious arranger for the band, transcribing all the then known symphonies of Mozart and Haydn, several of Beethoven's symphonies and numerous overtures and operatic excerpts. Krammer was also very active in recruiting talented new members for the band. He would visit ships bringing French prisoners from Spain to determine if there were any fine musicians on board and he once had a German clarinetist, named Eisert, extradited from a German prison to join the band. As a result a number of the band members were famous in their own right. It was said of the trumpeter, Schmidt, that he was the first trumpet of Europe and that 'his flourish was the most terrific and appalling thing ever heard from a musical instrument.' The horn players, the brothers Rehn and Hardy were celebrated as were the trombonists Albrecht, Schroeder and Berhns. Even the serpent player, Andre, was called one of 'the lions of the band,' and no distinguished visitor to the court departed without hearing Andre's performance of one of the trios of Corelli on the serpent.

A review of 1818 speaks of the musicality of this band and gives appropriate credit to Krammer.

> From the most delicate song to the magnificent symphonies of Haydn, Mozart and Beethoven, and even the grandest of Handel choruses, he has preserved the bearing of each class throughout in their pristine beauty and design, and with so nice an attention to the particular cast of expression appertaining to each instrument, that he has left nothing to be desired. Those are the daily services rendered to the Prince and to music by Mr. Kramer.

The coronation of George IV occurred in 1820 and then the band became known as the King's Household Band for ten years. From this period, there is a colored aquatint picturing a band of about twenty-five players, wearing uniforms with short blue coats, standing—although each player has a music stand, with the timpani, made of solid silver, placed in the front row center. The conductor, in evening dress, and his music stand face the audience, not the players. This followed a long court tradition that artists on stage should never turn their back on the aristocrats in the audience. A review of the band's performance in 1822 is again full of praise.

> It is impossible to exaggerate the perfection to which this band has been brought by the science and unremitting attention of Mr. Kramer. Their performance of arranged scores is inexpressibly fine, and their accompaniment is not less chaste, subdued and beautiful.

The band continued to exist under Queen Victoria until 1840, although beginning with her reign it was much smaller (seventeen players).

20 Church Wind Bands

DURING THE NINETEENTH CENTURY the civic militia band took over many of the duties of the civic wind bands of the ancient tradition, most of whom had disappeared by the end of the eighteenth century. Therefore now one finds the militia band performing in the church, including the accompaniment of polyphonic choral music.

There was, however, an entirely new church festival which necessitated an appearance by the military bands of the nineteenth century and this new purpose resulted in an extraordinary body of original band literature, much of which is still extant in European libraries. An early example of the references to this new ceremony can be seen in the diary of Vincent Novello, who was touring the continent in 1829. During his visit to Antwerp, he made a notation which today might seem rather enigmatic.

> Military Mass at 12. Overture Zauberflöte.

In a Jesuits Church in Munich, Novello heard a similar service with a military band playing music even less traditional for a Catholic Church.

> The service began at half past Ten with the Sermon (which was a tedious affair) and at 11 the Band commenced the Salute with a crash of all the Instruments and a furious Roll on the Drums—the effect was very striking and novel to me in the Church.
>
> Next came a light Movement in B flat, quite in the Dance style and would have been very appropriate as Ballet music. The second piece was an air in E flat followed by a Rondo and Polonaise—the whole was more like a Bravuro air for the Prima Donna in an Opera than anything else.

Bizarre as such an account reads, similar references can be found throughout the century. Apparently throughout Europe, the Catholic Church, as one of its many colorful special festivals, began setting one Sunday each year aside for the purpose of the commemoration of the military. On such a day it was often a military band who played during the Service and sometimes provided the entire music of the Mass.

Vincent Novello by Edward Petre Novello (d. 1836)

Opposite page: Anton Bruckner by Wilhelm von Kaulbach, 1885

There is no way of documenting how frequently such performances of operatic and ballet selections during the Mass by a military band, such as those quoted above, were heard. The extant music in European libraries suggests that more often the military band participated by playing music more in character with the occasion. In many cases composers wrote full length Masses with chorus for the military band to accompany. The military band also appeared in the Protestant Church in Germany during the nineteenth century, resulting in extant compositions ranging from cantatas to the extraordinary Protestant 'monster' concert performed by seven thousand singers and four hundred trombones in Ravensberg in 1877!

The extant band literature for the church in Austria includes numerous compositions by Neukomm, Schiedermayr, Liszt, and of course Bruckner. Every musician knows Bruckner's *E Minor Mass* for double chorus and band, but there are six additional major works which are not published or available in scholarly editions. One of these, his *Germanenzug*, is scored for TTBB and a full military band, with parts for two Bb soprano cornets, euphonium, four trumpets, four horns, three trombones, and tuba! (see Plate 34, p. 404–405)

In France, during the first half of the nineteenth century accounts mention the same kinds of appearances of military bands in the church mentioned above with respect to Germany. The somewhat baffled Lowell Mason, an American visiting Paris in 1852, recalled,

> The *religious* exercises commenced by a grand voluntary, by the military band in attendance, which was nothing more or less than the overture of the *Caliph of Bagdad*, by Boieldieu. The grand military mass now followed, and it consisted of a succession of popular operatic airs, played by the band, with an occasional roll of the small drum, an 'order,' or a 'present' by the old soldiers … [and] a few words chanted by the drummers, towards the close of the *solemnities*.

In any case, the second half of the nineteenth century was quite a different story! There are extant literally hundreds of *published* works for large band, with and without voices, composed for use in the church. One of these, a *Messe solennelle* by Louis Welter, identifies the parts of the Service where the military band played, thus giving us a valuable insight into how this large body of music was used. In this case, the five movements were performed as music for the

1. Entrée (Tempo di Marcia)
2. Offertoire (Maestoso)
3. Élévation (Andante)
4. Communion (Moderato)
5. Sortie (Allegretto)

Finally, it is interesting to find that some monasteries continued to maintain their own wind bands and wind ensembles during the nineteenth century. Novello reported hearing such an ensemble during his tour of Germany in 1829.

> Tuesday, July 7th. Left Heilbronn at half past 7. In the morning we heard a very simple and melodious Chorale played by the small Band of wind Instruments which, as our Host afterwards informed us, belonged to a Monastery adjoining our Inn. It was tastefully played and well in tune.

The monastery at Melk apparently maintained a similar ensemble at about the same time, as is suggested by the repertoire housed there.

The most detailed study of one of these monastery wind bands has been done by Jiří Sehnal, regarding one in Brno. Dr. Sehnal reports that the school for choir boys at this monastery, which dates from 1648, began to emphasize the playing of wind instruments during the end of the eighteenth century. By about 1816 there appears to have been established a regular *Harmoniemusik*. The selection of applicants for the boy's choir, judging by the results of examinations during 1816–1818, was closely related to the immediate needs for membership in the *Harmoniemusik*.

The *Harmoniemusik* had regular rehearsals, in addition to their rehearsals for church music, and when the occasion demanded special rehearsals were held. The general purpose of the Brno *Harmoniemusik* was to perform and uplift the usual music in the monastery church and to provide the opportunity for the monks, who were not allowed to frequent the theater, to hear whatever music was currently attracting the attention of the public. The *Harmoniemusik* also performed dinner music for the Abbot, especially when important visitors were present. Special concerts were sometimes given for visitors, in the refectory, the garden, or in the cloisters, who then were expected to make an appropriate donation to the ensemble. The *Harmoniemusik* also performed for occasions within the monastery, such as anniversaries, name-day celebrations, and for anniversaries for the reading of the first Mass by resident priests.

In addition to the *Harmoniemusik*, this monastery also organized a 'Turkish Musik band.' As this kind of wind band required a larger number of players, the instrumentation had to be completed with players brought in from the outside. The Turkish band also gave concerts, usually in the monastery garden or in the public square in front of the monastery.

PART VI
Plates

Plate 1

This is the title page for a multi-movement Baroque *Hautboisten* composition for 2 oboes, a lower oboe, an English horn ('taille') and 2 bassoons, a common *Hautboisten* instrumentation before the arrival of horns. The date of the first performance is given in the lower right hand corner, 6 July 1723. The composer, Venturini, is one of many Italian composers hired by German courts in the aftermath of the sweep of Italian opera across Europe.

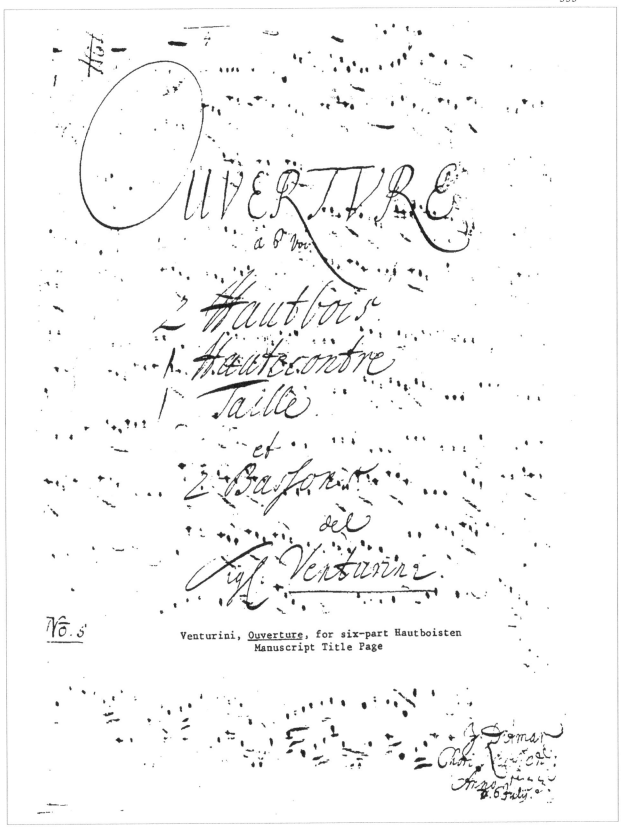

Venturini, Ouverture, for six-part Hautboisten
Manuscript Title Page

Plate 2

This is the first page of the oboe 1 part for the Venturini *Overture* mentioned in Plate 1. In the general style of the Ouverture form, the beginning would be *Adagio* (the *alla breve* meter symbol refers to placement of accents, not speed) with the music beginning in the fourth stave being *Allegro*.

The almost complete absence of articulation marks is typical before the nineteenth century. It was assumed the player would add slurs as appropriate. The symbol for a tie, a curved line through the bar line, rather than from note head to note head, is also common. The wavy line through a single note stem is a trill.

The symbol which looks like a question mark at the change of meter at the end of the third line is the point to which an eventual *Da capo* will return. The symbol at the end of each staff, looking like a fancy check mark, is called a *custos* and it shows the player the pitch of the first note of the first bar of the next line.

Venturini, Overture
First movement, Oboe I

Plate 3

This is the first page of the autograph score for a multi-movement Baroque *Hautboisten* composition for three bands and three trumpet choirs called *Concerto [da camera]* by Johann Fasch (1688–1758). The work was no doubt intended for some aristocratic gathering where nobles would bring their own ensembles.

Each *Hautboisten* band is scored for a typical early instrumentation in Germany, three oboes and bassoon.

Each trumpet choir consists of two clarino parts, a Principal part (traditionally the lowest trumpet voice of the trumpet choir) and the timpani which supplies the bass notes of the choir, not the rhythm.

Plate 4

This is the *Concerto* of Plate 3 in modern notation.

Plate 5

This is the first oboe part of a multi-movement *Hautboisten* work called *Sonata* by Johann Muller scored for three oboes, English horn and bassoon. As in all *Hautboisten* compositions doubling was expected, hence the use of '*Solo*' and '*Tutti*' in this page.

A number of Italian church instrumental forms of the sixteenth century moved North into Germany and the Low Countries during the seventeenth century where they became secular or court forms. None of these forms, such as the *sinfonia, sonata, concerto, canzona, aria*, etc., had as yet any agreed upon internal form.

This is a rare early example of written dynamics. It was expected the player would add all articulations and ornaments. The second beat of the second bar is a clear expectation of a trill and the composer has provided the after notes.

Johann Müller, XII Sonates, for Hautboisten
First edition [c. 1709], Solo Oboe

Plate 6

This *Ouverture* is one of several multi-movement *Hautboisten* compositions by Telemann which are currently found in the State Library at Darmstadt. They are in the hand of his copyist, the autographs having been moved to a secure location during World War II which was then bombed.

The symbol appearing as a cross over a note is a trill. Here the ties are from note head to note head, although hastily done so that the first one in the 9th stave looks like another note head. The notation for long rests are the first generation when numbers begin to appear over the rest symbols. The symbols themselves are in the earlier tradition. In the 4th stave, for example, the placement of the rest vertical bars meant 4 bars, 4 bars, 2 bars, for a total of 10 bars.

At the end of the first movement, five staves from the bottom of the page there is a first ending with an *alla breve* symbol which tells the player that the repeat is back to the beginning of the *allegro* of the 4th stave. The use of the common time symbol in the second ending indicated the slower tempo of the beginning, in other words a long note final note.

In the second movement, a 'Passepied,' there is a fermata symbol at the end of the second line. This indicates that on the *da capo* the music ends with this note, but it does not mean a longer note. The fermata in early music meant only 'stopping place,' as one sees today in Milan, where the fermata symbol is seen on signs for bus stops.

Telemann, Ouverture for Hautboisten
Copyist's manuscript, Oboe One

Plate 7

This is a Classic Period *Serenade* by Mozart's rival in Vienna, Antonio Salieri. The work is scored for the typical *Harmoniemusik* scoring of pairs of clarinets, oboes, horns and bassoons.

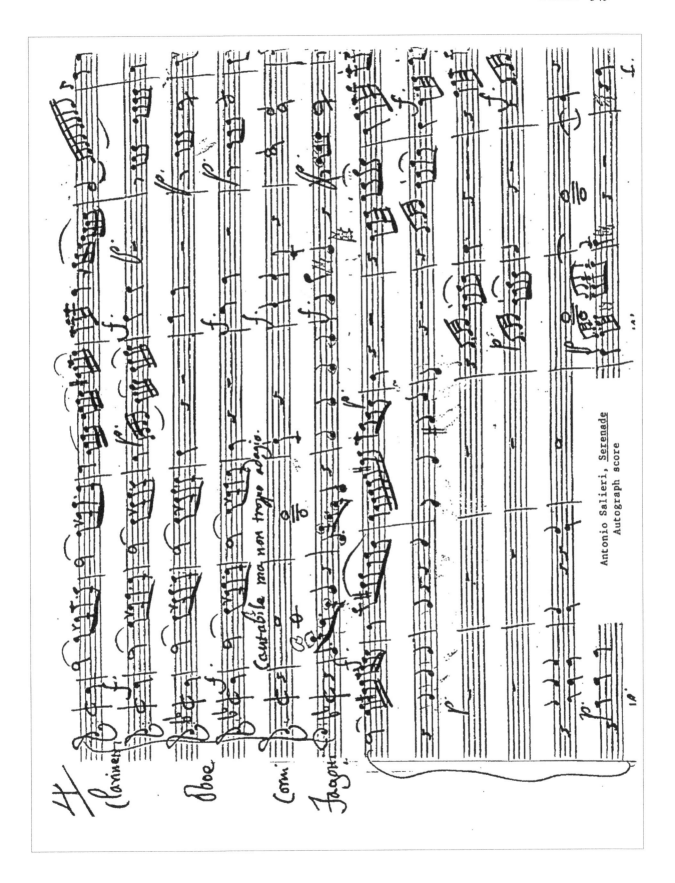

Antonio Salieri, Serenade
Autograph score

Plate 8

This is the first page of the autograph score for the Mozart *Gran partita* for 12 winds and string bass. The name and date are not in Mozart's hand and the date is incorrect. An ultrascopic examination reveals that there was a geniune Mozart signature underneath the present one.

Since it was assumed at this time that the first movement would begin *forte*, Mozart does not bother to notate that but notice how carefully he notates each change of dynamic in each voice which follows. In the fifth bar of the Bb horn parts one can see a rare Mozart mistake (in transposition) which he has corrected.

The *dolce* in Mozart meant 'solo part,' which is obvious here. Mozart uses the *custos*, which in the first oboe is under a tie.

N.23 gran Serenata. Del Sig:r Wolfgang Mozart.

Plate 9

This is an arrangement of Mozart's opera, *The Marriage of Figaro*, for *Harmoniemusik* by Johann Wendt, an oboist in the Emperor's *Harmoniemusik* in Vienna. This is the cover for the 2nd Bassoon part and it was customary to use that part as a cover page for all the parts. Scores were not sold. This set of parts was sold by one of two shops in Vienna which dealt in making customers individual manuscript copies of music. The number 6 1/2 under Lausch, one of the copy dealers, refers to the cost to the customer on a per page basis.

Mozart, The Marriage of Figaro
Arranged for Harmoniemusik by Johann Wendt
Title page

Plate 10

This is the cover page from a French publication of a *Harmoniemusik* arrangement of Mozart's *Magic Flute* opera. The arranger is not given, only the publisher Ignaz Pleyel of Paris. Since Pleyel himself composed a number of works for *Harmoniemusik*, this may also be his work.

Pleyel was born in a small village in upper Austria and was the twenty-fourth child of a poor school teacher. The local aristocrat felt sorry for the family and announced he would educate the twenty-fourth child, Ignaz. After his education in a local school, Pleyel, who wanted to leave the village but had no idea where to go, climbed on the top of his father's barn and threw a feather into the air, resolving to go in whatever direction the feather blew. The feather blew West, so off Pleyel went, ending in Paris where he became rich and famous as a publisher and manufacturer of pianos.

Once, in 1977, I conducted an outdoor concert of the partitas for *Harmoniemusik* by Pleyel in his home town, on his birthday, with a group of professional players from Vienna. We staged the event so that the music would drift across a river to be heard in then Communist Hungary.

XLII A 3   Graf Clam Gall

DOUZE AIRS
Choisis
de la Flûte Enchantée
de MOZART

Arrangés en Harmonie

Pour deux Clarinettes deux Oboe deux Bassons deux Cors

Prix

Gravé par Favrot

A PARIS

Chez Pleyel Rue Neuve des Petits Champs N.º 24. entre les rues S.ᵗᵉ Anne et celle de Chabannais.

Mozart, The Magic Flute, Arranged for Harmoniemusik
First Edition, Title Page

Plate 11

This is the first page of the first oboe part for a *Harmoniemusik* composition by Joseph Triebensee, then the leader of the *Harmoniemusik* ensemble for Prince Liechtenstein in Vienna. Typically each variation featured a different pair of instruments and one can see that in this case the oboe part is difficult even by modern standards. Oboists today, for example, do not often see a high F.

In the second bar of the third stave one sees a typical Viennese notation in which it was expected that the oboist would fill in the intervening notes.

The dynamic marking at the beginning, *m.v.*, means *mezzo voce*, or in today's notation *mezzo forte*.

Joseph Triebensee, <u>Variations on a Theme by Mozart</u> for Harmoniemusik, Autograph Manuscript, Oboe One

Plate 12

This is the title page of an arrangement for *Harmoniemusik* of Beethoven's *Seventh Symphony*. The work was published by Beethoven's publisher in Vienna and was sold at the same time as the first edition of the orchestral score.

Plate 13

This is the title page of a published arrangement of music from Beethoven's *Fidelio* by Wenzel Sedlak, who was the successor of Triebensee as leader of Prince Liechtenstein's *Harmoniemusik*. This arrangement, together with an arrangement for piano, were the first forms of *Fidelio* ever published. Beethoven himself took out an ad in a Vienna newspaper announcing that this publication not only had his approval, but was done under his personal supervision.

Plate 14

This score, written for a civic militia band in England late in the eighteenth century, represents the very first generation of published full scores in Europe. Of particular interest in these early published full scores is the percussion parts, themselves among the earliest percussion parts ever published. The wavy lines in the Tamborine are supposed to represent a roll. It is true graphic notation, attempting to put on paper what the editor heard.

This edition also included a separate version of this march for keyboard and flute, so the customer could perform the composition in his home and thereby vicariously participate in the Napoleonic wars.

Salner, St. Helena Slow March
First Edition score, page one

Plate 15

This is the autograph score for the *Te Deum* of Gossec, first performed by three hundred winds in a great outdoor celebration in Paris one year after the beginning of the French Revolution. This performance led to many more publications of band music used in similar ceremonies. Some writers date the modern band from the performance of this *Te Deum* on 14 July 1790.

The part marked 'altos' was for the taille, the English horn. The Serpent continued to be used in French church music well into the nineteenth century.

Gossec, Te Deum [1790]
Autograph score, first page

Plate 16

This is a very rare manuscript full score from the French Revolution period, an outstanding early band work by Méhul. Note the title says 'for full harmonie, without violins, etc.'

Of particular interest are parts for Buccin and Tuba curva, two instruments found on ancient Roman monuments and which the artist David, who was a member of the committee who planned the Revolutionary festival concerts, insisted that local instrument makers manufacture to help capture the (imagined) spirit of democracy in ancient Rome.

Méhul, Ouverture for Band
Eighteenth Century Copyist's score, page one

Plate 17

This is the autograph score for the *Symphony* for band by Anton Reicha, composed in Paris in 1815. Reicha wrote the symphony as a work for one large band, but, thinking this work might be used in one of the great outdoor Revolutionary festivals in Paris he created optional parts for two additional bands, in the old *concertato* style, on the the three lower staves of the score page. Reicha included in the score a number of pages in his own manuscript discussing performance problems, beginning with the need for a good conductor.

Anton Reicha, Commemoration Symphony
Autograph score, page one

Plate 18

This a modern realization of the Reicha *Symphony* making the three bands apparent.

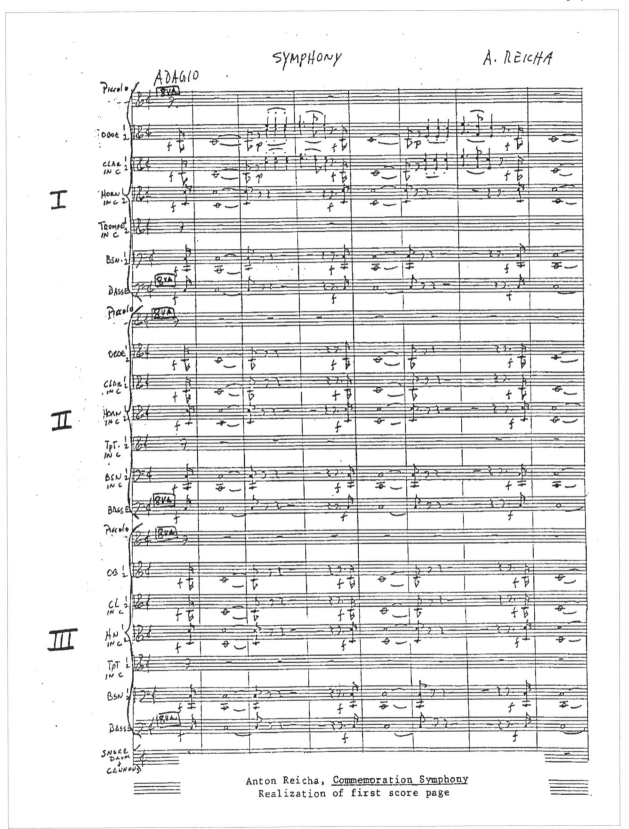

Anton Reicha, Commemoration Symphony
Realization of first score page

Plate 19

This is the cover page in Beethoven's own handwriting for his *Siegessinfonie*, his only composition for large wind band. His handwriting reads,

> On Wellington's Victory, at Victoria, 1813
> Written for Mr. Maelzel
> Ludwig van Beethoven

Beethoven never hesitated to use the paper nearest at hand to figure his daily expenses, hence the numbers on this title page.

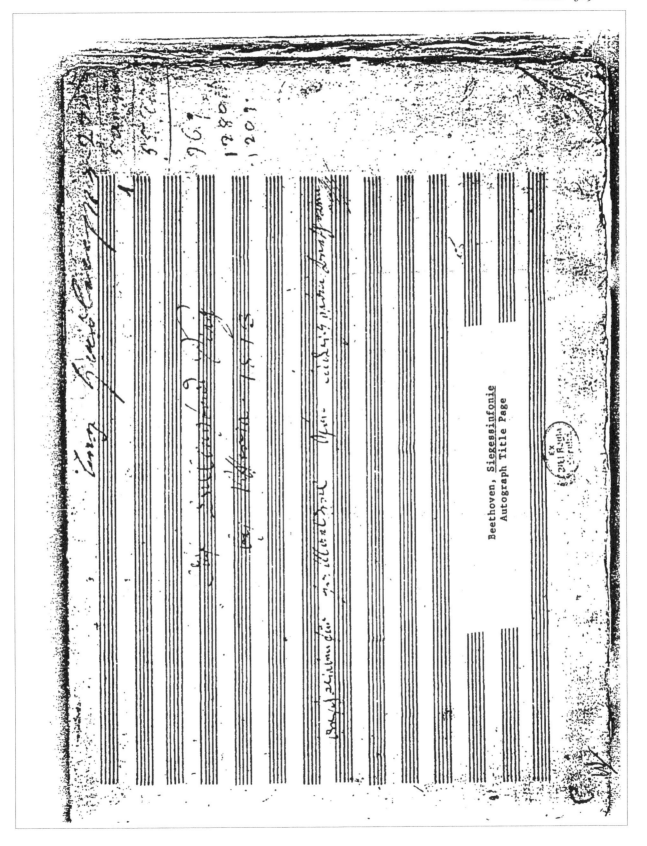

Beethoven, Siegessinfonie
Autograph Title Page

Plate 20

This is Beethoven's copyist's full score for the *Siegessinfonie*. Throughout it has additional markings made by Beethoven while he was proofing, as for example the '8va' here in the flute part. Beethoven has also written at the top *Allegro con brio* with the half-note metronome marking given as 128.

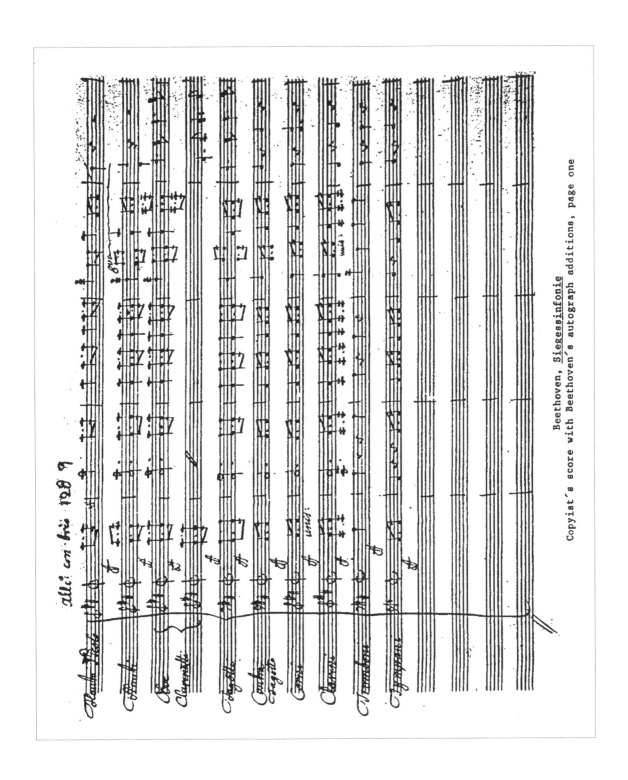

Beethoven, Siegessinfonie
Copyist's score with Beethoven's autograph additions, page one

Plate 21

An early nineteenth-century German arrangement of Weber's opera *Oberon* arranged for military band. Note that the military band with percussion here is called 'Turkische Musik,' to distinguish it from the earlier tradition of early nineteenth-century German military band music called *Harmonie*.

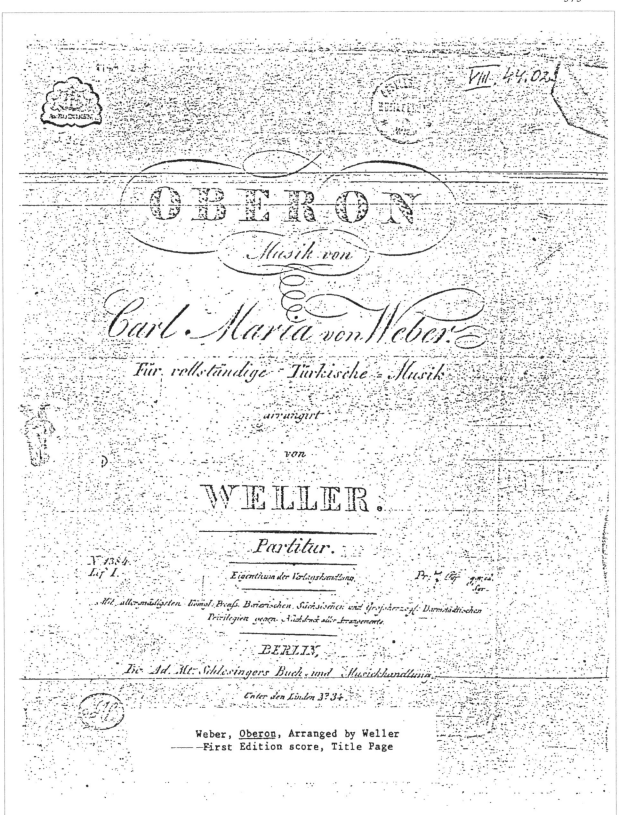

Weber, Oberon, Arranged by Weller
— First Edition score, Title Page

Plate 22

This is the first page of the full score for the *Oberon* music seen in the title page in Plate 21. Note that although the title page clearly specified the Turkish percussion instruments, large bass drum, cymbals, schellenbaum and trumpet, none are seen in the score itself as publishers still had not arrived at an agreed upon manner of notating the music for these instruments.

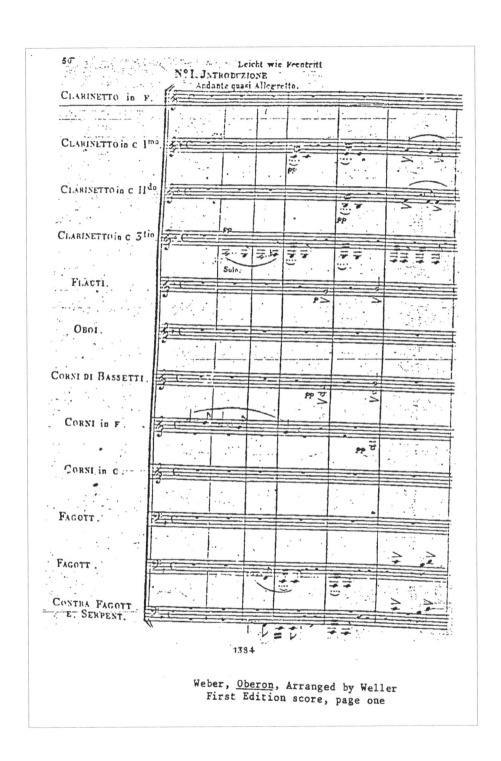

Weber, Oberon, Arranged by Weller
First Edition score, page one

Plate 23

This is the first page of the original autograph score of the *Notturno* for *Harmoniemusik* by Mendelssohn. It was later arranged by Schubert's brother for large military band in the version best known today.

The lowest part is for 'Corno di Basso,' which many later writers have incorrectly confused with 'Corno di Basetto.'

Mendelssohn, Notturno, for Harmoniemusik
Autograph score, page one

Plate 24

This is the first movement, of fifteen, of the *Requiem for Louis XVI* (1815) by Charles Bochsa who was then the Director of Music for one of the regiments of Napoleon's *Mousquetaires*. This is one of a number of full Masses composed with military band during the nineteenth century and this one is quite beautiful.

Bochsa was instrumental in the development of the modern harp and his name is known to all harpists today. He eventually fled Europe, made his way to San Francisco where he performed and then on to Australia where he just had time to compose his own requiem before dying. He was a great composer whose name has been left out of history books due to various personal problems.

Charles Bochsa, Requiem for Louis XVI [1815]
First edition score, page one

Plate 25

This is a large scale original band work composed by the head of the court music in Berlin, Spontini.

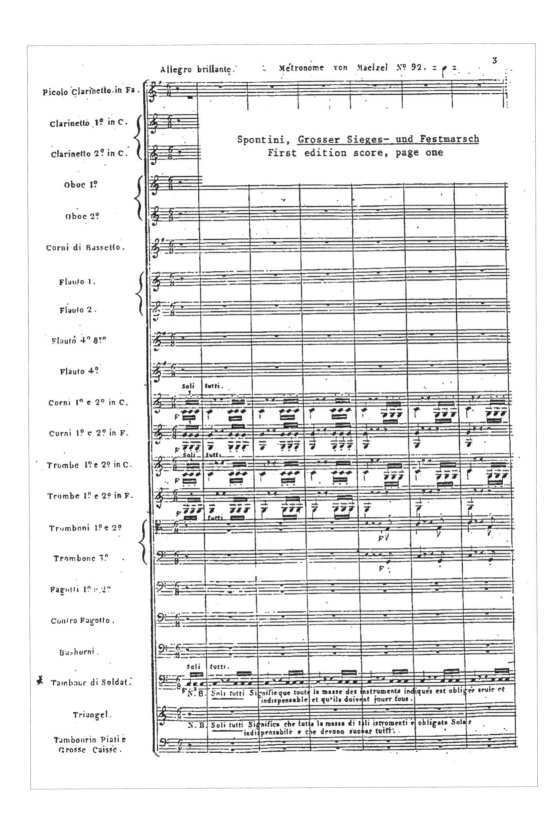

Spontini, Grosser Sieges- und Festmarsch
First edition score, page one

Plate 26

This is one of four original band compositions by Meyerbeer called *Fackeltanz*, or *Torch Dance*. All four survive in the full score made by Wilhelm Wieprecht from the composer piano versions. The *Torch Dance* was associated with royal weddings and was a dance performed indoors.

Wieprecht was the primary person responsible for inventing the modern tuba and one can see his enthusiasm at finally solving the long need for a flexible bass wind instrument by his use here of an entire family of five of the new tubas.

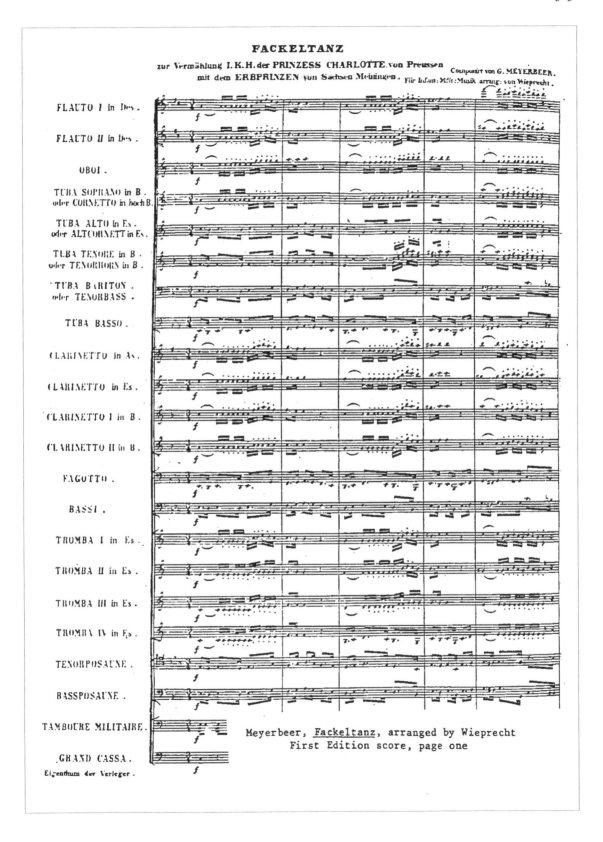

Meyerbeer, Fackeltanz, arranged by Wieprecht
First Edition score, page one

Plate 27

This is the title page of the Berlioz *Symphony* for Band, in the composer's handwriting.

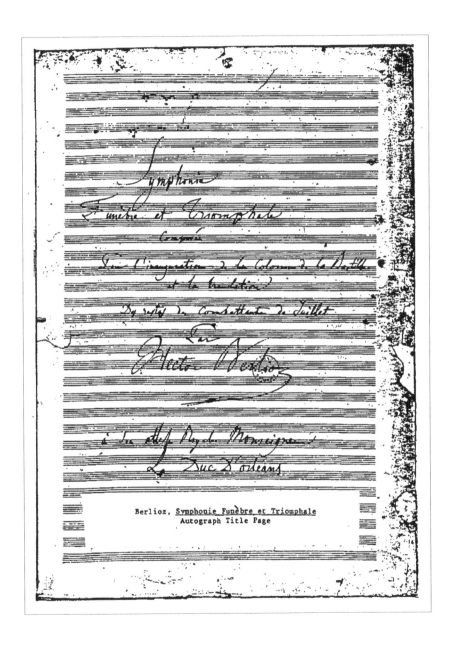

Berlioz, Symphonie Funèbre et Triomphale
Autograph Title Page

Plate 28

This is the first score page of the Berlioz *Symphony* for Band, in the composer's handwriting. His tone at the bottom refers to the fact that only the first few pages are autograph and the rest are in the hand of his copyist. This is the final version, of many, and includes additional strings. The tempo is given as quarter-note = 72.

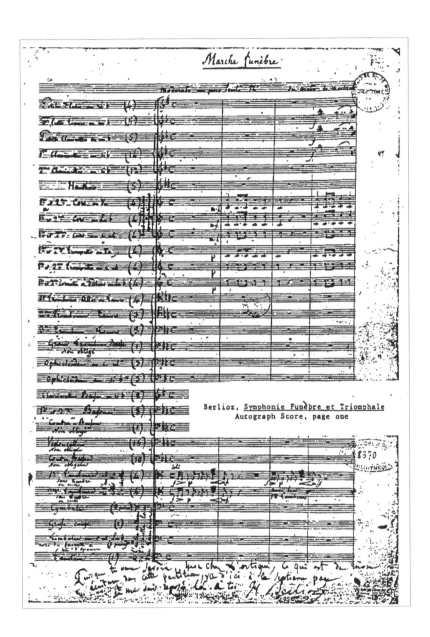

Berlioz, Symphonie Funèbre et Triomphale
Autograph Score, page one

Plate 29

This is the first score page of the *Fantasie* by Fessy composed for a 'battle of the bands' in Paris in 1845. It contains the very first published music for the new saxophone and the work was published by Adolph Sax himself who for a time included publishing among his many activities. This score has his publisher plate number '1.'

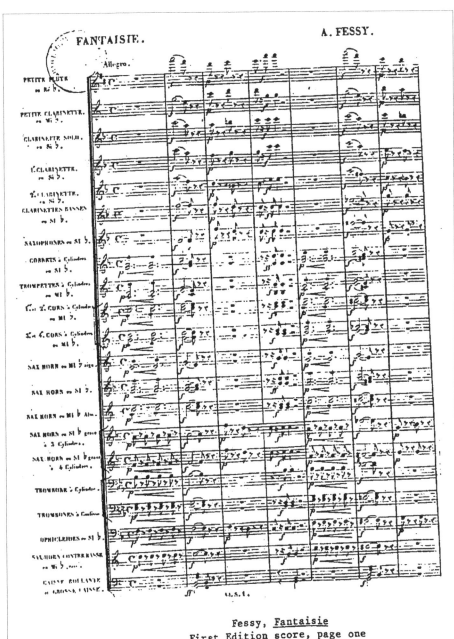

Fessy, Fantaisie
First Edition score, page one

Plate 30

This is a representative of thousands of large scale original band compositions published in Paris in the second half of the nineteenth century. These works are often characterized by surprising virtuosity, as can be seen in this saxophone part.

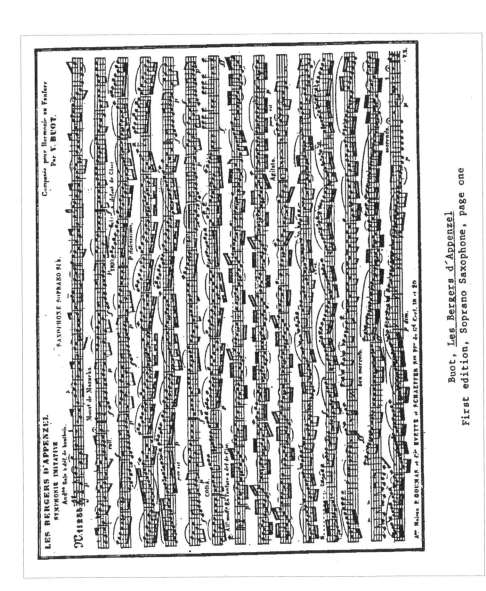

Buot, Les Bergers d'Appenzel
First edition, Soprano Saxophone, page one

Plate 31

This is the original autograph score, for piano, of the *Trauermusik* for wind band by Wagner. Note that the original conception did not include the introduction music we know today.

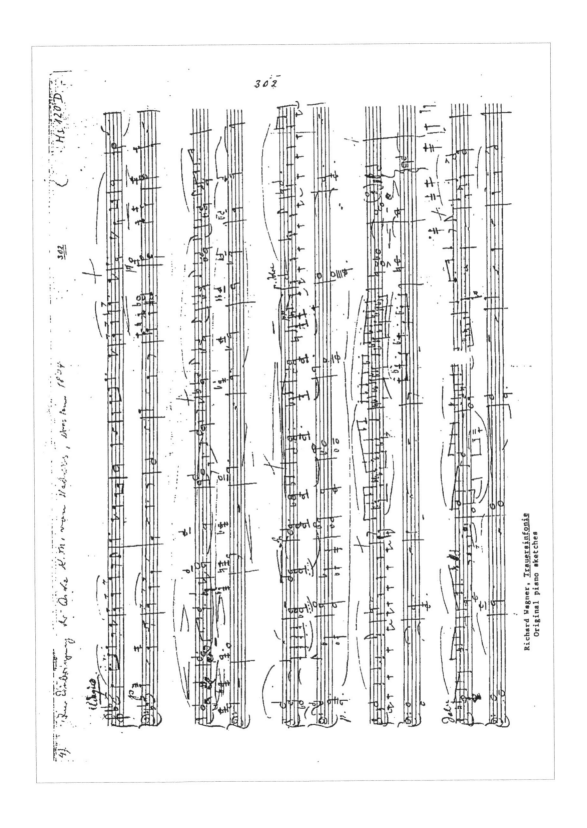

Richard Wagner, Trauersinfonie
Original piano sketches

Plate 32

This is the first autograph score for the *Trauermusik* by Wagner with designation of the instruments. It is typical of Wagner's autograph large scores that these sweeping slur marks go across the entire page. The intent is that the music is legato, not that it is a literal slur.

Wagner, <u>Trauersinfonie</u>
First [?] Autograph Score, with instrumentation, page one

Plate 33

This is the first score page of a massive arrangement for band by Arthur Seidel of about 30 minutes of music from Wagner's opera. Seidel was also commissioned by Wagner's publisher, Schott, to make similar arrangements of excerpts from *Die Walkure* and *Siegfried*. It was Schott's way of attempting to gain profit to repay loans they had made to the composer. We must assume Wagner approved of this entire idea for Seidel was making his arrangements from Wagner's now lost autograph scores. These scores for band were all published and performed long before the orchestral scores were.

The instrumentation reflects the German military bands at the end of the nineteenth century after they had also adopted the new saxophones.

Seidel, Grosse Fantasie aus Götterdämmerung [Wagner]
First Edition score, page one

Plate 34

This is one of a number of little known major works for band or large brass ensemble with voices by Bruckner. This example is scored for a typical German civic band of the late nineteenth century.

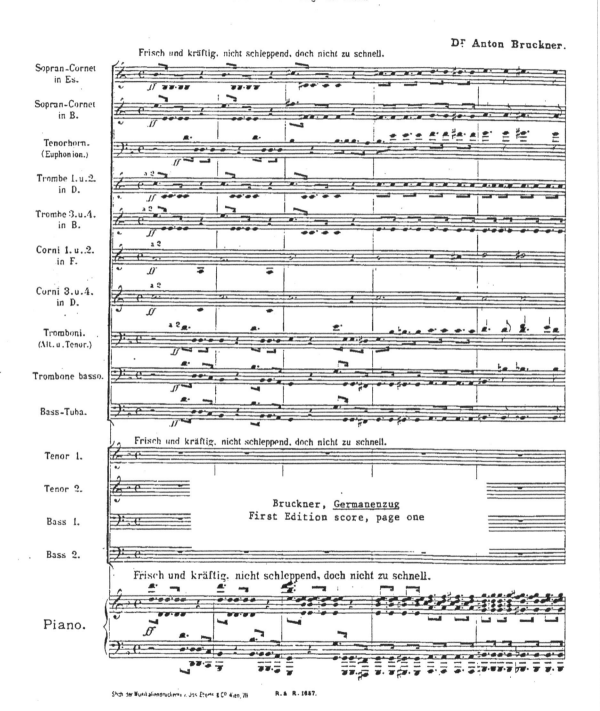

Bruckner, Germanenzug
First Edition score, page one

Illustrations

All artwork, illustrations, and photographs are either in the public domain or covered by a Creative Commons licence. Details of each illustration are below.

COVER
A trio of trombone and two trumpets in a woodcut titled *The Brass Players (Die Posaunisten)* by Heinrich Aldegrever from the series *The Great Wedding Dances*, 1538, public domain

PART I ANCIENT AND MEDIEVAL WIND MUSIC
1 WIND MUSIC BEFORE THE CHRISTIAN ERA
An Egyptian aulos player and dancers, Thebes, public domain • Bone flute dated in the Upper Paleolithic from Geissenklösterle, a german cave on the Swabian region, replica, licensed under the Creative Commons Attribution-Share Alike 2.5 Generic license, José-Manuel Benito Álvarez • Arch of Titus, Rome, License: GNU Free Documentation License, Version 1.2, Creative Commons Attribution-Share Alike 3.0 Unported, Creative Commons Attribution-Share Alike 2.5 Generic, 2.0 Generic and 1.0 Generic license • Coin from Jewish Bar Kokhba revolution, License: GNU Free Documentation License, Version 1.2 • Schnorr von Carolsfeld, public domain • Warrior playing the salpinx. Attic black-figure lekythos, late 6th–early 5th century BC, License: Marie-Lan Nguyen (User:Jastrow), Creative Commons Attribution 2.5 Generic license • Youth playing the aulos, detail of a banquet scene. Tondo of an Attic red-figure cup, ca. 460 BC–450 BC, Source/Photographer Jastrow (2008), Wikimedia Commons • Stitched Panorama, Amphitheatre at Delphi, Greece, 24 November 2008, Author: Luarvick, License: Creative Commons Attribution-Share Alike 3.0 Unported • The Reliefs of Trajan's Column by Conrad Cichorius, public domain • Reliefs on the Columna Traiana in Rome, 21 April 2008, Author: Wknight94, License: GNU Free Documentation License, Version 1.2 • Roman soldiers, players of the cornu, from the cast of Trajan's column in the Victoria and Albert museum, London, public domain • Funerary inscription about members of the guild of the tibicens (collegium tibicinum). Stone, first half of the 1st century BC. From the Esquiline Hill in Rome, 1875, Source/Photographer: Marie-Lan Nguyen (User:Jastrow) 2009, License: Creative Commons Attribution 2.5 Generic license.

2 WIND INSTRUMENTS AND THE EARLY CHRISTIAN CHURCH
A fanciful engraving of a musician's costume from a series by Nicholas de Larmessin I and II, late seventeenth century, public domain • Miniature from 'Jongleurs'; Ms. latin 1118; f. 112. Bibliothéque National de Paris, Source http://prehistoiredufolk.free.fr/images/ClemencicConsort.Troubadours1.jpg, public domain • *Tacuina sanitatis (Tables of Health)*, fouteenth century, public domain • A painted panel on the organ balcony at Abbey Eglise Saint-Pierre et Saint-Paul, public domain

3 CIVIC WIND BANDS
Heinrich Aldegraver (1502-1555), Crumhorn players, 1551, possibly Stadtpfeifer, public domain • Carroccio in the course of the historic parade of 2007, Author: Simo ubuntu, public domain • The Pifferari playing before the Virgin, Rome, unknown artist, 19th century, Library of Congress, public domain • Gentile Bellini, Processione della Vera Croce a Piazza San Marco a Venezia, 1496, public domain • Detail from the Adimari Cassone Wedding, attributed to Giovanni di Ser Giovanni (1406–1486), public domain • Les Très Riches Heures du duc de Berry, Mai the Musée Condé, Chantilly, public domain •

4 COURT WIND BANDS
Basse-dance at the court of Burgundy, uploaded by User:Esp2008, License: GNU Free Documentation License. • Colored plates from The Triumph of Maximilian I, public domain • Bible de Borso d'Este, Taddeo Crivelli, Biblioteca Estense, Modène, 1460, public domain

PART II THE RENAISSANCE
5 COURT WIND BANDS
Silvestro Ganassi, *La Fontegara*, 1535, public domain • Michael Praetorius, *Syntagma Musicum*, 1620, public domain • Johann Christoff Weigel, Abbildung der Gemein-Nützlichen Haupt-Stände, 1698, Deutsches Museum München, Germany, public domain • King Henry VIII's wind band in the musicians' gallery at Whitehall, public domain • *The Field of Cloth of Gold*, James Basire, 1774, public domain • Portrait miniature of Elizabeth I, ca. 1580, Nicholas Hilliard, public domain • Kenilworth Castle by Wenzel Hollar (1607–1677), public domain • Title page of Anthony Holborne's *Pavans, Galliards, Almains and other short Aeirs* (1599) imprinted by William Barley, 1599, public domain • Thoinot Arbeau, *Orchesographie*, 1546 • King Francis I of France, ca. 1538, previously attributed to Joos van Cleve, public domain • *The Engagement of St. Ursula and Prince Etherius*, ca. 5420, public domain) • Lucas van Valckenborch, *Frühlingslandschaft (Mai)*, 1587, public domain • Moritz (Hessen-Kassel), 1662, Matthäus Merian, public domain • Portrait of Giulio de' Medici (1478–1534) Pope Clement VII, ca. 1530, Sebastiano Luciani, public domain • Raffaello Sanzio (1483–1520), Portrait of Pope Leo X and his cousins, cardinals Giulio de' Medici and Luigi de' Rossi, 1518-1519, public domain • Portrait of Pope Paul III Farnese by Titian (1543), public domain • Giuseppe Zocchi (1711–67), View of the Tiber Looking Towards the Castel Sant'Angelo, with Saint Peter's in the Distance, ca. 1721–67, public domain

6 CIVIC WIND BANDS
Raimund Fugger by Vincenzo Catena, 1525, public domain • Collegium musicum from 'Gymnasium illustre', 1590, public domain • Sir Francis Drake by Marcus Gheeraerts the Younger, 1591, public domain • Portrait of Tielman Susato, License: Creative Commons Attribution 3.0 Unported license • De vier Leuvense pijpers in de jaalijkse ommegang (W. Boonen, Geschiedenis van Leuven, 1594, deel 2), public domain • An image from the Heldt'schen Trachtenbuch, ca. 1560–80, public domain • Augsburger Geschlechtertanz by Abraham Schelhas, ca. 1600, public domain • Basilica Di San Marco by Carlo Grubacs, 1849, public domain •

7 CHURCH WIND BANDS
Bernardino Pinturicchio, Coronation of Pius III, ca. 1503, Siena, Italy, public domain • Philippe Galle after a work by Johannes Stradanus, Antwerp, Belgium, 1595, public domain • Fran-

cisco Guerrero by Francisco Pacheco, 1599, public domain • A bronze medallion by Juan Marin and Bautista Vazquez, Seville Cathedral, 1564, public domain • Maurice, Elector of Saxony by Lucas Cranach the Younger, 1578, public domain • Matteo Pagan's Procession in St. Mark's Square on Palm Sunday, 1556–59, Venice, Italy, public domain • Giovanni Gabrieli by Annibale Carracci, ca. 1600, public domain

PART III   THE BAROQUE
8   THE BIRTH OF THE HAUTBOISTEN AND HARMONIEMUSIK
Harmoniemusik, public domain

9   COURT WIND BANDS
Jean Le Pautre's engraving *La Pompeuse et Magnifique Cérémonie du sacre de Louis XIV*, 1654, public domain • Coronation of Louis XIII, Peter Paul Rubens, public domain • *Les Grand Hautbois*, public domain • Girolamo Fantini, public domain • Portrait of Henry Purcell by John Closterman, 1695 •

10   MILITARY BANDS
Military version of the Hautboisten, Band of the First Foot Guards, 1753, public domain • Colored engraving of an Ottoman mehter band from 1839, public domain • Portrait of Frederick William I of Prussia by Antoine Pesne (1683–1757), ca. 1733, publci domain • Die Feldmusik (Hautboisten) Regiment, 1720, Nürnberg, public domain • Zurich infantry and Hautboisten, 1758

11   CIVIC WIND BANDS
Denis van Alsloot, *Procession en l'honneur de Notre-Dame du Sablon a Bruxelles le 31 mai*, public domain • Gottfried Reiche, copperplate engraving by C. F. Rosbach, 1727 (after portrait by E. G. Haussmann), public domain • Title page of Johann Hermann Schein's *Fontana d'Israel*, 1623, public domain • A civic wait band, ca. 1700, public domain • Archduchess Isabelle and Archduke Albert at the procession of the maids of the Sablon, Antoon Sallaert (1615), public domain

12   CATION OF THE FUTURE MUST EDUCATE ALL CHILDREN
Grazzi Chapel of Santissima Annunziata, Baldassare Franceschini, 1644, Florence, Italy, public domain • God the Father and the nine angelic choirs, Joan Gascó, 1503–1529, public domain

PART IV   THE CLASSIC PERIOD
13   COURT WIND BANDS
Harmoniemusik, 1751, public domain • Franz Fahrenschön, Bildnis Graf von Pachta, 1765, public domain • Joseph Haydn by Thomas Hardy, 1791, public domain • Nikolaus Esterházy by Martin Knoller, 1790, public domain • Archduke Maximilian Franz of Austria, eighteenth century, public domain • The Pouplinière portrait, engraving by J.J. Bachelou after Louis Vigée, ca. 1750, public domain

14   MILITARY BANDS
Fredercik the Great by Anton Graff, public domain • Ludwig IX von Hessen-Darmstadt, unknown painter, before 1790, public domain • Portrait of Louis XV, public domain • Johann Christian Bach by Thomas Gainsborough, public domain

15   CIVIC WIND BANDS
The Syren of the Stage, from The Musical Entertainer, London, public domain • Vauxhall Gardens, public domain • *The Monastery of Melk on the Danube*, 1845, Jakob Alt, public domain

16   MUSIC OF THE FRENCH REVOLUTION IN PARIS
François Joseph Gossec by Antoine Vestier, public domain • Photograph of a miniature portrait of Bernard Sarrette by Jean-Baptiste Isabey, public domain • Funeral procession designed by Jacques-Louis David on the death of Voltaire, public domain • Jacques-Louis David, self-portrait, 1794, public domain • The Fountain of Regeneration, public domain • Pierre-Antoine Demachy, *Fête de l'Etre suprême au Champ de Mars (20 prairial an II - 8 juin 1794)*, 1794, public domain • Robespierre, unknown painter, ca. 1790, public domain • Étienne Méhul by Antoine Gros, 1799, public domain • Charles-Simon Catel by Louis-Léopold Boilly, 1817, public domain • Luigi Cherubini, unknown artist, ca. 1815–1824, public domain

PART V   THE NINETEENTH CENTURY IN EUROPE
17   MILITARY BANDS
Georg Abraham Schneider, public domain • Wilhelm Wieprecht, unknown photographer, public domain • Josef Gungl, 1874, public domain • Josef Gungl, 1874, public domain • Philipp Fahrbach Jr , public domain • Julius Fucik, public domain • Michele Carafa by Antoine Maurin, public domain • Adolphe Sax, public domain • Kneller Hall, public domain • Nikolai Andreyevich Rimsky-Korsakov by Valentin Serov, 1898, Tretyakov Gallery, Moscow, commissioned by Pavel Tretyakov, public domain • Portrait of Eduard Hanslick, 1894, public domain

18   CIVIC WIND BANDS
Charles Bochsa, 1842, public domain • Hector Berlioz by André Gill, nineteenth century, public domain • Paul Taffanel, public domain • The civic band of Cioia, Italy, public domain • The front entrance of the Crystal Palace, Hyde Park, London, public domain

19   COURT WIND BANDS
Franz Krommer by Karel Maixner, 1871, public domain • Johann Simon Hermstedt, Source: Leaflet of the cultural department of the City Sondershausen, public domain • The Mecklenburgian Grand-duke Friedrich Franz I by Matthieu, 1776, public domain • Leopoldo II by Pietro Benvenuti, 1828, public domain • Jean-François Lesueur, public domain • King George IV when Prince Regent by Henry Bone, 1816, public domain

20   CHURCH WIND BANDS
Anton Bruckner by Wilhelm von Kaulbach, 1885, public domain • Vincent Novello by Edward Petre Novello (d. 1836), public domain

About the Author

Dr. David Whitwell is a graduate ('with distinction') of the University of Michigan and the Catholic University of America, Washington DC (PhD, Musicology, Distinguished Alumni Award, 2000) and has done post-graduate study at the University of Vienna and has studied conducting with Eugene Ormandy and at the Akademie fur Musik, Vienna. Prior to coming to Northridge, Dr. Whitwell participated in concerts throughout the United States and Asia as Associate First Horn in the USAF Band and Orchestra in Washington DC, and in recitals throughout South America in cooperation with the United States State Department.

At the California State University, Northridge, which is in Los Angeles, Dr. Whitwell developed the CSUN Wind Ensemble into an ensemble of international reputation, with international tours to Europe in 1981 and 1989 and to Japan in 1984. The CSUN Wind Ensemble has made professional studio recordings for BBC (London), the Koln Westdeutscher Rundfunk (Germany), NOS National Radio (The Netherlands), Zurich Radio (Switzerland), the Television Broadcasting System (Japan) as well as for the United States State Department for broadcast on its 'Voice of America' program. The CSUN Wind Ensemble's recording with the Mirecourt Trio in 1982 was named the 'Record of the Year' by The Village Voice. Composers who have guest conducted Whitwell's ensembles include Aaron Copland, Ernest Krenek, Alan Hovhaness, Morton Gould, Karel Husa, Frank Erickson and Vaclav Nelhybel.

Dr. Whitwell has been a guest professor in 100 different universities and conservatories throughout the United States and in 23 foreign countries (most recently in China, in an elite school housed in the Forbidden City). Guest conducting experiences have included the Philadelphia Orchestra, Seattle Symphony Orchestra, the Czech Radio Orchestras of Brno and Bratislava, The National Youth Orchestra of Israel, as well as resident wind ensembles in Russia, Israel, Austria, Switzerland, Germany, England, Wales, The Netherlands, Portugal, Peru, Korea, Japan, Taiwan, Canada and the United States.

He is a past president of the College Band Directors National Association, a member of the Prasidium of the International Society for the Promotion of Band Music, and was a member of the founding board of directors of the World Association for Symphonic Bands and Ensembles (WASBE). In 1964 he was made an honorary life member of Kappa Kappa Psi, a national professional music fraternity. In September, 2001, he was a delegate to the UNESCO Conference on Global Music in Tokyo. He has been knighted by sovereign organizations in France, Portugal and Scotland and has been awarded the gold medal of Kerkrade, The Netherlands, and the silver medal of Wangen, Germany, the highest honor given wind conductors in the United States, the medal of the Academy of Wind and Percussion Arts (National Band Association) and the highest honor given wind conductors in Austria, the gold medal of the Austrian Band Association. He is a member of the Hall of Fame of the California Music Educators Association.

Dr. Whitwell's publications include more than 127 articles on wind literature including publications in Music and Letters (London), the London Musical Times, the Mozart-Jahrbuch (Salzburg), and 39 books, among which is his 13-volume *History and Literature of the Wind Band and Wind Ensemble* and an 8-volume series on *Aesthetics in Music*. In addition to numerous modern editions of early wind band music his original compositions include five symphonies.

David Whitwell was named as one of six men who have determined the course of American bands during the second half of the 20th century, in the definitive history, *The Twentieth Century American Wind Band* (Meredith Music).

A doctoral dissertation by German Gonzales (2007, Arizona State University) is dedicated to the life and conducting career of David Whitwell through the year 1977. David Whitwell is one of nine men described by Paula A. Crider in *The Conductor's Legacy* (Chicago: GIA, 2010) as 'the legendary conductors' of the 20th century.

> 'I can't imagine the 2nd half of the 20th century—without David Whitwell and what he has given to all of the rest of us.' Frederick Fennell (1993)

Made in the USA
Monee, IL
28 August 2019